D1737878

Narrating Poverty and Precarity in Britain

Culture & Conflict

Edited by
Isabel Capeloa Gil and Catherine Nesci

Volume 5

Narrating Poverty and Precarity in Britain

Edited by
Barbara Korte and Frédéric Regard

DE GRUYTER

ISBN 978-3-11-036793-5
e-ISBN 978-3-11-036574-0
ISSN 2194-7104

Library of Congress Cataloging-in-Publication Data
A CIP catalog record for this book has been applied for at the Library of Congress.

Bibliographic information published by the Deutsche Nationalbibliothek
The Deutsche Nationalbibliothek lists this publication in the Deutsche Nationalbibliografie;
detailed bibliographic data are available on the Internet at http://dnb.dnb.de.

© 2014 Walter de Gruyter GmbH, Berlin/Boston
Cover image: Universal Images Group/GettyImages
Printing and binding: CPI books GmbH, Leck
♾ Printed on acid-free paper
Printed in Germany

www.degruyter.com

MIX
Papier aus verantwor-
tungsvollen Quellen
FSC
www.fsc.org   FSC® C003147

Table of Contents

Acknowledgments

The editors would like to thank Katja Bay, Natalie Churn, Kathrin Göb and Malena Klocke for their help in getting this book ready for publication, and Georg Zipp for co-organising a symposium which gave the contributors a first opportunity to discuss their ideas.

Barbara Korte
Narrating Poverty and Precarity in Britain: An Introduction

Poverty is commonly understood today as material deprivation that goes hand in hand with social exclusion and lack: of agency, opportunities and access to knowledge, traditions, rights or capabilities. Precarity, as discussed in this book, refers to insecure existential conditions that result from economic and social circumstances. In the early twenty-first century, the themes of poverty and precarity – along with related topics such as inequality, social justice and class antagonism – have gained a new societal and political presence in many countries of the world. While poverty has long been treated as a problem of developing countries, it is now also widely perceived as an urgent issue and source of conflict in American and European advanced economies, and this is reflected in the news media as well as in cultural production across media and genres. The emerging field of 'poverty studies' (Gandal 2009) therefore encompasses not only such disciplines as economics, the social sciences and moral philosophy, but also various branches of the study of culture, with a special interest coming from literary studies. While much of this research impulse originates in the United States and some European countries,[1] the representation of poverty and precarity in the United Kingdom has only recently begun to receive the attention of literary and cultural studies.[2] The present volume therefore focuses on Britain, with some comparative glances at the situation in other countries and cultures, and its chapters divide their attention between current cultural production and earlier instances of poverty representation that have retained significant relevance today. Its interest in the Victorians in particular is motivated not only by

---

[1] See the studies by Gandal (1998) and Jones (2008) on poverty in the US, and Brüns (2008) for European literature.

[2] Simon During has recently proposed that "the terms under which the subaltern problem have long been understood no longer hold" in a context where "politics of subalterneity were largely absorbed into the machinery of emergent neo-liberal state capitalism" and where "new, more extensive and less visible patterns of global dispossession are gaining ground. Relatively geographically and cultural stable relations of dominance and subordination are being replaced by relatively unstable and dispersed conditions of deprivation and insecurity" (1). In During's understanding, precarity "effectively invokes the insecurity of all those who live without reliable and adequate income or without papers. And it also applies to those with no, or unstable, access to the institutions and communities best able to provide legitimacy, recognition and solidarity" (1– 2).

the pioneering ethnographic and sociological research conducted in that period (such as Henry Mayhew's *London Labour and the London Poor*, 1851, and Charles Booth's monumental *Life and Labour of the People in London*, first 1889; complete 1902–1903), and the vast and varied amount of literature and journalism – as well as visual representations[3] – that the mid- and late-nineteenth century produced about poverty. It is also explained by the fact that Victorian representations still have a firm hold over today's public imagination of poverty. 'Dickensian' poverty (Yousef 2009) has remained iconic, continually producing many echoes in contemporary cultural production. Today's media also abound with remarks about how newly Victorian the UK's current treatment of poverty and precarity is, with speculation as to what Dickens might have written about today's unequal society, or how 'Dickensian' a young 'underclass' lives.[4]

The chapters in this book are concerned with literary representations of poverty in the widest sense: novels, short stories and narrative journalism, but also plays for the stage and scripted television. All of these representations tell stories, attesting that the struggle "with the meanings and consequences of our actions", which characterizes our being human, is "most often understood in narrative structures as we tell others and ourselves about what has transpired or what we fear will transpire in the future" (Davis and Womack 2001, ix). A special relevance of literature for the study of poverty has not only been claimed by representatives of literary studies, but has also been emphasized by sociologists, economists and moral philosophers. Pierre Bourdieu, for instance, has demanded that novels, and specifically complex ones, should become a model for the sociological representation of social suffering in order to replace "simplistic and one-sided images" and "the single, central, dominant, in a word, quasi-divine, point of view that is all too easily adopted by observers". Instead, he argues, social misery should be described "with the multiple perspectives that correspond to the multiplicity of coexisting, and sometimes directly competing, points of view" (1999, 3). Since literature is attentive to the particular and can render characters' inner worlds, it is an important complement to the general categories and statistics of the social and economic sciences. Literature gives faces and voices to poverty, and asks readers to see situations from the perspective of those who are afflicted (Sedmak 2003, 48). From the perspective of devel-

---

3 These included engravings such as Gustave Doré's for *London: A Pilgrimage* (1872), paintings (by artists such as Thomas Benjamin Kennington and William Strang) as well as photography (most famously John Thomson's *Street Life in London*, 1877) and screen entertainments such as *laterna magica* shows and early film (see *Screening the Poor*, 2011).

4 A search on the internet easily yields examples, see Metrowebukmetro (2009), Channel 4 News (2012), Hoggart (2010), Hunt (2008) or Butler (2011).

opment studies, social scientists at the London School of Economics also contend that "literary works sometimes have a stronger Geertzian 'being there' quality than certain academic and policy works"; furthermore, because they are "written in a more engaging and accessible manner", they will "often reach a much larger and diverse audience than academic texts" and have greater influence on public knowledge and understanding (Lewis, Rodgers and Woolcock 2008, 209). Not least, they foreground the human dimension of social misery and its ethical challenge. The economist Amartya Sen (2007), a leading authority on international poverty and inequality, has cited George Bernard Shaw's *Major Barbara* and concluded that the playwright "was right, a hundred years ago today, to point to the connection between poverty and evil and crime". To Sen, the fact that this insight came "from a dramatist and literary giant fits in well with [his] general thesis that the economics of poverty involves much more than just economics. Human lives in society are interlinked through economic, social, political and cultural associations." Martha Nussbaum notes the power of literature to "energize [people] with some urgency towards productive social action" and find it "plausible to think what Dickens clearly thought: that you can't really change the heart without telling a story" (2011, 3). The historian Gertrude Himmelfarb claims that the novels of Dickens's age "were undoubtedly one of the most important means by which the 'anonymous masses' [...] were brought to the attention of the public, assimilated into the social consciousness, and made the concern of an increasingly sensitive and vigilant social conscience" (1984, 405). The power of literature – and other forms of representation – to help people imagine and understand poverty, and to enquire what individual and social reactions it should provoke, is not only affirmed by academics, however. It is also suggested by the mere fact that literature has articulated and interpreted poverty in all periods and, in the English language, since the middle ages. The following section highlights some stages of this history and combines it with a sketch of the scholarly attention that certain periods and individual texts have attracted.

1 Poverty in English and British Literature: Conjectures and Trajectories in Research

The representation of poverty in literature – as well as other forms of representation – has distinctive trends that coincide with periods of a heightened societal awareness of poverty. The later middle ages are a case in point, when a generally precarious life could easily lead into destitution. Poverty was still widely interpreted in terms of Christian – Roman Catholic – doctrine, and the church and monasteries were the main institutions on which organized charity depended. *Piers Plowman*, an allegorical poem from the last quarter of the fourteenth century, is given a reading by Anne Scott (2004) that takes account of the medieval status of poverty between social exclusion and a status of special divine favour. While the poem does not envisage a situation in which poverty could be eradicated, it claims that the rich are obliged to give to the poor. The failure of contemporary society to provide the poor with appropriate care is a major theme in *Piers Plowman*, and it is unsurprising that the poem circulated amongst the participants of the Peasants' Revolt of 1381. However, the late-medieval literary treatment of poverty was far from uniform. Dinah Hazell (2009) shows how different genres reflected different social and moral facets of the relationship between "the meene and the riche", and Kate Crassons investigates how Middle English texts shaped the imaginary of poverty and projected possibilities for an ethical response with a complexity of signification that characterizes the literary treatment of poverty until today:

> Shaped by aesthetic forms, rhetorical strategies, and linguistic slippages, literary texts place the signs of poverty before readers; and they demand that readers both interpret these signs and assess their ethical implications, in the same way that an almsgiver would evaluate the signs of need in the body and speech of the poor themselves. When viewed in this light, literature becomes far more than the repository of shifting historical attitudes toward poverty. Rather, a text's complex use of signs embodies the very anxieties around representation that are at the heart of poverty itself. (2010, 13)

A significant shift in attitudes towards poverty and the treatment of the poor was occasioned by the Reformation. In England it led not only to re-interpretations of poverty, but also had drastic material consequences when the old system of charity lost its foundation in the wake of Henry VIII's dissolution of the monasteries. William Carroll's new-historicist study (1996) examines this re-negotiation of poverty for the age of Shakespeare, with special attention to the consequences of the Elizabethan Poor Laws. Discussing poems, pamphlets, plays, official documents and other types of texts, Carroll differentiates between various modes of representation and their aesthetic, political and socio-economical uses in Tudor and Stuart times, showing how the discourse on poverty was increasingly characterized by a protestant and specifically puritan ethos that perceived poverty more and more as a threat to the social order. Carroll diagnoses "a post-Reformation transformation of the very idea of charity" and "the painful transformation of a feudal economy into early modern capitalism" (1996, 4).

The Restoration and the long eighteenth century constitute a phase in which capitalism took a firm hold in England, with concomitant precarity and poverty.

A comprehensive anthology compiled by Steven King and others illustrates the multiple literary reactions to these developments. These reactions were both satirical (Frank 1997) and more often sentimental. A sentimental response to poverty – one of whose main intentions was to foster charitable attitudes in the upper and middle classes – gained speed with the spread of romanticism and maintained its influence in Victorian times (Tobin 1993).

Ever since the Poor Law Amendment Act of 1834, which aggravated the harsh laws originating in Elizabethan times, Victorian literature participated in a lively discussion about poverty and its management in politics and in social-reformist circles. The poor occasionally had their own literary voice in this debate, for instance in ballads (Hepburn 2000), but the novel, predominantly written by writers from the middle classes and for readers from these classes, was the most potent genre in which the contemporary 'social question' was negotiated. Indeed, it became a major instrument for stimulating the social emotions of those on whose individual philanthropy the Victorian welfare system essentially depended.[5] In a brief overview of English fiction from the 1840s to 1950s, the historian Krishan Kumar (1995) contends that until the early twentieth century, and in spite of Britain's change from a pre-industrial to an industrial-urban society, a pastoral pattern of representing poverty was perpetuated in the British novel, i.e. a tendency to harmonize the relationship between the rich and the poor with the aim of generating sympathy in the more privileged classes.

As Kumar points out, the 1930s produced a new significant peak of poverty literature in Britain: "The 'hungry thirties' echo the 'hungry forties' of the last century. There is fear of the working class. Communism has replaced Chartism. The mood on both sides of the industrial divide is one of anger and bitterness" (1995, 19). The economic collapse in the late 1920s and the political radicalism it brought forth inspired a wave of poverty-themed narratives in documentary as well as fictional modes. The period seems inseparable from George Orwell, whose *Down and Out in Paris and London* (1933) remains one of the most influential twentieth-century treatments of poverty and specifically homelessness, even though the fact that it was written by an author originating from the middle classes has elicited views that see *Down and Out* as an instance of dubious class-passing or even slumming.[6] Nevertheless, underlining a common humanity and

---

5 See the major studies by Smith (1980), Williams (1987), Lenard (1999), Himmelfarb (1984, 1991) and Betensky (2010).

6 On the questionable ethics behind narratives of actual class passing, see Betensky in "Princes as Paupers": "People of means who pass for poor or homeless play with, script, and dramatize relations of power" (2004, 148). She further contends that "[i]t is important to understand that the problem with dominant-class simulations of powerlessness lies *not* in the bourgeois sub-

defining poverty as a lack of income rather than 'civilization', Orwell articulates an enlightened view of poverty which is as topical today as it was in 1933. Apart from Orwell, Kumar identifies an "outpouring" of "dole-queue literature" (1995, 20), some of which was also produced by middle-class authors. But a distinctive mark of the 1930s is a substantial number of novels about poor and precarious lives by working-class writers such as Walter Greenwood, whose accounts were still predominantly read, however, by a middle-class reading public (1995, 22). Kumar concludes his survey with the observation that the main difference in the view on the poor's situation between the 1840s and the 1930s was the message that "[c]hange is possible; the choices are there; it is up to the poor to seize their chances" (1995, 23).

With the establishment of the post-war Welfare State, however, poverty as such appears to have become a less urgent topic for British writers and has been replaced with a dominant concern with working-class life. Nevertheless, texts by angry young women such as Shelagh Delaney's play *A Taste of Honey* (1958) and Nell Dunn's novel *Poor Cow* (1967) reminded audiences that poverty still needed to be addressed, and new media joined the debate. The BBC television play *Cathy Come Home* (1966), for instance, directed by Ken Loach, was a landmark intervention on homelessness that even led to a change in legislation. But poverty and precarity also became a (sub-)theme in new contexts, with a focus on the situation of women and on the life of migrants from the Commonwealth. With the termination of the 'post-war consensus' under Thatcher, mass unemployment, social descent and precarity re-emerged as urgent social problems, most visibly during the Miners' Strike of the mid-1980s. Yet, as during the 1950s and 60s, poverty was rarely treated as a separate topic but rather as a collateral issue in the context of such wider concerns as class, feminism and racial conflict in the multi-ethnic society. It seems that only renewed harsh debate about poverty and its causes under New Labour and the economic slump of the early twenty-first century have prompted new attention to poverty and precarity *per se*. This is most visible, perhaps, in the news media and documentary programmes on British television, but the book market and other fields of cultural production have followed suit (Korte and Zipp 2014).

---

ject's enjoyment, but in the customary and uncritical conflation of this enjoyment with the promotion of social justice. The *misrecognition* of 'powerlessness' for powerlessness is what transforms these middle-class experiments from role-playing rituals (with meaning for the middle-class role-player and those to whom the role-playing fantasy speaks) into something that gets taken for activism" (2004, 151). On the history of class-passing since the nineteenth century, see also Freeman (2001).

2 Leading Research Premises and Questions

The research conducted on the representation of poverty in English or British literature – and more rarely on representation in other corners of the arts – is usually focused on specific historical contexts. Nevertheless, some shared premises and research questions emerge (Korte 2012), and most can be transferred from literary representation to other media. First and foremost, literary representation is held to have significant impact on its audiences' ideas and potential responses concerning poverty and precarity. Representations feed the public imagination, or the "social imaginary" (Taylor 2004), and may be an influence in shaping people's opinions and perhaps even affect their behaviour towards poverty and the poor. How literature 'configures' poverty for its readers hinges on the lifeworlds and characters it portrays, on the ways it utilizes genre and literary modes, and particularly on how it makes choices in terms of voice and perspective.

Within the textual world, poverty is configured with reference to specific characters and the milieus in which they are situated, their 'representativeness' or individuality, the precise nature, causes and consequences of the deprivation they experience, and how their poverty intersects with gender, age, ethnicity and class; as well as what judgements, anxieties or perhaps positive qualities are associated with a poor life; and the degree to which poverty is depicted as other to the life of a middle-class readership.

In part, such choices on the content level are influenced by genre and mode: a predominantly realist text presents poverty with different facets than one with a sentimental, sensational, satirical or humorous orientation, and such modes have consequences for reader response. Most essentially, perhaps, this response – from paternalism or voyeurism to compassion and outrage – depends on perspective, and in the case of narrative texts this means agents of narration and focalization: Do we read a subjective self-narrative, or a seemingly objective third-person account? Is poverty seen from one perspective only, or are we confronted with multiple perspectives? Is the narrative in general contained in established ways of seeing, or does it break with them and defamiliarize accustomed modes of perception?

The voice in which a text speaks about poverty is another crucial element: Are the poor merely spoken about, or are they given a voice of their own? Simulated and authentic self-presentation at first sight suggests empowerment, but this is no automatism, because first-person narration can also be used to express a victimized position. The decision in favour of a specific voice, and also the kind of language in which this voice speaks,[7] is in any case entangled with the ethics

---

7 See for instance Salamon, who discusses the controversial view expressed, for instance by

of narration because it implies the agency of representation. This agency has been discussed in literary and cultural studies in such frameworks as subaltern speaking (Spivak 1988) and the politics of representation (Hall 1987), and in terms of authority as well as subversion and resistance. However, the agency of representation does not only concern the intratextual dimension of voice, but also the extratextual 'circuit' of production, dissemination and reception (du Gay et al. 1997) to which each representation is submitted.

One pitfall of representation emphasized in several recent contributions to poverty studies is the lack of agency over representation of those who actually experience poverty. The American critic Walter Benn Michaels (2006), for instance, has pointed out that literary treatments of poverty are rarely authored by the poor themselves and that, when they write themselves, their output will normally be marketed for, and read, by people of a higher class.[8] One can transfer this to the UK, where authors and readers of literature are also predominantly middle-class (Head 2006, 243). Of course, an author's own experience of poverty will not ensure either the quality or the credibility of his or her text. Nevertheless, what a reader knows about an author and his or her relation to poverty may affect this reader's response, and some texts reflect and comment on asymmetries of representation. It is therefore important to be sensitive to the social (a-)symmetries between those represented as poor, and the agents in a text's circulation: its authors and distributors, and of course its readers. For the question as to who listens to what is being articulated, and how one listens, is, in social terms, at least as important as the question of voice: "Voice as a social process involves, from the start, both speaking *and listening*, that is, an act of attention that registers the uniqueness of the other's narrative" (Couldry 2010, 9). Representing the misery of others can raise sympathy and awareness, and perhaps even trigger measures that may relieve this suffering, but it can also, more dubiously in ethical terms, fulfil needs of the recipient rather than the represented. Carolyn Betensky has discussed this as an ambiguous aspect of Victorian social-problem novels that, in her view, offered their bourgeois audience "the experience of their own reading as a viable response to conflicts that seem daunt-

---

William Vollmann, that "complexity of language [is] morally suspect when describing poverty, and complexity that is aesthetically appealing is doubly so" (2010, 170). To Salamon, "[t]he contention that linguistic complexity invites or enacts a kind of corruption on the part of the writer and that language describing the poor must be mimetically impoverished, as bare and minimal as the lives of the poor themselves, is both a misrecognition of the lives of the poor and inattentive to the complexities of languages of poverty" (2010, 171).

8 See also Jones (2008) and Brüns, who states that "literature tends to talk *about* the poor rather than have them speak for themselves" (2008, 11).

ing or irreconcilable" (2010, 1), and they thus used the suffering of the dominated to promote the dominating classes' *self*-understanding. Betensky returns to this issue in her contribution to this volume.

3 The Chapters

The book opens with a chapter that links current forms of political speaking about social inequality with a tendency which Carolyn Betensky identifies as an ethic dilemma of poverty representation in nineteenth-century social problem novels. Of late, right-wing observers in the US and Europe have characterized social movements that challenge capitalist entitlement as being motivated by 'envy'. At the same time, however, the right has come to stress the victimization of the *wealthy* at the hands of the same poor who envy them. With the preponderance of power on their side, those in whose hands wealth has concentrated have developed a compelling rhetoric of resentment from above that vies, in an emotional economy, with claims for redress from below. Betensky reads this as a legacy of discursive configurations first made available in nineteenth-century reformist novels: the same narrative strategies that attempted to humanize the poor before a middle-class readership invited this middle-class readership to feel what the poor felt as if they were poor – and in so doing, these strategies expanded the range of subject positions available to the middle-class imagination.

Joanna Rostek turns to the Victorian writer Harriet Martineau, whose *Illustrations of Political Economy* appeared between 1832 and 1834, i.e. immediately before the coming into effect of the Poor Law Amendment Act in Britain. Martineau was a writer highly sensitive to the social issues of her day, and the twenty-five tales of her *Illustrations* were meant to convey economic lessons by way of fictional short stories. The texts scrutinize the principles of the distribution of wealth, but also their underside – the growing numbers of destitute labourers striking for higher wages, women suffering from hunger, or orphaned children being forced to go to the workhouse. Rostek analyses Martineau's blend of literary discourse, with its emphasis on particular cases of poverty, and a more abstract scientific discourse about how poverty and precarity should be managed. This is linked with the essential question of what scope of agency is given to people in misery in the *Illustrations*, and to what extent Martineau considers the implications of her attempt to speak for those who cannot speak for themselves. This is finally connected to the question as to the gendering of Martineau's representation, and notably the role of a woman as political scientist vs. a woman as helper of the poor. Martineau's *Illustrations*, although hugely popular upon their publication, met with frequent criticism by reviewers who felt that the female author had violated established gender norms by not showing the due amount of compassion for the poor, and they point to limitations of Martineau's own agency as a female writer within the male discourse of economics.

On the stage, poor characters speak with a voice of their own, and they are spoken about; the poor are also literally exhibited to the gaze of an audience. Stage melodrama was a form of theatre that enjoyed particular popularity in Victorian times. Joachim Frenk's chapter investigates the genre and the narratives it developed for thinking about poverty in the Victorian period – and beyond. As Frenk claims, the melodrama of the nineteenth century merits fresh scholarly attention with a view to its contribution to the formation and transformation of what Gertrude Himmelfarb has termed, in her classic study of 1984, "the idea of poverty". A quasi-precarious genre in the literary canon (particularly in terms of the scholarly attention it has received), the melodrama addresses contemporary issues of precarity and poverty according to its own market-oriented and Manichean code. As a consequence, it oscillates uneasily between a deeply ingrained escapism and moments of highly stylized realism. For all its instability and irrationality, melodrama is able, now and then, to address the discourse of poverty in surprisingly 'direct' forms, only to give prevalence to its generic codes in the next emotionally charged stage moment. The chapter focuses on two plays, Dion Boucicault's *The Poor of New York* (1857) and George Robert Sims's *The Lights o' London* (1881) with a view to their constructions, deconstructions and reconstructions of poverty. As Frenk shows, both plays produce insights into how poverty could be culturally processed and subjected to a multi-vocal discussion that, in many aspects, was not so different from poverty debates of the twenty-first century. It is a crucial feature of the plays' generic and ideological matrices that neither of them offers anything approaching a consistent analysis of Victorian poverty. Instead, poverty hovers precariously between a possibly incendiary extradramatic topic and a mere plot convention.

Frédéric Regard's chapter is dedicated to strategies of representation in a notorious case of late Victorian reportage. *The Maiden Tribute of Modern Babylon* was a series of newspaper articles on child prostitution which appeared in the *Pall Mall Gazette* in July 1885. A pioneer in investigative journalism, William Thomas Stead exposed the lives of young underprivileged girls in London and other European brothels, and his portrayal created an international moral panic. Instead of simply presenting facts by reporting *on* them, Stead chose to *represent* the social injustice he unveiled. As a 'new journalist' he conceived of himself as a detective whose very presence in the heart of darkness re-established a demarcation line between humanity and inhumanity, democracy and tyranny, and it was such a line which provided the thread of the narrative, the only way to escape from the complex maze of the Minotaur's labyrinth. Like Theseus, the new journalist advanced to the centre of the labyrinth playing out his thread. Regard also argues, however, that one of the major characteristics of *The Maiden Tribute* was the paradoxical effect of instability its narrative strategy produced on the reader. Stead brought into light the concealed vices of Victorian respectability while simultaneously gesturing towards the victims left in obscurity, and exposed the scandal of innocence violated while signalling the impunity of the *débauchés*. Stead offered a striking metaphor for his technique when he invited his readers to think of themselves as the spectators of a shipwreck, and compared his own mission as a journalist to "throwing a rope into the abyss". The narrative thread should be construed as some such rope, repeatedly thrown into the darkness, affording only a very limited number of poor souls to manifest their presence to the straining eyes and ears of the rescuers, with no second opportunity being afforded to the multitude of other drowning characters, whose ghosts inevitably come back to haunt the readers, to re-present themselves in representation.

Marina Remy Abrunhosa's chapter also turns to reportage and reads a piece of investigative immersion journalism of the Victorian period, James Greenwood's "A Night in a Workhouse" (1866), against George Orwell's 'classic' literary reportage in *Down and Out in Paris and London* (1933). Tracing back the lineage between Greenwood and Orwell allows Remy to seize the ways in which both exposed the day-to-day living and sleeping conditions of the most precarious amongst the precarious: casuals forced to move from one ward to another. Behind both Greenwood's and Orwell's texts lies the will to find out, from the inside, the unofficial version of things. With their clear focus on sensation and experience, the texts question the ethical positioning at work in exposing the lives and the pain of others, a positioning which is at the crossroads between the rendering of an experience of dejection, abjection and even dehumanization and also, at times, of potential solidarity and reconfiguration of the self and the other. By bringing the other to the forefront, they may also point to a certain "politicity" of literature in the words of Jacques Rancière, calling for another "distribution of the sensible" and prompting a reflection on who speaks in a common space.

Marie-Luise Egbert's discussion of a novel by the Irish writer Flann O'Brien has its place in our book not only because its English version deconstructs stereotypes which British audiences had about Irish poverty, but also because it raises important general questions about hegemonies involved in representing the poor. *The Poor Mouth* (1973) is a satire of clichés about the West of Ireland. Originally written in Gaelic and translated into English three decades later, it parodies the false romantizising of supposedly quintessential characteristics of country-dwellers in the West, notably their precarious material circumstances. The title of this mock-autobiography derives from the Irish English proverb "to put on the poor mouth", which means to exaggerate one's own poverty. The tale itself is indeed one of exaggeration and excess: the narrator tells of the perennial suffering of his community under preposterous conditions. But it transpires from his tale that the simple-minded villagers fatalistically accept their dreary existence because it makes them the more authentically Irish. While it must thus be noted that O'Brien criticizes the Irish themselves for effectively living up to the stereotypes that exist about them, his main object of satire is the small urban elite of writers and self-proclaimed experts of culture based in Dublin, who praised the Western coastal regions as the area where authentic Irish culture had survived but did not themselves know Gaelic well enough to gain an adequate idea of that culture. *The Poor Mouth* provides a template for the formulation of questions which have to be asked when poverty and precarity become the object of literary representation. One such question is that of the audiences being targeted – a point of considerable complexity in the present case since the Gaelic original of the book excluded those whom it satirized. Shifting the point of view from readers to writers, one must also pose the question of who is empowered to articulate the experience of poverty; given the particular language situation of post-independence Ireland in which O'Brien was writing, this question can be addressed with the help of approaches from postcolonial studies.

The subsequent chapters all explore modes of representing poverty, inequality and precarity in the late twentieth and twenty-first centuries. The first three of these chapters analyze narratives in contemporary 'literary' production that make the ethical *and* narrative challenges of such representation explicit. Eveline Kilian's chapter analyzes Rose Tremain's *The Road Home* (2007) and Kate Clanchy's *Antigona and Me* (2008) from an explicitly theoretical position. It investigates the productivity of Judith Butler's concept of recognition for the analysis of the two narratives' presentation of Eastern European migrants in Britain, thus addressing the new economic inequalities in post-1989 Europe and the question as to how refugees and economic migrants from the 'East' cope with Western capitalism as a now global frame of recognition. Kilian proposes a dialogue between a theoretical model and her literary examples whose purpose is twofold: to use the theory as a critical tool for the analysis of the epistemological and ethical concerns raised in the literary texts, and to use the results of this analysis to reflect back on the model itself in order to detect its strengths, but also its potential oversights and weaknesses. Clanchy's narrative about the author's relationship to her Kosovan nanny addresses problems of recognition in the face of unequal economic and power relations in a manner that also finds expression in the author's self-reflexive considerations and in the narrative handling of the text. It thus becomes clear that the terms of recognition are by no means universal, but particular, and that the centrality of recognition in Western philosophical thought might itself be a prerogative of the privileged. The same applies to the normative frames that regulate the recognition of the subject and are appealed to as standards of judgement.

Romain Nguyen Van likewise 'tests' theoretical assumptions – by Butler and Bourdieu – on a literary text: the novel *Morvern Callar* (1995) by the Scottish writer Alan Warner. Nguyen Van proposes to investigate the kind of connection that is established between precariousness, precarity and precariat under a neo-liberal economic order for a novel that gives voice to a low-paid female supermarket employee. As a neo-liberal job market and precarity are depicted, discontinuity emerges as a characteristic narrative matrix: *Morvern Callar* thematizes the discontinuous dynamics of precarity which inform its very narrative structure. In the same way as class consciousness and class politics seem to peter out in the nation of shoppers that Morvern, the main protagonist, seems to embody, so does the possibility of regarding the precariat as a class. Because precarity endangers collective dynamics of solidarity, the recognition of the shared precariousness of all life in the novel is in fact not presented as a cohesive and constant mode of being for the main protagonist, but rather as sudden flickering moments and fragile narrative constructs.

Following Slavoj Žižek, Georg Zipp employs a visual concept when he reads John Berger's novel *King: A Street Story* (1999) 'paralactically'. A parallax is the apparent displacement of an object caused by a change in the point of observation. Zipp shows how Berger's novel experiments with accustomed ways of seeing homeless people by working with changed and constantly changing points of observation. Such parallaxes run deep through Berger's novel: they manifest themselves at various structural and interpretative levels and constitute attempts to make readers question their positions *vis à vis* poverty and to thus change the way they see poverty.

Aesthetically less complex representations of poverty are the focus of Barbara Korte's chapter, which is specifically concerned with contemporary literature about poverty produced in popular genres. More widely understood, however, popular treatments of poverty are not restricted to genre, and they have an important legacy in Victorian forms of popular representation. Since popular representation is meant to be accessible and attractive to its audiences, it has a high potential for shaping the public imagination. With respect to poverty, this may have the advantage of promoting the public awareness of social suffering, but since popular literature also has a special affinity to the market and to 'entertainment', its treatment of poverty raises ethical concerns, especially when it encourages stereotypical ways of seeing the poor and their conditions of life.

That such concerns can be justified is discussed in relation to historical romance and crime fiction. Yet, popular fiction in literature or film can also effectively subvert patterns of perception and formulas of representation.

The pros and cons of popular engagements with poverty and precarity are also addressed in the book's final chapter, in which Helen Hester investigates contemporary British 'reality TV'. In particular, Hester examines the emergence of the so-called 'poverty porn' phenomenon, and considers how and why certain forms of non-sexually explicit imagery are currently associated with the pornographic. She interrogates the manner in which reality TV representations of 'welfare culture' and the urban working classes have come to be entangled with a particular set of cultural anxieties about pornography. Not only are 'poverty porn' texts criticized for reducing real-life economic hardships to a series of affecting spectacles, but they are also seen as courting some highly dubious forms of viewer engagement. Hester argues that prurience is frequently positioned as a barrier to ethical engagement, as the viewer is distanced from the images on screen and need not confront the reality or the politics of that which is depicted. But poverty porn can also refuse viewer passivity and actively invite intervention. Drawing upon Leo Bersani and Ulysse Dutoit's work on the inherently dysfunctional nature of the sympathetic impulse, this chapter stages a reclaiming of prurience, arguing that a lascivious interest in enjoying the spectacle of suffering may, in fact, play an unacknowledged role in facilitating social and political change.

Several trajectories make these chapters speak to each other: A historical line runs from the Victorian period to the present cultural moment, and several essays indicate connections between various phases in the representation of poverty and precarity in British cultural production. All chapters are concerned in various ways with the agencies of representation; social asymmetries between representing agencies and represented subjects; ethical implications of 'voice' and 'listening'; limits of enunciation and narratability; the dangers of stereotyped representation and ways of countering them, the pitfalls of sensationalism, voyeurism and sentimentalism in the portrayal of social suffering; potentials and restrictions inherent in certain narrative techniques, genres and representational modes; performative functions of representation and the configuration of audience response; and, finally, cultural markets for poverty representation. It is no coincidence that, in terms of a wider theoretical framework, several essays reference Judith Butler's discussions of precarious life – one of the most influential and widely debated contributions to ethical, biopolitical and literary-political criticism in recent years in which poverty and precarity have an obvious place.[9] Overall, however, the chapters suggest that analysis of poverty narratives requires not only theorization, but an intersection of theoretical reflection and a close reading of texts. Close readings demonstrate how general issues associated with poverty combine in specific ways in specific texts, and how individual texts develop an idiosyncratic aesthetic to negotiate poverty. By nature of the phenomenon it represents, poverty representation is conflicted, contradictory and resists generalization, and this should be brought out by critical scrutiny.[10]

Works Cited

Betensky, Carolyn. *Feeling for the Poor: Bourgeois Compassion, Social Action, and the Victorian Novel.* Charlottesville: University of Virginia Press, 2010.

──. "Princes as Paupers: Pleasure and the Imagination of Powerlessness." *Cultural Critique* 56 (2004): 129–157.

Bourdieu, Pierre, ed. *The Weight of the World: Social Suffering in Contemporary Society.* Stanford, CA: Stanford University Press, 1999. [Translation of *La Misère du monde.* Paris: Seuil, 1993].

Brüns, Elke. "Einleitung: Plädoyer für einen social turn in der Literaturwissenschaft." *Ökonomien der Armut: Soziale Verhältnisse in der Literatur.* Ed. Elke Brüns, München: Fink, 2008. 7–19.

Butler, Patrick. "London: An Urban Neo-Victorian Dystopia." *The Guardian* 2 December 2011. www.theguardian.com/uk/2011/dec/02/uk-2017-london-dystopia (20 September 2013).

Carroll, William C. *Fat King, Lean Beggar: Representations of Poverty in the Age of Shakespeare.* Ithaca, NY: Cornell University Press, 1996.

Channel 4 News. "What Would Dickens Write about If He Were Alive Today?". 7 February 2012. http://www.channel4.com/news/what-would-dickens-write-about-if-he-were-alive-today (29 October 2013).

Couldry, Nick. *Why Voice Matters: Culture and Politics After Neoliberalism.* London: Sage, 2010.

Crassons, Kate. *The Claims of Poverty: Literature, Culture, and Ideology in Late Medieval England.* Notre Dame, IN: University of Notre Dame Press, 2010.

Davis, Todd F., and Kenneth Womack. "Preface: Reading Literature and the Ethics of Criticism." *Mapping the Ethical Turn: A Reader in Ethics, Culture, and Literary Theory.* Eds. Todd F. Davis and Kenneth Womack. Charlottesville: University Press of Virginia, 2001. ix–xiv.

du Gay, Paul et al. *Doing Cultural Studies: The Story of the Sony Walkman.* Milton Keynes: Open University Press, 1997.

---

9 For the centrality of narrative in other forms of 'precarious life' than poverty and economically-induced precarity see the contributions in Korte and Regard (2014).

10 Note that the authors' preferences for British or American spelling have been respected in the following chapters.

During, Simon. "From the Subaltern to the Precariat." *Academia.edu.* https://www.academia. edu/4547447/From_the_subaltern_to_the_precariat (11 April 2014).

Frank, Judith. *Common Ground: Eighteenth-Century English Satiric Fiction and the Poor.* Stanford, CA: Stanford University Press, 1997.

Freeman, Mark. "'Journeys into Poverty Kingdom': Complete Participation and the British Vagrant, 1886–1914." *History Workshop Journal* 52 (Autumn 2001): 99–121.

Gandal, Keith. "Poverty Studies." *Inside Higher Education* 29 June 2009. http://www.insidehighered.com/views/2009/06/29/gandal (23 April 2013).

——. *The Virtues of the Vicious: Jacob Riis, Stephen Crane, and the Spectacle of the Slum.* New York: Oxford University Press, 1998.

Hall, Stuart. *The Politics of Representation.* Minneapolis, MN: Silha Center for the Study of Media Ethics and Law, 1987.

Hazell, Dinah. *Poverty in Late Middle English Literature: The Meene and the Riche.* Dublin: Four Courts Press, 2009.

Head, Dominic. "The Demise of Class Fiction." *A Concise Companion to Contemporary British Fiction.* Ed. James F. English. Oxford: Blackwell, 2006. 229–247.

Hepburn, James. *A Book of Scattered Leaves: Poetry of Poverty in Broadside Ballads of Nineteenth-Century England.* Lewisburg, PA: Bucknell University Press, 2000.

Himmelfarb, Gertrude. *Poverty and Compassion: The Moral Imagination of the Late Victorians.* London: Faber, 1991.

——. *The Idea of Poverty: England in the Early Industrial Age.* London: Faber, 1984.

Hoggart, Simon. "Work and Pensions Cuts Take Inspiration from Dickens." *The Guardian* 19 October 2010. http://www.guardian.co.uk/politics/2010/oct/19/work-pensions-cuts-simon-hoggart (28 October 2013).

Hunt, Tristram. "Why Dickens Is so Relevant Today." *The Guardian* 12 October 2008. http://www.guardian.co.uk/books/2008/oct/12/charlesdickens (28 October 2013).

Jones, Gavin Roger. *American Hungers: The Problem of Poverty in U.S. Literature, 1840–1945.* Princeton, NJ: Princeton University Press, 2008.

King, Steven et al., eds. *Narratives of the Poor in Eighteenth-Century Britain.* 5 vols. London: Pickering and Chatto, 2006.

Korte, Barbara. "Dealing with Deprivation: Figurations of Poverty on the Contemporary British Book Market." *Anglia* 130.1 (2012): 75–94.

Korte, Barbara, and Frédéric Regard, eds. *Narrating 'Precariousness': Modes and Media.* Heidelberg: Winter, 2014.

Korte, Barbara, and Georg Zipp. *Poverty in Contemporary Literature: Themes and Figurations on the British Book Market.* Basingstoke: Palgrave Pivot, 2014.

Kumar, Krishan. "Versions of the Pastoral: Poverty and the Poor in English Fiction from the 1840s to the 1950s." *Journal of Historical Sociology* 8.1 (1995): 1–35.

Lenard, Mary. *Preaching Pity: Dickens, Gaskell, and Sentimentalism in Victorian Culture.* Frankfurt am Main: Peter Lang, 1999.

Lewis, David, Dennis Rodgers, and Michael Woolcock. "The Fiction of Development: Literary Representation as a Source of Authoritative Knowledge." *Journal of Development Studies* 44.2 (2008): 198–216.

Metrowebukmetro. "Young Underclass Living in 'Dickensian' Poverty." *Metro* 9 September 2009. metro.co.uk/2009/09/09/young-underclass-living-in-dickensian-poverty-397788 (20 September 2013).

Michaels, Walter Benn. *The Trouble with Diversity: How We Learned to Love Identity and Ignore Inequality.* New York: Metropolitan, 2006.

Nussbaum, Martha. *Creating Capabilities: The Human Development Approach.* Cambridge, MA: Harvard University Press, 2011.

Rancière, Jacques. *The Politics of Aesthetics: The Distribution of the Sensible.* Trans. Gabriel Rockhill. London: Continuum, 2004.

Salamon, Gayle. "Here Are the Dogs: Poverty in Theory." *Differences: A Journal of Feminist Cultural Studies* 21.1 (2010): 169–177.

Scott, Anne M. *Piers Plowman and the Poor.* Dublin: Four Courts Press, 2004.

Screening the Poor 1818–1914. DVD. Deutsches Filminstitut, Medienwissenschaft Universität Trier and Filmmuseum München, 2011.

Sedmak, Clemens. *Dichte Beschreibungen: Erzählte Armut. Vom Wert der Literatur für die Armutsforschung.* Working Papers "Facing Poverty": University of Salzburg, 2003. http://www.uni-salzburg.at/pls/portal/docs/1/1909249.PDF (23 April 2013).

Sen, Amartya. "Poverty, Evil and Crime." *UNDP* 5 October 2007. http://content.undp.org/go/newsroom/2007/october/amartya-sen-poverty-evil-and-crime.es (28 May 2013).

Smith, Sheila. *The Other Nation: The Poor in English Novels of the 1840s and 1850s.* Oxford: Clarendon Press, 1980.

Spivak, Gayatri Chakravorty. "Can the Subaltern Speak?". *Marxism and the Interpretation of Culture.* Eds. Cary Nelson and Lawrence Grossberg. Urbana: University of Illinois Press, 1988. 271–313.

Taylor, Charles. *Modern Social Imaginaries.* Durham, NC: Duke University Press, 2004.

Tobin, Beth Fowkes. *Superintending the Poor: Charitable Ladies and Paternal Landlords in British Fiction, 1770–1860.* New Haven, CT: Yale University Press, 1993.

Williams, A. Susan. *The Rich Man and the Diseased Poor in Early Victorian Literature.* Basingstoke: Macmillan, 1987.

Yousef, Nancy. "The Poverty of Charity: Dickensian Sympathy." *Contemporary Dickens.* Ed. Eileen Gillooly. Columbus: Ohio State University Press, 2009. 53–74.

Carolyn Betensky
Envying the Poor:
Contemporary and Nineteenth-Century
Fantasies of Vulnerability

Few literary topoï reflect back on their generators more than representations of the poor. If an author's subject position is always a determining factor in her or his representations of character, voice, setting, mood, etc., how much more so it is – or seems to be – when the author engages in descriptions of poverty and characterizations of the poor. Since at least as far back as the days of the nineteenth-century social-problem novel in Britain and France, representations of poverty and the poor have seemed to invite their readers to question their authors' familiarity with the conditions and people they are writing about, not to speak of their intentions and ideological affiliations. Nineteenth-century novelists who wrote narratives featuring poor characters regularly anticipated and responded to such questions in the prefaces to their works[1] as well as in their novels themselves. And if we moderns have been trained by everyone this side of Barthes and Foucault to be mindful of how we make use of the concept of 'the author', we are not very different from 'naïve', pre-Saussurean readers, for all that, when it comes to reading representations of the poor. My point is that thinking about the author of a novel about poverty when one reads it is not strange. Thinking about the author is the norm.

   I want to begin with the way the notion of 'the author' tends to loom so inescapably over representations of 'the poor' because I am interested in holding in focus, for a bit, the authorial subject position. It may seem counterproductive or at least counterintuitive to suggest, in a volume about representations of poverty and precarity, that it might be helpful to think more, not less, of the particulars of the position of what, in the case of the nineteenth-century texts I study, is the focalizing class. After all, there is something obscene about the way narratives by people of means that represent poverty almost always end up being at least as much about the interesting conscience of the caring rich as they are about the suffering of the poor. Yet this attention to the subjectivity of the caring rich is, in these narratives, doled out through the back door, as it were, by way of an attention to the suffering of the poor. It is a kind of attention that denies its own centrality (and hence novels with fairly scarce representation of poverty in

---

1 See Joanna Rostek's chapter in the present volume.

proportion to their length and plots can be known as novels 'about' poverty). Such a refusal to engage this subjectivity directly and seriously in non-normative ways[2] has consequences not only for understanding representations of poverty from the perspective of the non-poor (which still dominate the literary poverty-representation market), but also for defining strategies that could challenge the class structures that allow poverty to flourish.

This chapter considers the way the vulnerability of less privileged subjects – 'the poor' – gets packaged by the more privileged – 'the rich' – as something to be envied in a transatlantic cultural tradition that goes back at least as far as the nineteenth century. In my discussion of contemporary politics of this envy and its nineteenth-century literary antecedents in Britain and France, I will not be suggesting that the rich truly want to be poor, obviously, but I will be arguing that the rich want something very badly that they identify (and have historically identified) as a privilege of the poor. They want it for themselves only, moreover, and they do not want the poor to have it. Envy of the poor frames the poor as having a special kind of power that, from the perspective of the envious, they do not deserve. This envy goes hand in hand with a sort of resentment from above. It is the resentment of the Wall Street traders who rage against those who dare single them out for causing the global economic meltdown and tell the ninety-nine percent to just go and get a job.[3] It is the claim that my victim status equals or outweighs yours, and that you do not merit the power that comes with your powerlessness.[4] Dominant-class envy of the vulnerability of the poor is far from new. It is, rather, baked into the very tropes that structured early social-problem narratives in Britain and France in the nineteenth century. They structured social-problem narratives in the United States as well, and no doubt in other economically unequal locales where the novel dominated the cultural field and where the novel was understood to be a philanthropic emissary that mediated class conflict. Envy of the poor – of the vulnerability of the poor perceived as the power of the poor – is contained in the very narrative strategies that made it possible for rich people to feel, while reading novels, for the poor.

---

2 By "non-normative ways", I mean in ways that move beyond a very understandable urge to condemn or celebrate it.
3 See, for example, Maureen Farrell's "Why Wall Street Hates Obama" (2013) for a summary of the reactions of former Obama supporters with deep pockets who turned against him in the wake of remarks they perceived as being insufficiently respectful of them.
4 On the phenomenon of the putative prestige of the oppressed, see my "Princes as Paupers" (2004).

I

The difficulty of considering the subjectivity of the relatively, let alone extremely, well-off in connection with representations of precarity may be seen clearly in critical responses to some of Judith Butler's recent work. In "Violence, Mourning, Politics", the second essay in her collection *Precarious Life: The Powers of Mourning and Violence* (2004), Butler writes of some of the ways the US responded to the attacks of September 11, 2001. In her view, the events could have provided the US with an opportunity to rethink our relations with nations of similarly vulnerable others who have long lived under such conditions of violence. Our vulnerability could have become, in Butler's words, the "basis of claims for nonmilitary political solutions" (2004, 29). But instead of recognizing the corporeal vulnerability US subjects share with all other humans, instead of seeing how this vulnerability is what makes us inescapably interdependent as subjects, the US opted for the usual show of might. Plenty of Americans protested the war in Afghanistan, the war in Iraq and the ongoing 'war on terror', but by far the dominant response among Americans was not to reflect on this vulnerability, but rather, to do just the opposite: to both deny it and claim it as our own sacred property. In the course of denying our vulnerability through what Butler calls an "institutionalized fantasy of mastery" (2004, 29), we have managed simultaneously to idolize our own dead and to dehumanize, or as Butler explains, to re-dehumanize, the many thousands of dead Iraqi and Afghan others killed by our armies and mercenaries and drones.

In *Frames of War* (2009), Butler extends her focus on precariousness to consider precarity. "Precariousness and precarity are intersecting concepts", she writes, "Lives are by definition precarious; they can be expunged at will or by accident; their persistence is in no sense guaranteed" (2009, 25). Yet although Butler is claiming that precarity is a kind of precariousness, she is by no means saying that everyone is equally precarious. Some humans suffer under exceedingly precarious conditions, as she makes very clear:

> Precarity designates that politically induced condition in which certain populations suffer from failing social and economic networks of support and become differentially exposed to injury, violence, and death. Such populations are at heightened risk of disease, poverty, starvation, displacement, and of exposure to violence without protection. Precarity also characterizes that politically induced condition of maximized precariousness for populations exposed to arbitrary state violence who often have no other option than to appeal to the very state from which they need protection. (2009, 25–26)

Precariousness defines us all, but not all of us are as thoroughly and systemically challenged by precariousness as others. If we are all vulnerable, in other words, some of us are considerably more vulnerable than others. In "Butler's Biopolitics: Precarious Community" (2012), Janell Watson takes Butler to task for promoting a politics of universal vulnerability. While allowing that she distinguishes between "precariousness" and "precarity", Watson (2012) maintains that Butler is subsuming poverty under the aegis of precariousness all the same, and further, that Butler sees this all-for-one, one-for-all precariousness as some kind of idealistic *program* for social justice:

> Corporeal fragility both equalizes and differentiates: all bodies are menaced by suffering, injury, and death (precariousness), but some bodies are more protected and others more exposed (precarity). Precariousness is shared by all; precarity is 'distributed unequally' (Butler 2010, xvii, xxv, 25). Butler's egalitarian remedy to the social ills of unequally imposed precarity? Precariousness for all. Vulnerability will serve as the basis for a new kind of community. Precariousness will save the world from precarity. These are Butler's precarious propositions.

Watson contends that Butler's focus on the vulnerable subject rules out a collective, social approach to social change. Her choice to direct her attention to the precarious existence of the relatively well-to-do is itself the sign of her abandonment of the poor: "Rather than seeking to empower the weak – those who are living in precarity – Butler instead insists on the vulnerability of those who deny their precariousness" (2012).[5] Julian Reid, meanwhile, faults Butler for reproducing, in her focus on this shared vulnerability, the very conditions of liberal subjectivity that she wishes to counter: "the subject's vulnerability, based on exposure to an unknown and dangerous domain of relations, instantiates the very demand for protection on which liberal governance depends for its legitimation in relation to the subject" (2011, 773). He contrasts her dependent and vul-

---

5 Butler seems to have Watson's critique in mind when she clarifies her position on vulnerability as a central point from which to organize political change in an interview conducted via email round-table by Jasbir Puar: "[W]hat is at stake is a way of rethinking social relationality. We can make the broad existential claim, namely, that everyone is precarious, and this follows from our social existence as bodily beings who depend upon one another for shelter and sustenance and who, therefore, are at risk of statelessness, homelessness, and destitution under unjust and unequal political conditions. As much as I am making such a claim, I am also making another, namely, that our precarity is to a large extent dependent upon the organization of economic and social relationships, the presence or absence of sustaining infrastructures and social and political institutions. In this sense, precarity is indissociable from that dimension of politics that addresses the organization and protection of bodily needs. Precarity exposes our sociality, the fragile and necessary dimensions of our interdependency" (Puar 2012, 170).

nerable subject to a fantasized "hubristic" subject that can "transcend its vulnerabilities, destroy their sources, and free itself from them" (2011, 775).

Watson's and Reid's arguments rejecting Butler's positioning of vulnerability at the center of her political vision are flawed in a number of ways.[6] But what concerns me here is the way they both call her out for focusing on the liberal subject. In Watson's either/or formulation, Butler had a choice between the weak and, by implication, the strong – and she problematically opted to theorize from the position of the strong. Reid, on the other hand, does not see his liberal-subject-in-the-making among the vulnerability-deniers, as Watson does, but rather, among those Watson labels weak, and thus discounts the importance of acknowledging and analyzing it in those who are already reaping the benefits of liberal subjectivity. The bourgeois subject, with all of the imperatives and prerogatives and entitlements the term implies, needs to be engaged directly. Not engaging directly with the vulnerable bourgeois subject will not make it go away. Not engaging directly with the vulnerable bourgeois subject allows an especially pernicious side of its vulnerability – its envy of the other's vulnerability – to remain unmarked.

Vulnerability *denied* (and simultaneously idolized as victimhood) is intimately connected to vulnerability *envied*. The refusal to acknowledge our vulnerability gives it tremendous power over us. Disavowing it, we split it off from ourselves and locate it in the other, where we can both hate it and (secretly) love it.[7]

---

6 Watson ignores the disciplinary context in which Butler is making her intervention and suggests Butler's use of personal pronouns betrays her "general mistrust of the collective". Yet Butler is writing in a philosophical tradition in which such use of pronouns is commonplace. Watson also disregards the specifically *gendered* philosophical approach Butler is working from: Butler's focus on vulnerability puts her in conversation with a broader ethics of care that is gaining prominence among politically engaged feminist philosophers (Ann V. Murphy's "Corporeal Vulnerability and the New Humanism" (2011) for an overview). While Reid's critique of Butler eschews her notion of the subject for its always already liberal formulation, his own preferred "hubristic" rhetoric is highly masculinist and individualistic in ways that recall not only a bootstraps-ready, can-do liberalism but also a more nefarious neo-liberalism.

7 My understanding of the phenomenon of envy has been profoundly influenced by the writings of Melanie Klein. For Klein, envy implies more than just wanting what the other has: it also, crucially, implies projection onto that other. It is not just that I resent the good stuff the other has and want it for myself; I split off the hateful parts of myself – what I do not or cannot abide in myself – and ascribe them to that other. Once my "badness" is projected into the other, I can safely hate – or destroy – that other for manifesting (as I have constructed her) the hatefulness I feel toward her. In this way, the other (or rather, the other as what Klein calls the "internalized persecuting object") can be seen as "grudging and envious owing to the individual's envy being projected onto it"; and now I may perceive this other, furthermore, as dangerous to me (Klein 1987, 224).

If we fail to consider the envy of the poor other's vulnerability as a constituent component of the logic of late-stage capitalist hegemony (and the security state), we will be bewildered by the sheer profusion of rage that any demand for redress and equity evokes in the vulnerability-disavowing 'rich'. Further, and more importantly, we will be struck by the irony of claims of victimhood on the part of the relatively powerful, but we will not be able to appreciate them as additions to the hegemonic arsenal.

If envy on the part of the dominant classes goes underreported, there is no shortage of coverage when it comes to representing the envy and rage of the poor. In the 2012 US presidential campaign, for instance, multimillionaire Republican candidate Mitt Romney (2012) let loose at President Obama and other critics who had charged him with callousness to the plight of the economically struggling majority. Upon winning his party's primary in New Hampshire, he proclaimed:

> President Obama wants to put free enterprise on trial. In the last few days, we have seen some desperate Republicans join forces with him. This is such a mistake for our Party and for our nation. This country already has a leader who divides us with the bitter politics of envy. We must offer an alternative vision. I stand ready to lead us down a different path, where we are lifted up by our desire to succeed, not dragged down by a resentment of success.

The next day Romney was asked by television reporter Matt Lauer in an interview on NBC's *Today* show what he had meant by 'envy': "Do you suggest that anyone who questions the policies and practices of Wall Street and financial institutions, anyone who has questions about the distribution of wealth and power in this country, is envious? Is it about jealousy, or is it about fairness?" And Romney answered,

> You know, I think it's about envy. I think it's about class warfare. I think – when you have a president encouraging the idea of dividing America based on 99 percent versus one percent, and those people who have been most successful will be in the one percent – you have opened up a whole new wave of approach in this country which is entirely inconsistent with the concept of 'one nation under God'. Everywhere we go – or he goes – we hear him talking about 'millionaires and billionaires and executives and Wall Street'. It's a very envy-oriented, attack-oriented approach and I think it will fail. (Lauer 2012)

The rhetorical casting of the Obama administration and critics of capitalism as 'envious' manages to put on the defensive those who protest the impoverishment of vast numbers of people. Cast as unruly children who have not mastered the emotional conduct that might render them fit to join the grownups at the table, the 'envious' find themselves in the absurd position of having to demonstrate that they do not, in fact, want what the 'envied' have. Thus Obama (2012) proclaimed in his State of the Union speech, two weeks later: "When Americans talk about folks like me paying my fair share of taxes, it's not because they envy the rich [...]. It's because they understand that when I get a tax break I don't need and the country can't afford, it either adds to the deficit, or somebody else has to make up the difference." And liberal *New York Times* columnist Charles Blow (2012) wrote that "this has nothing to do with envy and everything to do with fairness." No envy here – as if envy would be an unreasonable response to deprivation and gross inequality. Even *Rolling Stone* reporter Matt Taibbi (2011) rejected the notion of envy when he wrote:

> Think about it: there have always been rich and poor people in America, so if this is about jealousy, why the protests now? The idea that masses of people suddenly discovered a deep-seated animus/envy toward the rich – after keeping it strategically hidden for decades – is crazy. Where was all that class hatred in the Reagan years, when openly dumping on the poor became fashionable? Where was it in the last two decades, when unions disappeared and CEO pay relative to median incomes started to triple and quadruple? The answer is, it was never there. If anything, just the opposite has been true. Americans for the most part love the rich, even the obnoxious rich.

Taibbi is right, of course, that adoration of the rich prevails among Americans of all classes – but since when did love preclude envy?

Needless to say, the idea that you should not have any hostile feelings toward people who have what you want for yourself is bewildering in its own right. But it is important to pay attention to the rhetorical operations Romney deploys in the passage quoted above. When he speaks of the need to come together and not dwell on what divides us, he is actually keying into a theme of liberal reformist discourse. It is not for nothing that the right wing in the US has been busy over the last few years trying to claim that Martin Luther King was really a free market capitalist.[8] 'We' are not the haters; we love and respect and tolerate each other. 'They' – the misinformed dividers, haters, enviers who foster class warfare – must be overcome.[9]

---

8 See Peter Montgomery, "Co-opting King: Why the Right Tries to Reclaim MLK" (2012), for a brief summary of attempts on the far right to portray King as one of their own.

9 It should be remarked, incidentally, that this rhetoric is not just limited to the American scene. Nicolas Sarkozy sounded the same note in France on May 1st, 2012: "Regardez les cortèges. Ils ont choisi de défiler avec le drapeau rouge, nous avons choisi de nous rassembler sous le drapeau tricolore. Nous voulons de grands projets pour un grand pays qui s'appelle la France. Nous ne voulons pas de l'égalitarisme, nous ne voulons pas de la haine, nous ne voulons pas de la lutte des classes, nous ne voulons pas du socialisme" (Euronews 2012).

Claiming the moral authority of the abused minority, Romney's speech framed the rich and successful as victims: victims of envy, victims of resentment, victims of class warfare. This is precisely where the envy of the rich for the vulnerability of the poor comes in. For Romney's contention that the poor envy the rich cloaks an expression of envy for a position the poor and disenfranchised have historically occupied: the rich quite literally envy the poor for being able rightly to call attention to themselves for being vulnerable.[10] As I said before, the rich do not envy the poor for their material conditions, nor do they envy the poor for being vulnerable within the material conditions the poor inhabit. Rather, the rich envy the poor for having an experience they themselves would like to have – without having to forfeit their position of relative privilege. Being vulnerable is thus an impossible dream, a seductive alternative reality, for those who have committed themselves to the "institutionalized fantasy of mastery" that Butler describes.

You can see right here that if the institution of the novel did not already exist, it would have had to be invented to give voice to the terrible ambivalence of this classed position. And you can see why nineteenth-century novels that address poverty would so frequently arrange for the rich to experience some of the same mistreatment as the poor objects of their sympathy. Contemporary claims to sympathy and expressions of resentment issued by agents of the 'one percent' are a legacy of discursive configurations first made available in nineteenth-century British and French reformist novels. As I have argued previously in *Feeling for the Poor*, the same narrative strategies that attempted to humanize the poor before a middle-class readership invited this middle-class readership to feel what the poor felt *as if they were poor* – and in so doing, these strategies expanded the range of subject positions available to the middle-class imagination. The power of narratives that draw attention to the oppression of the working classes, in other words, has not been lost on the dominant classes. Even as agents of the 'one percent' discount the claims of the dispossessed, they pay tribute to the power of the narrative structures that have come to typify such claims by restyling them into demands for sympathy for themselves – and only for themselves. I want to suggest that the right-wing ascription to the poor and their supporters of a "bitter politics of envy" in the US might better be understood as a screen for an expression of profound envy on their own part, an envy not of the conditions of

---

10 The pioneering British Object-Relations psychoanalyst Joan Riviere remarks a similar envy of the suffering of women on the part of men: "It appears [...] that, just as women envy men's initiative, conversely men envy women's capacity for passive experience, especially the capacity to bear and to suffer. Suffering relieves guilt; especially is the pain that brings life into the world double enviable unconsciously to men" (1964, 34).

poverty that propel claims to justice but of the perceived power of the narrative structures and subject positions from which such claims are made.

II

George Sand's novel *Le Compagnon du Tour de France* came out in 1840. It is very different from Benjamin Disraeli's *Sybil, or the Two Nations*, which appeared in 1845. Set in the time of the French Restoration of the Bourbon monarchy (1815 – 1830), the Sand novel is the story of a romance between an aristocratic woman named Yseult and a carpenter named Pierre; they fall in love while Pierre is restoring her grandfather's ancestral mansion, and although Yseult is all for abandoning her class and family privilege to be with Pierre, Pierre rejects her. It is not that he does not love her; rather, it is that he feels that class barriers are insuperable. The aristocratic and bourgeois characters he meets all go out of their way to treat him with reverence for being an artist and man of the people, and he continually and proudly insists on his place – his place as a worker, not as an exceptional, artistic friend of the house. The Disraeli novel, on the other hand, is also a romance, but here it is an aristocratic man named Egremont who falls in love with a woman of the people, the eponymous Sybil. Egremont goes undercover as a journalist among the poor and working classes after suffering disappointments in his personal life. Sybil, who is training to be a nun, is the daughter of a popular leader and militantly opposed to the continued rule of the landed classes (the novel is set in the era of the Reform Bill but defends itself against the arguments of the Chartists). Unlike the aristocratic Yseult in Sand's novel, the upper-class Egremont does succeed in his quest for the heart of the woman of the people, even though she rejects him the first time round with vehemence. Egremont is ultimately elected to Parliament, where he makes a speech expressing sympathy for the poor and working classes but suggesting that they are not ready yet for a greater share of power. Things do not go so well for the other poor and working class characters in the novel, but by observing Egremont, Sybil ends up learning that rich people really can be good. (She also learns that she is the rightful heiress to a fortune and an old family line, independently of Egremont).

Even though both of these novels feature courtship plots that hinge explicitly on overcoming class difference, they take very different positions on class difference. Politically, George Sand and Benjamin Disraeli could probably not have been further apart. Sand was an inveterate rebel, a strong proponent for the rights of women and a fervent socialist (in the 'romantic socialist' sense common among radical French intellectuals in this period) who went on in 1848 to participate in the formation of the short-lived Second Republic. Disraeli was, at the time he published this novel, thickly involved in the affairs of the conservative and nationalist Young England movement. He was a lifelong Tory who would go on to be a two-time Prime Minister and one of Queen Victoria's most trusted advisors. Sand's sympathies were clearly with the people, and the novel takes their side as well, whereas Disraeli's public position and his novel's premise were that the poor and working classes needed to be protected and guided by the aristocracy. Yet despite the fact that these authors and their novels are politically so dissimilar, both novels see fit to include scenes of backlash against the poor for whom they are at the same time trying to develop sympathy.

At one point in Sand's novel, Pierre finds himself confronted by an insecure bourgeois Carbonarist conspirator named Achille. Achille is unnerved when he mistakenly believes Pierre to know more about a revolutionary plot than he does. Angrily, he says to Pierre:

> Mon rôle est plus difficile que le vôtre [...] Vous êtes le peuple, c'est-à-dire, l'aristocratie, le souverain, que nous autres conspirateurs du tiers-état nous venons implorer pour la cause de la justice et de la vérité. Vous nous traitez en subalternes; vous nous questionnez avec hauteur, avec méfiance; vous nous demandez si nous sommes des fous et des intrigants; vous nous faites subir mille affronts, convenez de cela! Et quand nous ne poussons pas l'esprit de propagande jusqu'à l'humilité chrétienne, quand notre sang tressaille dans nos veines, et que nous prétendons être traités par vous comme vos égaux, vous nous dites que nous n'étions pas sincères, que nous portons au dedans de nous la haine et l'orgueil; en un mot, que nous sommes des imposteurs et des lâches qui descendons à vous implorer pour vous exploiter. (Sand 1988, 273)

> It's harder for me than it is for you. You are the people, that is to say, the aristocrats, the sovereign, whom we third-estate conspirators have to beg for help in our pursuit of justice and truth. You treat us like second-class citizens. You question us with haughtiness and disdain. You ask us whether we're lunatics or schemers. You make us endure all of your insults. But then, if we fail to toe the party line to the point of abject Christian humility, if we act like red-blooded human beings once in a while and expect you to treat us as equals, you come back and tell us we never were sincere in our feelings, that our hearts are full of hatred and pride. Then you go around and say we're impostors and cowards who are only interested in exploiting you. (my translation)

This is not the only time in the novel a rich character calls Pierre an uncaring aristocrat and demands a more sympathetic reception. Just a little before his encounter with Achille, Pierre gets lectured by Yseult's grandfather, a count who prides himself on being modern and free of class prejudice:

> Elle vous a fait, en mon nom, des offres de service, des promesses d'amitié; elle a parlé selon son coeur. Vous avez rejeté ces offres avec une fierté qui vous rend encore plus estimable à mes yeux, et qui me fait un devoir de vous servir malgré vous. Prenez donc garde

d'être injuste, Pierre! Je sais d'avance tout ce que votre vieux républicain de père a pu vous dire pour vous mettre en garde contre moi. J'estime infiniment votre père, et ne veux pas blesser ses préjugés; mais il y a cette différence entre lui et moi, qu'il est l'homme du passé, et que moi son aîné, je suis pourtant l'homme du présent. Je me flatte de mieux comprendre l'égalité que lui; et si vous refusez de me confier le secret de votre peine, je croirai comprendre la fraternité humaine mieux que vous aussi. (Sand 1988, 264–265)

She has offered you my help and promised you my friendship, just as I would have hoped. You have rejected our offers with a pride that makes me respect you even more and that makes me feel as if I am duty-bound to serve you whether you like it or not. Be careful not to be unjust, Pierre. I already know what your old republican father must have told you to put you on guard with me. I have only admiration for your father, and I don't want to disturb him in his prejudices, but you should know that there's a big difference between him and me. He's a man of the past, and I – even though I'm older than he is – am a man of the present. I believe that I know better than he does what equality is. If you don't open up to me, I'm going to think that I know what fraternity is better than you do, too. (my translation)

Of course Yseult's grandfather changes his tune the moment he learns that his granddaughter has been romantically interested in the laborer, and all of his professions of equality and fraternity get tossed aside pretty quickly.

When, in Disraeli's novel, Egremont reveals his true identity to Sybil and her father, he explains that he had deceived them in order to circumvent the prejudice he expected them to display upon encountering a man of his high social position. He had been instructed, he says, that "an impassable gulf divided the Rich from the Poor; I was told that the Privileged and the People formed Two Nations, governed by different laws, influenced by different manners, with no thoughts or sympathies in common; with an innate inability of mutual comprehension" (299).[11] He begs Sybil to forgive him and accept his friendship in spite of his family affiliation, but she refuses: "'Oh, sir!' said Sybil, haughtily; 'I am one of those who believe the gulf is impassable. Yes... utterly impassable'" (300). Egremont is forced to look "in despair upon this maiden walled out from sympathy by prejudices and convictions more impassable than all the mere consequences of class" (300). The following day, Egremont returns to see Sybil. Tempers have cooled on both sides, but he still faces an indomitable foe in her prejudice. This is how Sybil sees Egremont: "A Norman, a noble, an oppressor of the people, a plunderer of the church – all of the characters and capacities that Sybil had been bred up to look upon with fear and aversion, and to recognize as the authors of the degradation of her race" (333). He approaches her, saying, "You seemed to treat with scorn yesterday [...] the belief that sympa-

---

11 All page numbers for Disraeli's novel refer to the 1985 Penguin edition.

thy was independent of the mere accidents of position. Pardon me, Sybil, but even you may be prejudiced" (333). He continues a moment later: "You look upon me as an enemy, as a natural foe, because I am born among the privileged. I am a man, Sybil, as well as a noble" (333). Finally, he insists that the People need to trust the rising generation of aristocrats to work on their behalf:

> The new generation of the aristocracy of England are not tyrants, not oppressors, Sybil, as you persist in believing. Their intelligence, better than that, their hearts are open to the responsibility of their position. [...] Enough that their sympathies are awakened; time and thought will bring the rest. They are the natural leaders of the People, Sybil; believe me they are the only ones. (334)

Both of these cases contrive to pin prejudice, unfairness and closed-mindedness onto the poor, and feature good, humane, sensitive rich people who have themselves overcome the old class warfare habit. These novels reside, in official political terms, on opposite ends of the spectrum from each other, yet they are oddly in sync with one another in this respect. In Sand's novel, Pierre is a paid laborer who gets told again and again how he needs to understand how some rich people really care about the poor – and if he does not get that immediately, he is behaving like a new, topsy-turvy incarnation of Louis XVI. Disraeli's Egremont, in the meantime, is wronged, grievously wronged, by the woman of the people who cannot see that he is different from the rich people she has been taught about. In both of these novels, class conflict is maintained by the *poor* character. When Sybil claims ("haughtily") that she believes the "great gulf" between the classes is "impassable", Disraeli is delivering the responsibility for this great gulf into her lap – and by extension, at the door of the poor and working classes.

I have brought these two particular novels together because they provide very explicit examples of vulnerable, misunderstood, resentful, sympathy-craving rich characters facing down oppressive poor ones. But while these representations of the aggrieved rich and the stubbornly class-fixated poor are especially pronounced, the backlash structure that conditions them can be seen across the nineteenth-century social-problem novel genre. Middle-class social-problem novels – like Elizabeth Gaskell's *Mary Barton* (1848) and *North and South* (1855), Charlotte Brontë's *Shirley* (1849), Charles Dickens's *Hard Times* (1854), George Eliot's *Felix Holt, the Radical* (1866), Eugène Sue's *Les Mystères de Paris* (1842–1843), Victor Hugo's *Les Misérables* (1862), just to name a few – take for their themes or backgrounds the daunting economic and social abuses facing the newly urbanized and industrialized working classes in Britain and the relatively unindustrialized but much more revolution-prone poor of France. These novels purport to be novels about the problems of the poor, but they are at the same time novels about how the poor are a problem for the rich. And when I say problem, I mean opportunity: novels about poverty written from positions of relative privilege offer their readers a most compelling and seductive character with whom to identify – the one good rich person, and this character gives the reader the opportunity to learn about and feel for the suffering of the poor, right alongside her or him. The story of the development of the one good rich person's knowledge and feelings about the poor often provides the primary focus of these narratives, so that the inner life of the one good rich person tends to overtake poverty as their overriding theme.

But this one good rich person with the very interesting feelings is only part of the picture. Social-problem novels could not *be* social-problem novels if they did not represent the poor as being able to have feelings just like the rich. (Drawing their readers to grasp the idea that the poor have feelings is often touted as a great achievement of social-problem novels – their raison d'être.) These novels are said to humanize the poor, to make them more sympathy-worthy, by demonstrating that 'they' are like 'us'. But if 'they' are like 'us', 'we' can be like 'them'. If 'they' are just like 'us', 'they' can have rich inner lives as we like to think we do, lives worth respecting as we like to think we do our own – all very good. But even better is that if 'they' are just like us, then 'they' can be just as ignorant and oppressive as we are – and we can be as hurt by 'them' as 'they' are by us. The demonstration of affective commonality across the classes that emerges in the nineteenth century for the consumption of a middle-class reading public produces a new and unfamiliar mode of being for bourgeois subjects – right up there alongside its production of sympathetic poor people. Ultimately, the 'discovery' of poverty that these novels collectively rehearse for their readers conditions another discovery – the discovery of the bourgeois subject with the potential to be vulnerable, misunderstood and blameless. And this bourgeois subject can be just as vulnerable, misunderstood and blameless as, and even more vulnerable, misunderstood and blameless than, the suffering poor upon whose plight such narratives are premised. Scenes featuring vastly underestimated, falsely blamed, unfairly branded rich victims of poor people's meanness or thoughtlessness abound in the novels I have been working on, and they are also found in others: Elizabeth Gaskell's *North and South* features several scenes in which the heroine, a preacher's daughter, gets to tell the poor people she has befriended that they are very presumptuous for thinking that her life is so good. Dickens includes a number of comeuppance scenes in his novels where a poor character learns that rich people suffer, too: in *Hard Times*, for example, Stephen Blackpool learns as he lies dying of how mistaken he was for having had suspicions about Louisa Gradgrind. Charlotte Brontë's Shirley, in the novel *Shirley*, has the pleasure of telling off a whole slew of ignorant, protesting laborers that they have been unjust to the mill owner who has dispossessed them. It is hard, in fact, to find an example of a novel in the genre that *does not* feature this sort of backlash. And it is hard to read this sort of backlash without seeing it as the expression of deep and otherwise inexpressible envy lurking in the bourgeois political unconscious – an envy of the poor for getting to be weak, vulnerable, sinned against and worthy of sympathy.

Of course, all of those well-meaning nineteenth-century social-problem novels are not responsible for the production of Mitt Romney or Nicolas Sarkozy or any of those venture capitalists who complain about the trials of the one percent. But what the narrative humanization of the poor in the nineteenth century accomplished, along with making the poor interesting enough for bourgeois readers to care about them, was to make vulnerability itself a condition of such intense fascination and appeal that the rich could not leave it alone, even as they pursued their institutionalized fantasies of mastery. The notion that in vulnerability lay power derived from the attention bourgeois readers themselves brought to the texts they read about the suffering of the poor. It was the vulnerability of the poor – the ability of the poor to suffer just like the rich – that made them interesting to middle-class readers, but it was this interestingness and this ability to marshal sympathetic attention that made the poor objects of envy at the same moment as they became objects of sympathy. And as objects of envy, they had to be put in their place at the same time as they were being invited to the table.

Analyzing the incredible and improbable success of the radical right wing in the United States since the election of Barack Obama, Thomas Frank writes of their strangely gleeful attitude toward their own vulnerability:

> It was the orgasmaclysm: They tingled to imagine the outrageous injustices that would be done to them by the coming 'death panels'. They purred to hear about the campaign of 'indoctrination' that the new president had planned for their innocent kids; their pulse quickened to think of the 'chains' he was preparing for their mighty wrists; and they swelled with imagined bravery to picture how they would be targeted by 'the coming insurrection'. (2012, 66)

The anger of people who occupy positions of relative privilege toward people who are demonstrably more vulnerable than themselves is in some ways a tribute to the power of narrative strategies of representation that made vulnerability compelling and enviable. But here is the problem with this tribute: the power of powerlessness – if ever such power existed as anything more than a ripe fantasy in the bourgeois imaginary – ends up getting recuperated not only by the institutionalized fantasy of mastery but also as a functioning element of a veritable *technology* of mastery. Billionaires and corporations and totalitarian regimes have learned, alas, to be shrewder at marketing themselves as victims and reaping the benefits of their own phony victimization than the poor or working classes or their middle-class sympathizers ever were. The economist Paul Krugman wrote in May 2012 in the *New York Times* of the aggrieved Wall Street bankers who objected to Obama's latest putative offense to capitalism; he said that all of their complaining would be very funny, if only they did not have so many cards in their hands to begin with: "If Wall Streeters are spoiled brats, they are spoiled brats with immense power and wealth at their disposal. And what they're trying to do with that power and wealth right now is buy themselves not just policies that serve their interests, but immunity from criticism." Such immunity from criticism is precisely what the envy of the poor aims to consolidate, which is why it is so important to think about fantasies of vulnerability along with fantasies of mastery, and about the many terribly complex negotiations that go into representations of poverty.

Works Cited

Betensky, Carolyn. *Feeling for the Poor: Bourgeois Compassion, Social Action, and the Victorian Novel*. Victorian Literature and Culture Series. Charlottesville: University of Virginia Press, 2010.
——. "Princes as Paupers: Pleasure and the Imagination of Powerlessness." *Cultural Critique* 56.1 (2004): 129–157.
Blow, Charles M. "Bitter Politics of Envy?". *New York Times* 13 January 2012. http://www. nytimes.com/2012/01/14/opinion/blow-bitter-politics-of-envy.html?_r=0 (4 August 2013).
Butler, Judith. *Frames of War: When is Life Grievable?* New York: Verso, 2010.
——. *Precarious Life: The Powers of Mourning and Violence*. New York: Verso, 2004.
Disraeli, Benjamin. *Sybil, or the Two Nations*. New York: Penguin, 1985.
Euronews. "Nicolas Sarkozy revendique un 1er mai loin des syndicats et de la gauche." 1 May 2012. http://fr.euronews.com/2012/05/01/nicolas-sarkozy-revendique-un-1er-mai-loin-des-syndicats-et-de-la-gauche/ (4 August 2013).
Farrell, Maureen. "Why Wall Street Hates Obama." *CNNMoney* 6 November 2012. http://money.cnn.com/2012/11/06/investing/wall-street-hates-obama/ (3 August 2013).
Frank, Thomas. *Pity the Billionaire: The Hard-Time Swindle and the Unlikely Comeback of the Right*. New York: Metropolitan, 2012.
Klein, Melanie. "A Study of Envy and Gratitude." *The Selected Melanie Klein*. Ed. Juliet Mitchell. New York: Free Press, 1987. 55–119.
Krugman, Paul. "Egos and Immorality." *New York Times* 24 May 2012. http://www.nytimes.com/2012/05/25/opinion/krugman-egos-and-immorality.html (4 August 2013).
Lauer, Matt. Television-Interview with Mitt Romney. *Today*. NBC. 11 January 2012.
Montgomery, Peter. "Co-opting King: Why the Right Tries to Claim MLK." *Right Wing Watch* 4 April 2012. http://www.rightwingwatch.org/content/co-opting-king (4 August 2013).

Murphy, Ann V. "Corporeal Vulnerability and the New Humanism." *Hypatia* 26.3 (2011): 575–590.

Obama, Barack. "State of the Union Address." *Whitehouse Press Office*. 24 January 2012. http://www.whitehouse.gov/the-press-office/2012/01/24/remarks-president-state-union-address (4 August 2013).

Puar, Jasbir, ed. "Precarity Talk: A Virtual Roundtable with Lauren Berlant, Judith Butler, Bojana Cvejić, Isabell Lorey, Jasbir Puar, and Ana Vujanović." *TDR: The Drama Review* 56.4 (2012): 163–177.

Reid, Julian. "The Vulnerable Subject of Liberal War." *The South Atlantic Quarterly* 110.3 (2011): 770–779.

Riviere, Joan. "Hate, Greed and Aggression." *Love, Hate and Reparation*. Eds. Melanie Klein and Joan Riviere. New York: WW Norton, 1964. 1–53.

Romney, Mitt. "New Hamphire Victory Speech." *National Journal* 10 January 2012. http://www.nationaljournal.com/2012-presidential-campaign/text-mitt-romney-s-new-hampshire-victory-speech-20120110 (4 August 2013).

Sand, George. *Le Compagnon du Tour de France*. Grenoble: Presses Universitaires de Grenoble, 1988.

Taibbi, Matt. "Wall Street isn't Winning – It's Cheating." *Rolling Stone* 25 October 2011. http://www.rollingstone.com/politics/blogs/taibblog/owss-beef-wall-street-isnt-winning-its-cheating-20111025 (4 August 2013).

Watson, Janell. "Butler's Biopolitics: Precarious Community." *Theory & Event* 15.2 (2012): n. pag.

Joanna Rostek

Managing the Unmanageable: Paradoxes of Poverty in Harriet Martineau's *Illustrations of Political Economy* (1832 – 1834)

1 Introduction

With the following words, Harriet Martineau, the nineteenth-century writer, jour-nalist and, as Susan Hoecker-Drysdale (1992) maintains, first woman sociologist, looks back on the composition of what would turn out to be an unexpected pop-ular success – her *Illustrations of Political Economy:*

> I wrote the Preface to my 'Illustrations of Political Economy' that evening; and I hardly think that any one would discover from it that I had that day sunk to the lowest point of discouragement about my scheme. [...] I was chilly and hungry: the lamp burned low, and the fire was small. I knew it would not do to go to bed, to dream over again the bitter disappointment of the morning. I began now, at last, to doubt whether my work would ever see the light. I thought of the multitudes who needed it, – and especially of the poor, – to assist them in managing their own welfare. I thought too of my own conscious power of doing this very thing. Here was the thing wanting to be done, and I wanting to do it [...]. I cried in bed till six, when I fell asleep; but I was at the breakfast table by half-past eight, and ready for the work of the day. (1877a, 171–172)

The circumstances in which Martineau set about her publication were anything but favourable. In 1831, aged 29, she had conceived of a daring plan: she would attempt to convey the main principles of the nascent science of Political Econo-my by way of didactic fictional stories, through which the lessons to be derived from writers such as Adam Smith, Thomas Malthus and James Mill were to be explained to the general public. The daily troubles of doctors and labourers, fish-ers and farmers, men, women and children would be presented in tales – each encompassing roughly 120 pages of a pocket-sized book – yielding economic les-sons. Convinced of her idea's utility, Martineau approached several publishers with her plan, but only one of them, Charles Fox, finally agreed to take on the series, and not without dictating demanding conditions to the young and hither-to unknown author.

It is to this moment of worry and doubt that Martineau returns in the excerpt from her autobiography quoted above. Yet time soon proved that she was right in her appraisal of popular taste. The *Illustrations*, consisting of twenty-four fictional tales and a final summary of their morals, became an instant success, attracting the attention of such prominent readers as the young Princess Victoria, John Stuart Mill and Edward Bulwer-Lytton. According to Caroline Roberts, one reason for the success was that the tales "were seen to provide realistic pictures of humanity and, in particular, of the lower classes [...]. [R]epresentations of poverty abound in the *Illustrations* and were praised by readers" (2002, 18–19). Suggestively, Martineau's representations of poverty proved to be the means of her own escape from impecuniousness, as from then on she was able to make a comfortable living with her writing. No longer hungry and chilly, no longer brooding over the prospect of failure, no longer forced to earn money with needlework, Martineau had become a respected and financially secure "teacher of the people", in the words of her later biographer R. K. Webb (1960, 91–133). Retrospectively, she concluded in her autobiography that "[a]ny one to whom that happens by thirty years of age may be satisfied; and I was so" (1877a, 181).

2 Politics and/of Poverty

Although in its modern guise economics is associated with quantitative and statistical methods, its origin is usually traced back to a text which is anything but that: Adam Smith's *An Inquiry into the Nature and Causes of the Wealth of Nations* (1776) proves that its author took seriously the denomination of the chair he was holding at the University of Glasgow for several years, namely that of Moral Philosophy. The investigation into concepts such as justice, virtue, sympathy and public good form the basis of Smith's works, even if today he is – somewhat tragically perhaps – mostly remembered for an expression that he used but twice within his entire oeuvre: the (in)famous "invisible hand" which has become a shorthand term for Smith's alleged endorsement of egoism and greed. The simplistic interpretation ignores that *Wealth of Nations* – not to mention what Smith arguably considered his actual *magnum opus*, i.e. *The Theory of Moral Sentiments* (1759) – is far more nuanced in its argumentation and sensitive to ethical questions. For Smith, the aim of Political Economy is "to enrich both the people and the sovereign" (2004 [1776], 141), and that the people are mentioned first is consistent with his overall line of thought: he bore in mind the interests of the less affluent members of society. To claim that he was a radical egalitarian would certainly overstate the case, but some critics have convincingly argued that "Smith's undeniable concern for the poor and working portions of society in fact make him rather a precursor to modern progressive liberalism than an icon of classical *laissez-faire* liberalism. Smith's strong general anti-interventionism in economics is problematic for this interpretation, but his concern for the least among us was real and palpable" (Otteson 2004, 6).

It is therefore significant that the only economic text Harriet Martineau explicitly refers to in the preface to her *Illustrations* is "Smith's Wealth of Nations" (x).[1] The conviction that questions of wealth distribution are inherently moral, that economic policies should benefit the whole of society, and that attention must be paid to the latter's destitute members places Martineau within a distinctly Smithian heritage – notwithstanding her somewhat cheeky remark that *Wealth of Nations* was "not fitted nor designed to teach the science to the great mass of the people" (x). Like Smith, Martineau conceives of Political Economy as a "moral science" (xiii) inquiring "into the principles which regulate the production and distribution of the necessaries and comforts of life in society" (iii). She asks rhetorically: "Can any thing more nearly concern *all* the members of any society than the way in which the necessaries and comforts of life may be best procured and enjoyed by *all?*" (iv; emphasis added). The question translates into her belief that all social classes must be taken into consideration within her tales. Martineau appears to have had equally high hopes that at the level of reception all social strata would be perfectly capable of following her stories and of putting her scientific lessons into practice. The preface deliberately downplays class differences: "We do not dedicate our series to any particular class of society, because we are sure that all classes bear an equal relation to the science, and we fear that it is as little familiar to the bulk of one as of another" (xiv). On that note, however, Claudia Oražem points out that "[i]t is uncertain [...] whether the Political Economy contained in her stories was actually absorbed to the extent Harriet Martineau hoped for" (1999, 103).

Martineau's literary-economic project should not be reduced to a modest popularization of doctrines formulated by Smith, given that it bears witness to the author's engagement in topical political questions. The tales adding up to the *Illustrations of Political Economy* appeared monthly between 1832 and 1834 – a period tellingly coinciding with the activity of the Royal Commission into the Operation of the Poor Laws that culminated in the passing of the Poor Law Amendment Act of 1834. In fact, following the success of the early *Illustrations*, Martineau was approached by Lord Brougham, chairman of the Society for the Diffusion of Useful Knowledge, who asked her to compose comparable novellas that would specifically focus on the desired reform of the Poor Laws. It was out of the missionary and slightly self-aggrandising spirit underlying Martineau's

---

[1] All page numbers for the preface refer to the 1834 edition of Martineau's *Illustrations of Political Economy*.

autobiography quoted above – "I thought of the multitudes who needed it, – and especially of the poor" – that she complied with Brougham's wish, producing four tales which were serially published as *Poor Laws and Paupers Illustrated* (1833–1834).[2] Even if this series did not match up to the success of the *Illustrations* and turned out to be a failure in financial terms (Oražem 1999, 164), it nonetheless stands for Martineau's sustained interest in the issue of poverty and her related political impetus. Poverty is to her not a private affliction, but a national challenge.

Consequently, the arguments that she provides in favour of her didactic project in the preface to the *Illustrations* build upon the idea that the present state of England is amendable, because despite being – as Martineau is anxious to emphasize in her very first sentence – "an enlightened nation" (iii), the country is riddled with excessive social disparities, leading to the discontentment of all classes: "the poor [...] are oppressed, and the rich are troubled" (vii). In an extended parable comparing the state of the English nation to that of a mismanaged medieval castle, Martineau complains of the waste abounding in the luxurious chambers of the masters, while "under servants [are] driven into a cold corner to eat the broken food which was not good enough for their masters' dogs" (vii). With the help of Political Economy such inequalities – whose principal existence Martineau, like Smith, nevertheless deems 'natural' and unquestionable – can be to some extent mitigated.

Poverty is therefore at the very heart of the *Illustrations*' politics: according to Martineau, it is only by understanding, managing and reducing it that England can live up to its full potential. This argumentation effectively recognizes the poor as an important group within the nation, as their destiny has direct implications for the well-being of the entire collective. Yet, as will be shown in the following with the help of examples from three narratives,[3] Martineau nevertheless remains reluctant to fully translate the crucial function she obviously accords to the poor into a comparable scope of their agency within the *Illustrations*. Her stories can be thus related to a general trend which Mary Poovey diagnosed for the mid-nineteenth century, namely the "paradoxical outcome where the value of the working poor to national progress is better recognized [...], but this recognition leads not to increased rewards, but greater surveillance and supervision"

---

2 For cogent analyses of *Poor Laws and Paupers Illustrated*, including their historical contextualization and a discussion of their ideological premises, consult Oražem (1999, 143–164) and Vargo (2007).

3 The three stories in question and the abbreviations that are subsequently used for them are: "A Manchester Strike" (*MS*), "Cousin Marshall" (*CM*) and "Sowers Not Reapers" (*SNR*). Another tale, "Weal and Woe in Garveloch", is referenced as *WW.*

(Hollis 2002, 381). Acting out of a genuine concern for the welfare of the indigent and evincing the well-meaning but patronising attitudes of Victorian social reformers, Martineau likewise attempts to perform in her texts what Political Economy set out to do in reality, namely to 'manage' the poor, as if they were passive entities that can be assessed, classified and fitted into a desired social model. Symptomatic of this attitude is a remark uttered by a character in the tale "Cousin Marshall" in the context of a discussion of the Poor Laws. Miss Burke, a sensible and gentle woman with whom the readers are meant to sympathize, ingenuously proposes: "It seems to me [...] that as wide a distinction ought to be made between temporary and lasting indigence, and between innocent and guilty indigence, within the work-house, as between poverty and indigence out of it; and as the numbers are, I believe, very unequal, I should think it might easily be done" (*CM*, 236). Paradoxically, however, the *Illustrations* demonstrate precisely the reverse, namely that classifying poverty may *not* "easily be done". No clear-cut taxonomy of poverty emerges from the tales; instead, diverse forms, reasons for and solutions to penury are presented, at times sustaining, at others contradicting each other. The complex nature of poverty thus compromises the wish for management: Martineau attempts to tame it, but her stories repeatedly frustrate her efforts by recording the complicated determining factors of destitution.

3 Paradoxes of Poverty

Poverty has for Martineau an economic, but above all a moral dimension. Already in the preface to the *Illustrations* she declares that "none will doubt whether a perpetuity of ease or hardship is the more favourable to virtue" (xvi), the implication being that economic hardship poses the biggest threat to morality. The tales are thus interspersed with memorable maxims that relate a lack of morals to a lack of money. To quote but a few illustrative examples:

> [N]one are so prone to quarrel as those who have nothing else to do, and whose tempers are at the same time fretted by want. (*MS*, 203)
>
> Hard times are the days of crime. (*WW*, 95)
>
> There is nothing so corrupting as poverty [...]. (*WW*, 114)
>
> I am sure I should find it difficult to assert that any set of vices could be more to be dreaded than those which arise from extreme poverty. (*WW*, 124)
>
> [D]estitution [...] is the cause of crime. (*SNR*, 308)
>
> [T]he pressure of want [is] the main spring of the vast machinery of moral evil by which society is harrowed and torn. (*SNR*, 378)

At the same time, the narratives abound in representations of characters who preserve their moral integrity despite economic hardship, and they include a significant number of affluent characters who are corrupt and unlikeable. The truthfulness of the simplistic equation 'poverty equals vice', i.e. of one of Martineau's major argumentative cornerstones, is thus called into question by the stories' content. But the implications of the posited correlation between poverty and vice are contradictory in yet another regard. On the one hand, the poor are placed under a general suspicion of moral depravity. On the other, any of their morally questionable deeds are partially excused when the poor are seen as mere victims of unfavourable external economic circumstances. This ambivalence gestures towards the greater question of accountability for both individual and collective economic and moral acts. Martineau, as will be shown presently, is ultimately unable to resolve this issue with certainty. While in some cases she deems the indigent capable of making their own decisions and clearly condemns them when they depart from the prescribed economic doctrines, at other times she casts them as passive and pitiful victims of a faulty system. Within the scope of individual tales the attribution of responsibility seems quite consistent, but the issue becomes more complicated when the *Illustrations* are viewed as a whole. If the poor are in some stories cleared of any responsibility, but in others shown as evidently having and urged to live up to it, it becomes difficult to abstract from the *Illustrations* reliable guidelines of economic behaviour. If responsibility variously rests with individuals, the government, the 'system' or God, the parameters for the allegedly easy distinction "between innocent and guilty indigence" so resolutely demanded by Miss Burke in "Cousin Marshall" become questionable.

As a devoted Malthusian, Martineau is particularly prone to placing the blame on the poor for their suffering when she deems it to be the result of overpopulation. Exemplary in this regard is her tale "A Manchester Strike", which describes the futile industrial action of the employees of a cotton mill. The story begins with a compassionate description of the lot of the workers, particularly the children, who have to toil during night shifts, risking their health and enduring unbearable heat and noise. The tale's protagonist is William Allen, a sensible, modest and principled labourer who, much against his will, leads the unsuccessful strike. It is his awareness of the material afflictions besetting him and his colleagues that makes him accept the unrewarding task. During one of the meetings of the strike committee he asserts:

> Some change, and that a speedy one, there ought to be in the condition of the working classes: they cannot go on long labouring their lives away for a less recompense than good habitations, clothing, and food. These form the very least sum of the just rewards

of industry; whereas a multitude are pinched with the frosts of winter, live amidst the stench of unwholesome dwellings in summer, have nearly forgotten the taste of animal food, and even sigh for bread as for a luxury. (*MS*, 168)

To render the image of industrial hardship more acutely, Martineau focuses on the pitiful lot of Allen's daughter Martha, whose health and spirits decline due to the drudgery at the factory. During one of her night shifts, the exhausted eight-year-old girl accidentally falls asleep, dreaming of walking "on broad roads or through green fields" (*MS*, 176), but awakening to the grim reality of her industrial existence – an episode calling to mind William Blake's "The Chimney Sweeper" from his *Songs of Innocence*.

These and other passages in "A Manchester Strike" reveal Martineau's genuine sympathy for the sufferings of the lower classes. Yet when it comes to the reasons for the destitution described in the tale, the dedicated Malthusian is adamant: the fault does not lie with the manufacturers, but with the workers whose large families reduce the wage-fund out of which they are to be paid.[4] This mechanism is laid down by the honourable manufacturer Mr Wentworth, a character whose good sense, fellow feeling and modesty are emphasized time and again, making him a trustworthy voice of economic wisdom. In a lengthy passage Mr Wentworth patiently explains the premises of the wage-fund theory to the attentive labourers, tellingly resorting to a quasi-biblical parable in which Adam hires planters in the Garden of Eden (*MS*, 158–162). Economic laws are thus cast in biblical terms and emerge as divinely ordained and indisputable. Acting against them is concomitant with committing a sin and therefore induces corresponding punishment: poverty, for example. This strategy of joining "God and science" (Freedgood 1999, 210) – which Martineau repeats in other tales – paradoxically leads the noble Mr Wentworth to a rather un-Christian conclusion. He refuses to relieve the workers' suffering through higher wages, because "[i]f you choose to bring a thousand labourers to live upon the capital which was once divided among a hundred; it is your fault and not mine that you are badly off" (*MS*, 161). This conviction is stressed further on in the story:

---

4 As James P. Huzel (2006, 70–78) demonstrates, Martineau's Malthusian beliefs met with fervent attacks by her contemporaries. Incidentally, whenever reviewers rebuked Martineau's alleged lack of compassion for the impoverished and for her radical stance toward the old Poor Laws, their criticism was distinctly gendered. George Poulett Scrope, for example, gave voice to his disbelief in the *Quarterly Review* (1833): "A *young woman* who deprecates charity and a provision for the *poor!!!*" (2004, 425). William Maginn (1832) found himself comparably appalled by "a book written by a *woman* against the *poor*" (2004, 420). It is therefore worth remembering that Martineau's own agency as a female writer within the male discourse of economics was at times just as limited as the agency that she granted to the poor in her stories.

> And how are the masters to help you if you go on increasing your numbers and undersell-
> ing one another, as if your employers could find occupation for any number of millions of
> you, or could coin the stones under your feet into wages, or knead the dust of the earth into
> bread? They do what they can for you in increasing the capital on which you are to subsist;
> and you must do the rest by proportioning your numbers to the means of subsistence. But
> see how the masters are met! In Huddersfield the masters are doing their utmost to extend
> their trade; but the multitudes who are to subsist by it increase much faster. (*MS*, 196–197)

The passage contrasts the hard-working and benevolent manufacturers with the heedless, ungrateful, animalistic and dangerously proliferating "multitudes" who are in apparent need of instruction by such eminent and superior figures as Mr Wentworth. The working-class hero Allen quickly understands the predicament of his employers and makes his fellow workers terminate the strike.

"A Manchester Strike" is therefore, as Claudia Klaver likewise argues focusing on different aspects of the narrative, a tale of unbalanced "sentimental economics" (2003, 61; 59–65): it begins with a sympathetic depiction of poverty, but merges into an outwardly well-meaning, yet ultimately accusatory narrative that deems the poor responsible for their own penury. This logic translates into the paradox that although "A Manchester Strike" is a tale about industrial action and thus a paradigmatic case of economic agency on the part of the underprivileged, the story fundamentally denies agency to those that suffer from economic want. This is brought home through such characters as Clack, a member of the union, who repeatedly demands that his colleagues take resolute measures against oppressive poverty. He challenges Mr Wentworth's Malthusian piece of advice by declaring that "the poor must raise themselves by such means as are in their own hands, and not wait for judgment of Providence" (*MS*, 173). On another occasion, he asks a manufacturer who prefers taking a ride to talking with his employees: "How would you get such a rein, I wonder, sir, if we did not grease our fingers in your service?" (*MS*, 156) The reader may at first feel inclined to agree with Clack's expostulations. Yet Martineau is persistent in discrediting Clack – whose telling name already points to the alleged erroneousness of his convictions – as an unlikeable, quarrelsome and self-important troublemaker. In the end, he is removed from the strike committee by the "general consent" (*MS*, 186) of his fellows: this rather unrealistic narrative twist makes the labourers voluntarily expel one of their most fervent spokesmen.

Clack's undesirable political action is opposed to the patience and reticence of William Allen, whom Martineau is at pains to set up as a positive role model. Despite his leading role in the strike, Allen remains a strangely passive figure, which is underscored by the fate he meets with in the end of the story. When his former masters refuse to re-employ him because of his commitment to the turnout, Allen asks the noble Mr Wentworth for work. But the manufacturer is sorry to report that he can hire no additional labourers and implies that the blame for the present predicament lies with the strikers. Martineau's working-class hero accepts the verdict with due submission: "Allen bowed and had no more to say. [...] [He] would trespass no longer on Mr. Wentworth's time" (*MS*, 214). Arguably, Allen would make formidable friends with Stephen Blackpool, the passively suffering worker in Charles Dickens' *Hard Times*, to whom life is a "muddle" that can only be grasped by those ranking above him.[5] One can interpret this as Martineau's general unwillingness to grant poor characters economic and political agency. But it is also worth considering that patience and submission are the most likely solutions that the Malthusian premises of the tale can offer. In the story, a former labourer reasonably interjects that "[i]t was poor comfort to tell the people that wages could not be any higher on account of their numbers, since it was not in their power to lessen those numbers" (*MS*, 197). The truthfulness of this observation is sanctioned by the authority of Mr Wentworth, who admits that the poor cannot expect "present comfort [...]. All that you can now do, is to live as you best may upon such wages as the masters can give, keeping up your sense of respectability and your ambition to improve your state when better times shall come" (*MS*, 197). This remark inadvertently exposes a major drawback of the science that Martineau seeks to promote: the apparent inability of Political Economy to fulfil the *present* needs of society.

One of the most overtly Malthusian tales in the *Illustrations* is "Cousin Marshall", a story that addresses upfront the purported deficiencies of the existing Poor Laws. Like "A Manchester Strike", it provides insight into the suffering caused by poverty and features likeable characters commiserating with the fate of the lower classes. The considerate and kind Mr Burke, for example, tells his sister Louisa of the hardship that he witnesses during his work as a surgeon:

> It is dreadful to see the numbers of poor women disappointed of a reception at the last moment, and totally unprovided. The more are admitted, the more are thus disappointed; and those who are relieved quit the hospital in a miserable state of destitution. [...] It would make your heart ache if I were to tell you how large a proportion of my Dispensary patients

---

5 In this regard it is somewhat ironic that Martineau's *Autobiography* reveals a certain disdain for Dickens's economic abilities: "Another vexation is his vigorous erroneousness about matters of science, as shown in 'Oliver Twist' about the new poor-law (which he confounds with the abrogated old one) and in 'Hard Times', about the controversies of employers. Nobody wants to make Mr. Dickens a Political Economist; but there are many who wish that he would abstain from a set of difficult subjects, on which all true sentiment must be underlain by a sort of knowledge which he has not" (Martineau 1877b, 378). For a substantial analysis of the disagreements between Martineau and Dickens, see Fielding and Smith (1970).

are children born puny from the destitution of their parents, or weakly boys and girls, stunted by bad nursing, or women who want rest and warmth more than medicine, or men whom I can never cure until they are provided with better food. (*CM*, 241)

Burke's experiences lead him to define the problem which is central to "Cousin Marshall": "The grand question seems to me to be this – *How to reduce the number of the indigent?*" (*CM*, 241). Given the story's Malthusian premises, the answer to this question turns out to be comparable to the one offered by "A Manchester Strike": the number of the indigent cannot be reduced presently, but only in the future, and the principal means of effecting this is by curbing the growth of the population. Yet in "Cousin Marshall", Martineau is less willing to place the sole blame for overpopulation on the poor, and instead draws attention to the wrong incentives being given by the Poor Laws. In other words, although in both stories the diagnosed economic and social problem is the same – i.e. poverty resulting from overpopulation – the responsibility for it is shifted to different quarters in each case. While in "Strike", the system is deemed correct and the lower classes are at fault, in "Cousin Marshall", the situation is virtually the reverse, as Louisa Burke's patronising remark makes plain: "It is rather hard upon the poor [...] that we should complain of their improvidence when we bribe them to it by promising subsistence at all events. Paupers will spend and marry faster than their betters as long as this system lasts" (*CM*, 249). Burke takes his sister's argumentation a step further when he claims:

There is harm enough done by the poor taking for granted that they are to be supplied with medicine and advice gratis all their lives; the evil is increasing every day by their looking on assistance in child-birth as their due; and if they learn to expect food and warmth in like manner, their misery will be complete. (*CM*, 251)

The reasoning might make sense in the context of Burke's disapproval of the Poor Laws, yet his statement draws at the same time the somewhat illogical (economic) conclusion that the combination of medical advice, family support, food and shelter adds up not to contentment and security, but to "harm", "evil" and "misery".

The contradictory lines of thought translate into a further paradox: the destitute in "A Manchester Strike", although they are presented as having economic responsibility, remain, as we have seen, passive and largely devoid of agency. In "Cousin Marshall", by contrast, the lower classes display a significant amount of economic activity, although they are conceived of as 'victims' of a faulty system. The role model of the story is the eponymous Cousin Marshall, a poor yet resilient woman who despite financial burdens and eventual widowhood manages not only to provide a decent living for her dear ones but also to support other persons in need. Self-reliance is to her "a far more natural and pleasant thing" (*CM*, 224) than the appeal to public support which she considers a disgraceful "degeneracy" (*CM*, 291). It is therefore not surprising that Cousin Marshall regularly falls out with Mrs Bell, the paradigmatic social parasite whose entire energy is directed to wheedling out benefits from the parish. That the reader is meant to feel contempt for Mrs Bell is obvious, yet it is likewise undeniable that Mrs Bell displays a remarkable degree of economic agency. Martineau devotes several pages to the description of her various petty frauds, which include claiming parish assistance for a deceased child. The narrator concludes each of Mrs Bell's successful schemes with her self-congratulatory remark that she "had truly managed the whole matter very 'cleverly'" (*CM*, 250). The phrasing is of course ironic, yet the irony is somewhat destabilized by the fact that from an economic vantage point, Mrs Bell is indeed a clever manager. Her conviction that "[i]f the law put such difficulty in the way of getting relief, we are driven to tell fibs; for relief we must have" (*CM*, 278) translates in her case into financially effective measures which help her to secure a relatively comfortable existence for her family.

A comparable ambivalence occurs in the portrayal of the two vagrants Hunt and Childe. Childe teaches Hunt the skill of begging, which, it turns out, includes wearing appropriate apparel, displaying particular behaviour, having a good knowledge of the surrounding area and its inhabitants, etc. Although Martineau seeks to discredit the two beggars as insolent impostors, they nonetheless emerge as purposeful, knowledgeable and strategic 'workers' within the economic domain they 'specialize' in. In fact, the two beggars involuntarily mimic a traditional economic relation, with Childe being the experienced master and Hunt the willing apprentice. After their day at 'work', the two retire to a public house where they enjoy food and drink with their merry fellows. The scene is obviously meant to arouse the readers' outrage, but, again, apart from the fact that the two beggars pursue a 'contemptible' economic activity, the close of their day resembles that of honest labourers who may likewise gather in a pub after a hard day's work. Childe, Hunt and Mrs Bell are thus not slothful parasites passively awaiting the benefits of the Poor Law system. Quite the opposite: they are systematic, diligent, strategic and resourceful, thus ironically displaying economic virtues that the *Illustrations* demand from the poor elsewhere. In Martineau's tales, "the ideal member of society [...] plans for the future and is intent on safeguarding capital in all its forms" (Oražem 1999, 118), which applies to the three characters in question. Their "Pauper Life" described in the eponymous subchapter of "Cousin Marshall" paradoxically emerges as bustling with effective economic agency, thus showcasing that economy and morals, of whose unity Martineau is generally convinced, may, in fact, part ways.

A vision of national decline hovers over "Cousin Marshall" with Burke predicting that unless the Poor Laws are abolished, "the nation [will] become a vast congregation of paupers" (*CM*, 247). The recurrent use of first-person plural pronouns invites the reader to partake in the fear that the "pauper system" might eventually "swallow up all our resources, and make us a nation of paupers" (*CM*, 247). "We are now borne down, we shall soon be crushed, by the weight of our burdens" (*CM*, 288), Burke foretells. The danger is also seen as imminent by Mr Effingham, another figure of authority in the story: "God help us! [...] our security is gone, as a nation, and as individuals" (*CM*, 282). "Cousin Marshall" establishes thereby a dichotomy of 'us' vs. 'them', presenting a portion of the poor as a threatening Other. This dualism is emphasized by the terminology of the story, with the "poor" and "indigent" being positively, and "pauper", "beggars" and "vagabonds" negatively connoted.

But the issue gets complicated insofar as the narrative presents many different forms of poverty, effectively demonstrating that there is no clear-cut 'them'. Cousin Marshall stands for heroic endurance, Mrs Bell for impertinent 'management', while in the case of the beggars, poverty is turned into a kind of performance: in the evening, "their beggar apparel [is] being thrown into a corner, and looking-glass, brushes and towels, [are] being all in requisition" (*CM*, 257). Further cases of destitution include the young Ned and his sister Jane: although both are temporarily forced to go to the workhouse, Ned manages to escape and to earn a living through honest, hard work, while Jane gets pregnant from – of course – a dishonest "pauper labourer" (*CM*, 272) and is in the end "quite lost" (*CM*, 290). Martineau explains their different outcomes with their differences of character, but this in turn undermines her argument that it is the Poor Law system and not an internal predisposition of the poor that leads to depravity. While within the bounds of the story Martineau has sufficient room to make the readers understand which of the poor characters mentioned above belongs to 'us' and which to 'them', the panoply of poverty she presents in "Cousin Marshall" has consequences for the representations of penury in other stories. The distinction between 'good' and 'bad' poverty relies on literary means, with Martineau providing the adequate background information for each of the representative characters. Yet in other tales – and, above all, in the real life to which Martineau lays claim – such background knowledge may not be always provided, and the question of whether the type of poverty at hand is of the heroic or of the insolent kind, whether it is self-induced or unjustly imposed, may then not be answered with any certainty. In other words, Martineau's wish to taxonomize poverty in "Cousin Marshall" requires the acknowledgment of the complexity of the phenomenon which then, however, taints the initial wish to categorize.

The failure of Martineau's project to offer a coherent and manageable representation of poverty within the *Illustrations* can be evidenced further with examples from a third tale. In "A Manchester Strike", the message given to the poor was: "it is your fault and not mine that you are badly off" (*MS*, 161). The reverse case of responsibility being shifted to external circumstances is provided in "Sowers Not Reapers", which supports the abolition of the Corn Laws. The story is set in a village in Yorkshire, near Sheffield, and depicts the dire consequences of the laws for the local community. The tale features the character of Margaret Kay, mother of several children and wife to John Kay, a worker at the local foundry. The readers learn fairly early on that Margaret suffers from alcoholism and hence regularly violates the code of behaviour expected from a 'decent' woman: as her addiction becomes worse, she is unable to take care of the household, look after her children and support her husband. Importantly, however, Martineau does not denigrate her female protagonist, but portrays Margaret's affliction with palpable sympathy, relegating the responsibility for the 'vice' she indulges in to external causes. She has Margaret ruefully explain: "O, it began long and long ago. When I was weakly as a girl, they used to give me things, and that was the beginning of it all. Then when I grew weakly again, it seemed to come most natural, especially because it was cheaper than bread, and the children wanted all we could get of that" (*SNR*, 352). The seemingly marginal comment that drink was "cheaper than bread" relates Margaret's lack of self-control not to her moral weakness, but to faulty economic policies. In the context of the Corn Law problem that is central to the story, the implication is that without the injurious laws, bread would have been cheaper and Margaret's addiction could have been prevented. It is thus not Margaret's intrinsic weakness, but, as the narrator sympathetically notes, "poverty which had seduced her into a fatal habit" (*SNR*, 374). In the words of Mary Kay, who is the voice of economic and moral authority in the story: "It was suffering, – it was hunger that did all that!" (*SNR*, 377).

The case of Margaret Kay sets the tone for the entire narrative, which vehemently condemns the Corn Laws as detrimental to all members of society. The statement closing the "Summary of Principles Illustrated in this Volume" makes this abundantly clear: "As it is in the interest of all classes that the supply of food should be regular and cheap, [...] it is the interest of all classes that there should be a free trade in corn" (*SNR*, 381). Consequently, the story features representatives of various social ranks – the labourers Kay and Chatham, the shopkeeper Mrs Skipper, the farmer Anderson, the manufacturer Oliver and the landowner Mr Fergusson – who all suffer from the injudicious laws and who therefore unite in their censure of the hardship they provoke. Martineau lingers particularly on the consequences that the laws have for the poor and she again draws on quasi-religious rhetoric to convey the intense suffering of "men possessed by the demon of want" (*SNR*, 335) – a demon that in this case can only be 'exorcized' through a Corn Law repeal. Chatham, a skilled labourer who is introduced as an intelligent and "very important personage in his village" (*SNR*, 337), repeatedly describes the difficult lot of the lower classes:

> To none is the sun so dark as to the dim-eyed hungerer. To none is the moon so sickly as to the watcher over a pining infant's cradle. Let man remove the shadow of social tyranny, let him disperse the mists which rise from a deluge of tears, and God's sun and moon will be found to make the dew-drops glitter as bright as ever on the lowliest thatch, and to shine mildly into humble chambers where those who are not kneeling in thanksgiving are blessing God as well by the soundness of their repose. (*SNR*, 335)

Drawing heavily on bathos and syntactic parallelisms, Chatham's descriptions of poverty read like sermons – an impression that is all the more intensified by his recurrent evocations of God. Martineau again conflates economic with religious discourse. But whereas in "A Manchester Strike", the poor were the 'sinners', in "Sowers Not Reapers" the poor are mere victims and it is the English government that cruelly and unnecessarily enacts suffering upon the people, thus acting against quasi-divine will. Chatham exhorts that "God giveth to all living things food in its season. This, like all other words of God, is true; but with his viceregents rests the blasphemy if shrunken lips whisper that it is a lie" (*SNR*, 335). The two tales thus contradict each other in their attribution of economic accountability.

This inconsistency leads Martineau to demand sympathy for certain (economic) deeds which she condemns as unacceptable in other tales. One of the issues raised in "Sowers Not Reapers" is Luddism, and the story features occasional descriptions of the nightly activities of machine breakers. It is easy to imagine that Mr Wentworth, the likeable manufacturer from "A Manchester Strike", would have no empathy for labourers destroying items from his factory; it is likewise hard to conceive that the respectable Mr Effingham from "Cousin Marshall", to whom "security of property [...] is the most precious of an independent man's right" (*CM*, 283), would welcome the destruction of industrial property by starving labourers. But in "Sowers Not Reapers", a different stance is taken. While the Luddites are not openly praised for their behaviour, they are nonetheless excused for their desperation, which is attributed to government-induced poverty. Chatham argues that these people "must be fed before they can effectually struggle for perpetual food" (*SNR*, 329), and his fiancée, instead of dreading, pities them as "[p]oor wretches" who look "as if they had no life nor spirit in them" (*SNR*, 329). While in some cases, therefore, destroying property out of poverty is an outright crime, in others, it seems pardonable.

Another example of contradictory economic reasoning emerges when the hungry villagers seek to ransack the shop of Mrs Skipper, the local baker. The attentive reader of "Cousin Marshall" will remember that providing the poor with bread for free only makes them more dependent and leads, as Mr Burke has put it, to their complete "misery". But "Sowers Not Reapers" suggests a different logic: Mrs Skipper chirpily gives away her produce, convinced that "God loves a cheerful giver" (*SNR*, 318). The "swarms of paupers" (*CM*, 278) that are on the brink of ravaging England in "Cousin Marshall" appear in a different light in the Corn-Laws story: "They do not seem creatures to be afraid of, when one comes close to them; – so tired and lagging!" (*SNR*, 316). Martineau shows, moreover, understanding for pilfering and explains it as resulting from "the scourge of want" (*SNR*, 307). She even somewhat mitigates the Malthusian stance that she so forcefully endorses in other narratives. Instead of cautioning against the threat of overpopulation, she has her hero Chatham optimistically proclaim: "There is room for myriads more of us, and for a boundless improvement of our resources; these resources are forbidden to improve, and these myriads to exist. Whence rulers derive their commission thus to limit that to which God has placed no perceivable bound, let them declare" (*SNR*, 333). In sum, the 'them' in "Sowers Not Reapers" are not the poor; here, they belong to the 'us' that is looked down upon by the government: "our people [are] brought low for want of food, driven to skulk and pilfer for it, and then disgraced and punished" (*SNR*, 308). While this line of reasoning makes sense in the context of the story, it sits squarely with, or even stands in opposition to, the doctrines commended in other tales.

4 Poverty and Science-Fiction

In "Sowers Not Reapers" Chatham complains that English legislators pay no heed to the sorrows of poor people but content themselves with "tales of victories abroad, and of rejoicings at home in places where no poor man sets his foot. [...] Thus they can forget our story for a while" (*SNR*, 330). This remark might be arguably read as a meta-comment on the *Illustrations* themselves, which are precisely stories that draw the public's attention to the needs of society's underprivileged members. In the same tale, John Kay, husband to the alcoholic Margaret, pronounces on behalf of his neglected children: "I speak plain, because it is about those who cannot speak for themselves" (*SNR*, 353) – an apt summary of Martineau's benevolent-patronising attitude towards the poor. In fact, the narratives at times read like *Illustrations of Poverty*, with destitute labourers striking for higher wages, women suffering from hunger and orphaned children being forced to go to the workhouse. The problem at the heart of Martineau's project remains, however, that the wish to represent the complex nature of poverty stands in opposition to the wish to manage and categorize it. The more facets of penury Martineau presents in her stories, the more it becomes obvious that the phenomenon is too intricate to be pressed into a taxonomy, to which the manifold contradictions outlined above bear witness.

Using the example of "Cousin Marshall", Brian P. Cooper argues that as regards female characters in the *Illustrations*, such "strains result from Martineau's attempts to realistically represent the lives of poor women, while simultaneously claiming that they should enjoy all the rights and responsibilities of a liberal political subject" (2007, 116). Martineau's representations of female emancipation are thus at odds with limitations grounded in class and gender. While Cooper's reading is persuasive as regards some of the female characters, it cannot account for all of the paradoxes of poverty mentioned above. Another possible line of inquiry is therefore to consider whether the inconsistencies may be attributed to Martineau's hybrid mode of presentation, i.e. her fusion of science with fiction. Claudia Klaver, for example, believes Martineau's popularising approach to be "riddled with tensions and contradictions that ultimately compromised its didactic message. More specifically, the very fictional forms that Martineau so successfully used to win an audience for political economy were also the source of the tensions that deformed her project" (2003, 53). Elaine Freedgood argues in a similar vein when she posits that Martineau's "fictions strive to be what is finally an impossible and inefficacious generic hybrid: realist myth" (1999, 212). Are then the contradictory requirements of the two discourses at the heart of Martineau's paradoxes of poverty?

Lana L. Dalley observes that "[w]ithin early nineteenth-century print culture, fiction – especially domestic fiction – was regarded as the domain of pleasures and emotions, while more 'serious' works – on such topics as history, politics or economics – were regarded as serving a higher intellectual purpose that contributed to the greater good in ways that fiction did not" (2010, 103). Martineau's texts, by combining fiction with economics, face the difficult challenge of doing justice to both realms. The most evidently scientific part of the tales are their "Summar[ies] of Principles Illustrated in this Volume" at the end of each story, which enlist the principal economic lessons in an 'objective' language, as self-evident and unavoidable truths: "In a society composed of a natural gradation of ranks, some must be poor; i.e. have nothing more than the means of present subsistence" (*CM*, 293). Martineau further regularly resorts to "lengthy, sometimes rather cumbersome conversations between two or three characters in which the issue at hand is explained and erroneous thinking is refuted" (Oražem 1999, 103). This device of fusing scientific argumentation with fiction met with criticism from none other than Edward Bulwer-Lytton, who in his review of 1833 regretted that Martineau's

> dialogue offends verisimilitude [...]. It is easy to see the benevolent and wise purpose in making the poor themselves speculate on truths, rather than be lectured by others into instruction. It opens to them what may be called 'Intellectual Independence', and teaches, on a large scale, the Lancaster system, that the best schoolmaster is the pupil himself. But while this purpose is a full excuse for her practice in drawing philosophical fishermen and Socratical cottagers, the practice cannot but interfere with the effect of the fiction, and the artist-like delineation of the characters [...]. (2004, 428)[6]

Incidentally, it is worth noting that Bulwer-Lytton reprimands Martineau on purely aesthetic grounds. He does not mind that the agency of the poor is limited by being made to articulate Martineau's convictions; quite the contrary, he even applauds this strategy as less patronizing than direct instruction would be.

Bulwer-Lytton's criticism emphasizes that in the *Illustrations*, the tendency to formulate abstract principles – be it through summaries or lengthy dialogues between well-informed characters – sits somewhat squarely with the requirements of nineteenth-century domestic fiction: a mere statement such as "[t]he subsistence-fund must be employed productively and capital and labour be allowed to take their natural course" (*CM*, 294) is unlikely to trigger any sort of emotion in the common reader, except maybe for boredom. To be successful, the scientific discourse underlying the *Illustrations* thus needs an emotive counterpoise, which is why Martineau envisages concrete situations in domestic settings and encourages readers to identify with individual characters. Some of the tales' titles themselves bear witness to this strategy. The stories "Ella of Garveloch" and the above-mentioned "Cousin Marshall", for example, depict how circumspectly the eponymous heroines manage the lives of their dear ones, despite unemployment, famine or death in the family. Martineau attempts to ensure that the readers' sympathies are directed toward those characters who act in accordance with the teachings of Political Economy, while those who sin against them arouse con-

---

6 Arguing from a contemporary perspective, Caroline Roberts interprets such dissonances between characters and their speech as a challenge to established gender norms: "Indeed, [Martineau's] retention of awkward-sounding economic jargon in the mouths of her characters testified to the awkwardness of 'masculine' discourse itself and was necessary for the demystification of this discourse and the instruction of her readers" (2002, 15). Dalley also reads the *Illustrations* as a subversion of prevalent gender norms: "[B]y employing and reconfiguring economic discourse, Martineau challenges the cultural limits imposed upon women's discursive and economic acts, stretches the boundaries of novelistic discourse, and assigns women writers and fiction greater cultural authority" (2010, 115).

tempt. We are thus meant to admire the widow Marshall for self-sufficiently bringing through her family and two orphaned children, but to be less sympathetic of a poor Irishman from Garveloch who, in appallingly stereotypical fashion, is idle and prone to drink, so that his poverty is presented as of his own making.[7]

However, Klaver convincingly shows that in some tales, Martineau is unable to fully functionalize the readers' sympathetic identification. When the emotive appeal of the literary strand contradicts the conveyed economic messages, "a kind of narrative violence" (2003, 68) ensues, which discredits the underlying scientific discourse. Yet while this is true of the examples Klaver quotes, it does not seem to account for the paradoxes within Martineau's representations of poverty. The central problem delineated above is that Martineau's wish to categorize poverty is compromised by her simultaneous portrayal of its manifold forms. It would be fairly easy to attribute the categorising impulse to science and that to render complexity to literature. But such an interpretation would presuppose an overly simplistic view of both discourses. Far from being automatically appreciative of the complex nature of reality, fiction can be manipulative, reductive and serve ideological needs. As to Political Economy: like any other science, it evidently strives to abstract from 'reality' certain applicable rules. But for these rules to be formulated, the antecedent complexity of the phenomenon must be taken into account first. Martineau's attempt to cover various forms of and reasons for destitution is therefore anything but unscientific. What is more, in the 1830s Political Economy may not (yet) be reduced to a merely quantitative discipline. In this context, Ella Dzelzainis and Cora Kaplan draw attention to "Martineau's conception of political economy, which she understood as a moral philosophy rather than as merely a science" (2010, 5–6). The inconsistencies besetting Martineau's representations of poverty are therefore not a proof of the failure of, as it were, her science-fiction, but rather a result of the complexity of the issue she had chosen to address.

5 Conclusion

In her Martineau biography of 1887, the author Florence Fenwick Miller praises her biographee with a truly Victorian epitaph: "[T]hose who lived with her loved her; she was a kind mistress, a good friend, and tender to little children;

---

7 For a discussion of stereotypes of Irish poverty, see the chapter by Marie-Luise Egbert in this volume.

she was truly helpful to the poor at her gates, and her life was spotlessly pure" (1887, 223). At a second glance, however, the compliment strikes one as dubious: was Martineau generally helpful to the poor, or only to those who happened to knock at her door? With a view to her *Illustrations*, a similar ambivalence creeps in. There is undeniably a wish to manage and control poverty (both in economic and in literary terms) which effectively denies agency to the underprivileged. Within this strand, poor characters do not act: they merely illustrate 'truths' to which they are subjected. In the preface, Martineau even turns this strategy into an asset of her project: one can, she notes, explain certain maxims "by stating them in a dry, plain way: but the same thing will be quite as evident, and far more interesting and better remembered, if we confirm our doctrine by accounts of the hardships suffered by individuals" (xii). This functionalistic approach to poverty is, however, offset by the fact that Martineau records in her narratives the complexities and afflictions of poverty, even if it bursts the purposes of her taxonomy.

Such contradictions can be cited to diagnose the failure of Martineau's project: in a way, the *Illustrations* almost tragically miscarry by inadvertently exposing that poverty is a far too complex issue to be managed and contained, i.e. by ultimately demonstrating the impossibility of the very task they promote. From a critical stance, one can object further that Martineau's inconsistent representations of poverty result from her drive to objectify the poor by casting them into various types which only serve to illustrate the discussed political-economic measure at hand. The subordination of realism to economic doctrines is what Elaine Freedgood deems problematic in Martineau's tales:

> It is this anti-realist credo that ultimately undermines the representational power of the *Illustrations*, and weakens the work's ability to assuage cultural anxiety: the bright side can usually take care of itself; it is the neglected dark side that demands explanation, and Martineau could not illuminate that darkness except by reference to economic laws that were guaranteed to be working, however invisibly, toward a happy equilibrium. (1999, 221)

Yet the reverse claim, namely that the existence of Martineau's paradoxes of poverty demonstrates her genuine concern for the situation of the underprivileged members of society, is just as plausible: from this standpoint, the inconsistencies imply that Martineau does not merely objectify the poor, turning them into a uniform, manageable entity, but that she remains attuned – whether consciously or not – to the complexity of the phenomenon she seeks to address. Steven Connor notes that "[d]estitution encodes a play between measurability and immeasurability, between the economic and the uneconomic" (2005, 19). It is precisely this 'play' that is (arguably inadvertently) evinced by the *Illustrations*. For certain, therefore, when looking at Martineau's writing from today's vantage point, it is important – if also fairly easy – to critically engage with her blind spots and ideological assumptions, which she mistook for self-evident truths. But it is equally vital to bear in mind Tomas Sedlacek's general admonition: "Today we take these truths reservedly and tolerantly put them inside quotation marks, but we must be aware that the next generations will just as unhumbly put today's truths into quotation marks as well" (2011, 41).[8]

Works Cited

Bulwer-Lytton, Edward. "'On Moral Fictions: Miss Martineau's *Illustrations of Political Economy*.' *The New Monthly Magazine and Literary Journal* 37 (1833): 146–51." *Illustrations of Political Economy: Selected Tales*. By Harriet Martineau. Ed. Deborah Anna Logan. Peterborough: Broadview, 2004. 427–429.

Connor, Steven. "Destitution." *Metaphors of Economy*. Eds. Nicole Bracker and Stefan Herbrechter. Amsterdam: Rodopi, 2005. 9–23.

Cooper, Brian P. *Family Fictions and Family Facts: Harriet Martineau, Adolphe Quetelet, and the Population Question in England, 1798–1859*. London: Routledge, 2007.

Dalley, Lana L. "Domesticating Political Economy: Language, Gender and Economics in the *Illustrations of Political Economy*." *Harriet Martineau: Authorship, Society and Empire*. Eds. Ella Dzelzainis and Cora Kaplan. Manchester: Manchester University Press, 2010. 103–117.

Dzelzainis, Ella, and Cora Kaplan. "Domesticating Political Economy: Language, Gender and Economics in the *Illustrations of Political Economy*." *Harriet Martineau: Authorship, Society and Empire*. Eds. Dzelzainis and Kaplan. Manchester: Manchester University Press, 2010. 1–11.

Fielding, K. T., and Anne Smith. "*Hard Times* and the Factory Controversy: Dickens vs. Harriet Martineau." *Nineteenth-Century Fiction* 24.4 (1970): 404–427.

Freedgood, Elaine. "Banishing Panic: Harriet Martineau and the Popularization of Political Economy." *The New Economic Criticism: Studies at the Intersection of Literature and Economics*. Eds. Martha Woodmansee and Mark Osteen. London: Routledge, 1999. 210–228.

Hoecker-Drysdale, Susan. *Harriet Martineau: First Woman Sociologist*. Oxford: Berg, 1992.

Hollis, Hilda. "The Rhetoric of Jane Marcet's Popularizing Political Economy." *Nineteenth-Century Contexts* 24.4 (2002): 379–396.

Huzel, James P. *The Popularization of Malthus in Early Nineteenth-Century England: Martineau, Cobbett and the Pauper Press*. Aldershot: Ashgate, 2006.

Klaver, Claudia C. *A/Moral Economics: Classical Political Economy and Cultural Authority in Nineteenth-Century England*. Columbus: Ohio State University Press, 2003.

---

8 I would like to thank the Institute for Advanced Studies in the Humanities at the University of Edinburgh for granting me a fellowship in the framework of which I could conduct research for this article.

Maginn, William. "On National Economy: Review of Miss Martineau's 'Cousin Marshall'. *Fraser's Magazine for Town and Country* (November 1832): 403–413." *Illustrations of Political Economy: Selected Tales.* By Harriet Martineau. Ed. Deborah Anna Logan. Peterborough: Broadview, 2004. 420–422.

Martineau, Harriet. "Weal and Woe in Garveloch." *Illustrations of Political Economy: Selected Tales.* By Harriet Martineau. Ed. Deborah Anna Logan. Peterborough: Blackwell, 2004. 22–136.

——. "A Manchester Strike." *Illustrations of Political Economy: Selected Tales.* By Harriet Martineau. Ed. Deborah Anna Logan. Peterborough: Blackwell, 2004. 137–216.

——. "Cousin Marshall." *Illustrations of Political Economy: Selected Tales.* By Harriet Martineau. Ed. Deborah Anna Logan. Peterborough: Blackwell, 2004. 217–294.

——. "Sowers Not Reapers." *Illustrations of Political Economy: Selected Tales.* By Harriet Martineau. Ed. Deborah Anna Logan. Peterborough: Blackwell, 2004. 295–381.

——. *Harriet Martineau's Autobiography: With Memorials by Maria Weston Chapman.* Vol. I. London: Smith, 1877a.

——. *Harriet Martineau's Autobiography: With Memorials by Maria Weston Chapman.* Vol. II. London: Smith, 1877b.

——. Preface. *Illustrations of Political Economy.* Vol. 1. London: Fox, 1834.

Miller Fenwick, Florence. *Harriet Martineau.* London: Allen, 1887.

Oražem, Claudia. *Political Economy and Fiction in the Early Works of Harriet Martineau.* Frankfurt am Main: Lang, 1999.

Otteson, James R. "Introduction." *Selected Philosophical Writings.* By Adam Smith. Ed. James R. Otteson. Exeter: Imprint Academic, 2004. 1–10.

Roberts, Caroline. *The Woman and the Hour: Harriet Martineau and Victorian Ideologies.* Toronto: University of Toronto Press, 2002.

Scrope Poulett, George. "'Review of *Illustrations of Political Economy.*' The Quarterly Review 49 (1833): 157–152." *Illustrations of Political Economy: Selected Tales.* By Harriet Martineau. Ed. Deborah Anna Logan. Peterborough: Broadview, 2004. 422–425.

Sedlacek, Tomas. *Economics of Good and Evil: The Quest for Economic Meaning from Gilgamesh to Wall Street.* Oxford: Oxford University Press, 2011.

Smith, Adam. *Selected Philosophical Writings.* Ed. James R. Otteson. Exeter: Imprint Academic, 2004.

Vargo, Gregory. "Contested Authority: Reform and Local Pressure in Harriet Martineau's Poor Law Stories." *Nineteenth-Century Gender Studies* 3.2 (2007): n. pag. http://www.ncgsjournal.com/issue32/vargo.htm (23 August 2013).

Webb, R. K. *Harriet Martineau: A Radical Victorian.* London: Heinemann, 1960.

Joachim Frenk

"We have learned the value of poverty": (Re-)Presentations of the Poor in Nineteenth-Century Melodramas

1 Poverty and Melodrama

One exemplary quotation that both describes and perpetuates the nineteenth century's singling out of the poor as a people – almost a race – apart is to be found in an 'industrial' novel, and it takes the form of a dialogue. In one of the most famous literary passages dealing with the condition-of-England question formulated by Carlyle, Benjamin Disraeli has two of his characters in *Sybil* (1845) arrive at the idea of the two nations that provides for the novel's subtitle:

> 'Well, society may be in its infancy', said Egremont slightly smiling; 'but, say what you like, our Queen reigns over the greatest nation that ever existed.'
> 'Which nation?' asked the younger stranger, 'for she reigns over two.'
> The stranger paused; Egremont was silent, but looked inquiringly.
> 'Yes', resumed the younger stranger after a moment's interval. 'Two nations; between whom there is no intercourse and no sympathy; who are as ignorant of each other's habits, thoughts, and feelings, as if they were dwellers in different zones, or inhabitants of different planets; who are formed by a different breeding, are fed by a different food, are ordered by different manners, and are not governed by the same laws.'
> 'You speak of –' said Egremont, hesitatingly.
> 'THE RICH AND THE POOR.'
> At this moment a sudden flush of rosy light, suffusing the grey ruins, indicated that the sun had just fallen; and through a vacant arch that overlooked them, alone in the resplendent sky, glittered the twilight star. The hour, the scene, the solemn stillness and the softening beauty, repressed controversy, induced even silence. (1980, 96)

The silence is then broken by the eponymous heroine's almost angelic singing, which creates the vision of a pre-industrial England the novel longs for: an England untouched by the divisive powers of a technological and urban modernity. Here as elsewhere, *Sybil or The Two Nations* suggests a simple division of an ever more complex Victorian society, a reductive division one would rather expect from the simplifying and diverting strategies of contemporary melodrama, both in its argument and in its aesthetic packaging. The binary opposition flaunted here, between a poor 'them', which was dreaded by middle- and upper-class readers alike, many of them plagued by a fear of social falling, and a rich 'us', which created a deceptive cohesion where actually there was none, was denounced as incredible and oversimplified even in the 1840s. The elitist social romanticism of Disraeli's Young England ideology was savagely attacked, for instance in Dickens's *The Chimes* (Frenk 1998, 107–109).

Sybil or The Two Nations was published in the year in which Friedrich Engels published *The Condition of the Working Class in England in 1844* (in German; the English translation followed in 1887), shortly before Henry Mayhew started collecting material for *London Labour and the London Poor*, and eleven years after the Poor Law Amendment Act, commonly referred to as The New Poor Law, had been passed through parliament. The divisive rhetoric of Disraeli's social daydream first isolates the poor (as a homogeneous group) and then seeks to reintegrate them into the concept of the one nation via a synaesthetic moment of sacralising pastoral and music that represses the controversy of the speakers. The musical element, the excessive rhetoric and the optical spectacle are all influenced by a melodramatic poetics that is here imported into the novel's poverty discourse. The discursive proximity between melodrama and other forms of the age's textual production was a common phenomenon at the time. As Elaine Hadley notes: "The characteristic mode of anti-Poor Law literature does share with stage melodrama many structural features and, to that extent, justifies the comparison and the common term *melodramatic*" (1995, 78).

The two classic main arguments against the analysis and interpretation of nineteenth-century melodrama can be traced back to that century itself: for one thing, melodramas were and are considered to be of such low aesthetic and artistic value, so rough-hewn and Manichean in their narrow presentation of a simplistic world-view, that the interpretive results they promised are claimed to be meagre.[1] For another, the sheer mass of melodramas in their own golden age seems to make it difficult to arrive at overarching conclusions concerning a genre of mass entertainment that was first and foremost produced to make a profit from whatever was of interest to its courted target group, which wanted to be affirmed in its views. However, the rise of critical interest in historical forms of popular culture over the last decades has changed this canonical and critical marginalization of the melodrama, and it has paved the way for an inclusion of the study of melodrama into the burgeoning field of poverty studies.

A. N. Wilson sums up the paternalizing Victorian attitude of those who, like Disraeli (Diedrich 1992), treated the poor like children: "The middle-class liberals, with their sanitation acts, education acts, board schools and churches,

---

[1] See for instance Nicoll (1947, 353–361) and for a historicizing discussion Schmidt (1986, 30) and Krug (2001, 6).

throughout the nineteenth-century and beyond, wanted not merely to improve conditions for the poor but wanted to improve the poor" (2003, 335). This impulse towards an often unquestioned 'improvement' according to middle-class norms and values was not necessarily a given in melodramas that followed their own, often markedly different agendas. At the same time, the stage of the melodrama was an area of cultural production that enabled an acting out of "a middle-class feeling and awareness that for some time the poor had been moving into and out of cultural domains that no act of settlement had so far been able to order successfully" (Tetzeli von Rosador 1997, 129). Containing 'the poor' via the exaggerated emotions, fantastic plots and clear-cut positive outcomes of the melodrama was one strategy of coping, at least fictionally, with the new forms of mass poverty and the problems adhering to them. It is therefore a matter of debate whether members of the nineteenth-century poor are re-presented in particular melodramas, or whether the stage fictions bear such little resemblance to anything outside the theatre that it would be better to say that imaginary poor are being presented. What melodramas may still make readable, visible, performatively accessible, though, are elements of a poverty discourse that could perhaps not have been easily formulated elsewhere at the time. Melodramas, the mass forms of entertainment whose popularity as a genre corresponded to that of the novel (the latter being largely limited to the literate), helped formulate the nineteenth century's ideas of poverty.

It is curious that in her classic study *The Idea of Poverty: England in the Early Industrial Age*, Gertrude Himmelfarb, despite using all kinds of sources to excavate her topic, does not mention the melodrama as a genre that should be studied to approach an understanding of the early nineteenth-century discourse on poverty:

> Embedded in the social milieu, the idea [of poverty] can only be extracted from that milieu, from the behavior of people as well as from their writings, from legislation and debates, popular movements and public issues, economic treatises and religious tracts, novels and 'penny dreadfuls'. 'Idea' in this sense is a shorthand expression for a complex of concepts, attitudes, values, beliefs, perceptions, images. (1984, 11)

While Himmelfarb includes for instance penny dreadfuls as a popular genre, she omits melodramas. She does not explicitly exclude them either, yet in her book she does not refer to a single melodrama.

Melodramas are full of 'poor characters' (in more than one sense). For all its occasional lack of aesthetic refinement, the melodrama very much merits scholarly attention with a view to its contribution to the formations and transformations of nineteenth-century ideas of poverty. However, the interpretation of what the melodramatic poor signified (or can signify today) hinges on the definitions of melodrama itself. As a dramatic genre, melodrama has been critically described within a wide critical spectrum. Here is Michael Booth's well-established definition from the mid-1960s: "Essentially, melodrama is a dream world inhabited by dream people and dream justice, offering audiences the fulfilment and satisfactions found only in dreams. An idealization and simplification of the world of reality, it is, in fact, a world its audiences want and cannot get" (1965, 14). For Booth, then, melodrama is the genre of escapism *par excellence*, far removed from any kind of social realism, let alone reality. In a much more recent approach, David Mayer argues that melodrama figures as a socially seismic genre:

> The decades immediately preceding the nineteenth century, the century itself, and the first two decades of the twentieth century, we must invariably remember as we consider melodrama, constitute a period of rapid and profound change. Concomitant with these changes is intense stress. As we study a melodrama, we must factor in the growth of a vast overseas empire, urbanization, industrialization, agricultural crises, emancipation and universal suffrage, the rise of new social classes and the enlargement or endangering of earlier ones. [...] Along with more immediate concerns, British melodramas frequently explored the major fault-line of class and status and the anxieties which these subjects engendered [...]. (2004, 147)

Booth's and Mayer's views can be taken to demarcate the end-points on a spectrum of critical perspectives on melodramas that extend from the irredeemably escapist to the politically engaged, from the rigidly formulaic to the elusively protean. Mayer's claim that melodramas, albeit in their own ways and within their own changing generic codes, often do address the problems of the age instead of ignoring them, has recently gained more critical acceptance. The fact that melodramas address the poverty of their time certainly does not mean that they analyze the issue in any thorough form. Melodrama tends to conjure up the demons of the age only to slay them in an inevitable happy ending which turns its back on any sense of plausibility reigning in the world outside the theatre.

   At the turn of the millennium, Michael Hays and Anastasia Nikolopoulou claimed that melodrama, as a shaping cultural factor of the nineteenth century, has so far not been analyzed thoroughly enough, particularly with a critical view to its politics:

> [T]he melodrama played an important role in the cultural dynamics of the nineteenth century, a role that was downplayed or outright denied by most earlier critics. Yet any attempt to define (or redefine) melodrama by turning away from a historical understanding of the genre and its uses and reinscribing it under an aesthetic category named after the adjective derived from it is bound to move critical discussion into a subjective arena that must inevi-

tably disregard the cultural dynamics underlying the actual production and reception of the melodrama. In order to get at the historical significance of the melodrama it remains important to ask, for example, about the implications of its 'illegitimate' status. Why did contemporaries attack it as a monstrous aesthetic configuration or, more interestingly, as Coleridge put it, 'a modern Jacobinical drama', and why were large segments of its audiences regarded as criminal elements? (1999, viii)

The vilification and marginalization of the melodrama from the beginning of its stage appearance thus point to the genre's subversive potential as a site of a politically dangerous culture of the silenced and disenfranchised. The poor were not only a stock element of the melodramatic personnel; they were also seen as a sizable part of the melodramas' audiences, assuming they were not too poor to buy a ticket – the poorest of the poor would hardly ever be able to see a play. The cultural dynamics of technological modernity that produced and sustained stage melodramas for more than a century derived much of its energy from the contested social distinctions of an ever more pluralistic society. The manners of speaking, writing and performatively actualizing current social questions were heavily influenced by the generic and ideological codes of the melodrama. The very 'acting out' of poverty was a hotly contested issue in the debates surrounding the New Poor Law of 1834, as Elaine Hadley explains:

The Royal Commission of Enquiry, which was deputed to capture the essence of the Old Poor Laws, filled its enormous volumes with instances of 'imposture' – the standard term used to describe individuals' dishonest, if not precisely illegal, attempts to get relief when they did not need it. 'Imposture', a conceptual imposition of deception and deceit, was the dirty underside of theatrical performance, the term used by the audience when it no longer was willing to believe in or indulge the actor. [...] By many, the poor were no longer considered to be poor; they seemed simply to be acting poor. (1995, 85 – 86)

Poverty was indeed acted out on a number of levels, and the melodrama of the time both used the cultural scripts of poverty to cater to its audiences' interests and developed these scripts according to the changing theatrical fashions and framing conditions. These constant adaptations in a century of radical changes were facilitated by melodrama's generic hybridity, its status as a dramatic form that alternated between different established genres instead of fusing them, a characteristic that was stressed already in the nineteenth century (Tetzeli von Rosador 1977).

2 *The Rent Day*

Poverty, both in the city and in the country, was not only the worrying subject of performative routines that purportedly created an impression of absolute misery merely to abuse ever more anonymous institutions of charity; it was also the object of the nineteenth century's pervasive fear of a French revolution on British soil. This fear found its way onto the melodramatic stage via the debates surrounding and leading up to the First Reform Bill of 1832. Douglas Jerrold's rural domestic melodrama *The Rent Day*, first performed in 1832, is one contribution to these debates. One of the events that fed into its story of misery and extortion among the agricultural population was the Captain Swing rebellion of 1830. This rebellion indicated dangerous and widespread unrest in the countryside which resulted from the introduction of ever more efficient agricultural machines and from the fact that parliament

> had responded inadequately to the hardship years which followed the end of the French wars, when the agricultural labour market was flooded by thousands of demobilized soldiers. [...] Violence spread from Kent to Surrey, Sussex, Hampshire, Wiltshire and further north through Essex, Bedfordshire and Cambridgeshire to Suffolk and Norfolk. (Thomson 2006, 175–178)

In Jerrold's melodrama, the small farmer Martin Heywood, impoverished because "[h]arvest after harvest's failed – flock after flock has died" (Jerrold 1847, 15), can no longer pay his rent to the absentee landlord. The landlord's steward Crumbs, a former street criminal, is relentless and, at the end of the second act, has his henchmen Bullfrog and Burly remove all portable property from the farm. Martin, reduced in his own house from a self-supporting farmer to one of the destitute poor, threatens to rebel against his tormentors while his wife Rachel and his brother Toby hold him back:

> RACH[EL]. Dear Martin, be calm!
> CRUM[BS]. You'll not oppose the law?
> MAR[TIN]. I know not that. I tell you, don't provoke me. [...]
> BURLY. [*Showing a paper*] What say you to our warrant, Master Heywood?
> MAR. I tell you not to tempt me. I cannot trust myself, for I am desperate! Leave the farm!
> CRUM. [*To Bull. & Bur.*] You know your duties [*Exit L.*
> BUL[LFROG]. [*On L., who has been looking over goods*] Business is business. [*Takes out pen, ink, and book.*] One bedstead!
> MAR. Let me come at them!
> TOBY. Nay, nay, brother!
> RACH. Husband!
> CHILDREN. Father! [*They all hang about* MARTIN, *keeping him from attacking* BURLY *and*

BULLFROG.]

MAR. (C.) [*After a struggle, sinks into the chair.*] Rachel! – my poor babes! – take all, take all.

BUL. [*Making out inventory.*] One bedstead – one table!

BEAN[STALK] AND NEIGHBOURS. [*who have entered, R., and come down, some remaining behind*]. Shame! Shame!

TOBY. Blood-suckers!

BUL. One toasting-fork, one bird-cage, one baby's rattle!

MAR. God help us! God help us! [*Buries his face in his hands.* (Jerrold 1847, 25 – 26)

Interestingly, the adjective "poor" is used here only by Martin when he addresses his little children. The "poor babes" are pitied by their father; "poor" is not used in its predominantly economic sense to describe Martin's state. The most ominous political statements in this crucial passage are Martin's replies ("I know not that [...] I cannot trust myself, for I am desperate!"), which for one dramatic moment leave open whether he will abide by the law or whether his poverty will turn him into a violent rebel. In typical fashion, the melodrama shows the ultimate containment of its protagonist's subversive tendencies: Martin's rebellious spirit is subdued, but the play makes it clear that the rural poor like him might once more act out their dissatisfaction as they had done in 1830 – 1831. The mercilessness of the steward-as-villain is materialized on the stage through the domestic objects that are being taken away from the family: the bedstead, the table, the toasting-fork, the bird-cage and, finally, the baby's rattle. The objects become ever more diminutive and less valuable while their 'human' signifying potential increases.[2] Taking away a baby's rattle from the 'deserving' poor is melodramatically condemned as a lack of human solidarity with the innocent. Bulldog's triumphant listing of the rattle marks the point when the despairing Martin turns to prayer, asking God for help in the face of the inhuman treatment of his wife and children. But before this conventional religious turn, the play has made it clear that, reduced to abject poverty, Martin might have resorted to other means. The scene, and the second act, famously end in a tableau that copies Sir David Wil-

---

2 With its focus on domestic objects and its hero who encounters problems he has not caused, *The Rent Day* is the melodramatic equivalent of the farce of the 1820s and 1830s. It is driven by the same plot mechanics: "[The farce's] comedy deals in misadventures with food, drink, and domestic paraphernalia of all kinds. Domesticity is the key word; no more utterly domestic drama has ever been written. In no other drama have furnished lodgings, articles of clothing, and the contents of kitchen cupboards and larders afforded so much opportunity for confusion, misunderstanding, and comic business of all kinds. The central character of such farce is usually a perfectly ordinary man, often married, who either through his own mistake, or through a combination of unfortunate circumstances of which he is in no respect the author, finds himself helplessly and inextricably involved in a sequence of disastrous events over which he has neither control nor influence" (Booth 1995, xvii-xviii).

kie's renowned painting *Distraining for Rent* (1815). One may interpret this either as emphasizing the social criticism of the scene or as weakening the scene's impact by retreating into an aestheticizing discourse (Rippl 2011; Krug 2014).

3 *The Poor of New York* and *The Lights o' London*

A look at two melodramas from the second half of the century can reveal that, in spite of their formulaic character, individual melodramas merit closer analysis for the ways in which they intervened in the discourse on poverty as one of the most central debates of the nineteenth century. The first of these is a play by one of the most successful playwrights of the century: Dion Boucicault, who was also, not unusually for the age, an actor-manager. *The Poor of New York* was written in 1857 during the time Boucicault lived in the United States (1854–1860) for the money and fame he hoped to get on the American market. Like many others at the time, this melodrama is based on a French play, namely *Les Pauvres de Paris* (1856) by Edouard-Louis-Alexandre Brisbarre and Eugene Nus. *The Poor of New York* "was a collaboration between Boucicault and three journalists, Seymour, Goodrich, and Warden – although the bulk of the writing was done by Boucicault – and was first advertised as being 'by the **** Club'. Popular with nineteenth-century audiences, but derided by critics, it was a play which Boucicault himself admitted was 'guano' rather than 'poetry'" (Dion Boucicault Collections 2012). After his return to Europe, Boucicault put the play on British and Irish stages; he revised its title according to the place of performance. The poor of New York highlighted in the premiere would, in the performance history of this melodrama, become the poor of, for instance, Liverpool, Dublin and London. Indeed, the play also became known under the title *The Streets of London* after it was performed in London in 1864. Next to its somewhat strange definition of 'the poor', which is to be discussed, *The Poor of New York*, set during the financial panic that occurred in the United States in 1837 (Act 1) and 1857 (from Act 2), features a sensation scene in which a house burns down on stage. This scene was the eye candy that was meant to pull audiences, which rather throws the play's social concern for the poor into relief.

The poor in the play are the Fairweathers, an impoverished family of the affluent middle class who, at the sudden death of the patriarch, are cheated out of their possessions by the corrupt banker Gideon Bloodgood, who lives in luxury with his family. Unbeknownst to the Fairweathers, Mark Livingstone, the hero, a former rich suitor to the heroine Lucy Fairweather, has meanwhile gone bankrupt as well and is now also one of the new poor. The play's title is therefore somewhat misleading since its poor of New York consist of fallen members of the middle class and a formerly rich man. None of them is reduced to an abject poverty comparable to the poverty of millions of others, which ensured that the Broadway audience at Wallack's Lyceum Theatre did not come into contact with the poorer poor. The first meeting between these not-too-poor shows everybody's awkwardness about their social position:

> MRS F[AIRWEATHER]. Mr Livingstone.
> PAUL. Good morning, Sir.
> LIV[INGSTONE]. Sir! – Mr Livingstone! – have I offended you?
> PAUL. We could not expect you to visit us in our poor lodging.
> MRS F. We cannot afford the pleasure of your society.
> LIV. Let me assure you that I was ignorant of your misfortunes – and if I have not called – it was because – a – because – [*Aside.*] What shall I say? [*Aloud.*] – I have been absent from the city. [...]
> LIV. And what would you say if I were no better off than yourselves – if I too were poor – if I –
> PAUL. You, poor, who own a square mile of New York? (16–17)[3]

The Fairweathers think that Livingstone has shunned them because of their poverty, while he really has done so because of his own. The shamed Livingstone cannot bring himself to confess his poverty to his former friends – a typical melodramatic plot twist. More importantly, poverty is represented as being more a cause for anxiety concerning one's social prestige than a life-threatening state of material insufficiencies.

By contrast, Livingstone's former family baker Puffy does not have any qualms about having fallen into the ranks of the poor:

> PUFFY. Down in the world now, sir – overspeculated like the rest on 'em. [...]
> LIV. So you are poor now, are you? [*Takes a potato, playfully.*
> PUFFY. Yes, sir; I ain't ashamed to own it – for I hurt nobody but myself. Take a little salt, sir. But, Lord bless you, sir, poverty don't come amiss to me – I've got no pride to support. Now, there's my lodgers –
> LIV. Ah, your second floor.
> PUFFY. A widow lady and her two grown children – poor as mice, but proud, sir – they was grand folks once; you can see that by the way they try to hide it. (14)

Puffy's acceptance of his poverty hinges on his only having brought ruin upon himself – overlooking the fact that his wife is also affected by his excessive speculations. Being the landlord of the modest house the Fairweathers live in, Puffy expresses respect for the Fairweathers' upholding of their pride in spite of their

---

3 All page numbers refer to the 1857 edition of *The Poor of New York.*

social degradation. The difference between Puffy's acceptance of his new position and the 'pride' of the Fairweathers is illustrated when Paul Fairweather searches for work which he needs to procure a living for his mother and sister in lieu of his deceased father. Having been repeatedly rejected by prospective employers, Paul gives vent to his frustration by differentiating himself from the poor – whom he perceives as another kind of people:

> PAUL. Livingstone, I begin to envy the common laborer who has no fears, no care, beyond his food and common shelter – I am beginning to lose my pity for the poor.
> LIV. The poor! – whom do you call the poor? do you see them? they are more frequently found under a black coat than under a red shirt. The poor man is a clerk with a family, forced to maintain a decent suit of clothes, paid for out of the hunger of his children. The poor man is the artist obliged to pledge the tools of his trade to buy medicines for his sick wife. The lawyer who, craving for employment, buttons up his thin paletot to hide his shirtless breast. These needy wretches are poorer than the poor, for they are obliged to conceal their poverty with the false mask of content – smoking a cigar to disguise their hunger – they drag from their pockets their last quarter, to cast it with studied carelessness, to the beggar, whose mattress at home is lined with gold. These are the most miserable of the Poor of New York. (18)

According to Paul, the poor of the working class are to be envied for the very fact that they are so poor that they cannot afford to worry about anything but the most elementary in the hierarchy of needs, "food and common shelter". As a (former) member of the aspiring middle class, Paul can no longer pity them because they do not share his longing for 'adequate' employment, a completely self-centred line of argument since it presupposes that the urban poor can and should share this aspiration. Livingstone supports Paul's curious rejection of the 'other' poor by identifying three prototypical struggling members of the middle class – a clerk, an artist, a lawyer – who are "poorer than the poor, for they are obliged to conceal their poverty". According to Livingstone, a formerly rich man, the costly performance of an adequate social appearance is the cause of 'true' poverty; the 'real' poor are the run-down members of the quasi-deserving lower middle class (all of Livingstone's *exempla* are men) who have to pretend that they are not poor while they are struggling to survive. At the end of the argument, paradoxically, the 'fake' poor at the bottom of the social ladder are not even materially poor; according to Livingstone (there is no indication that he has ever come into contact with the urban poor), their "mattress at home is lined with gold", and yet they receive alms from the 'true' middle-class poor. His argument, which amounts to a complete reversal of the idea as to who is to be considered poor, is not contradicted by anybody. The above-mentioned British discussion about "impostures" of the poor in order to get at support they do not really need is here turned on its head: the performative routines of the sunken middle class aim at the complete opposite of the much-criticized impostures – they seek to camouflage the desperate situation of no longer being able to function as an economically independent citizen and actually being in need of support.

In a brilliant flash of absurd social comedy, the sermonizing Livingstone is taken for a social propagandist by the citizens gathering around him. A champion of a silenced majority, he receives applause for passionately speaking up for the 'true' poor of the penniless middle class:

> [*A small crowd has assembled around* LIVINGSTONE *during this speech; they take him for an orator; one of them takes down what he says on tablets.*
> Enter POLICEMAN
> PUFFY AND CROWD. Bravo – Bravo – Hurrah – get on the bench!
> POLICE. Come – I say – this won't do.
> LIV. What have I done?
> POLICE. No stumping to the population allowed in the park.
> LIV. Stumping!
> REPORTER. Oblige me with your name, sir, for the Herald.
> LIV. Oh! [*Rushes off, followed by* PAUL. (18 – 19)

Livingstone first addresses himself to Paul, but in a melodrama it is not out of place to see him turning into a public orator and addressing his speech to the public; 'universal truths' would often be proclaimed in this manner. It is only when the policeman reminds Livingstone, who gets carried away with the inherent truth of his words, of the dangerous character of his speech that Livingstone switches off the orator mode and turns into a private man again. Here, the play comes to reflect on the poverty phobia of the middle classes, its ideological main topic. At the same time it subverts itself, that is, Livingstone's pose, by exposing the public discourse and some of the overblown, heard-it-all-before rhetoric surrounding the topic of poverty. For this dramatic moment, it even satirizes, in the minor figure of the avid reporter, the proliferation and the exploitation of the poverty discourse in the nineteenth century's budding media society. With so many layers exposed all at once, the play's poverty discourse threatens to get out of control. In typical melodramatic fashion, the play offers no solution by argument; Livingstone simply exits, and the show goes on.

The conventional ending of the play seeks to smooth out all the cracks that have become visible in the facade of the poverty discourse:

> BAD[GER]. [*speaking to the happy couple,* MARK LIVINGSTONE *and* LUCY FAIR-WEATHER] You have seen the dark side of life – you can appreciate your fortune, for you have learned the value of wealth.
> MRS F. No, we have learned the value of poverty.

[*Gives her hand to* Puffy.] It opens the heart.
Paul. [*To the public.*] Is this true? Have the sufferings we have depicted in this mimic scene, touched your hearts, and caused a tear of sympathy to fill your eyes? If so, extend to us your hands.
Mrs F. No, not to us – but when you leave this place, as you return to your homes, should you see some poor creatures, extend your hands to them, and the blessings that will follow you on your way will be the most grateful tribute you can pay to the
POOR OF NEW YORK. (68)

The conventional metadramatic appeal at the inevitably happy ending of the play falls short of Livingstone's previous speech. The poverty discourse that has been exposed as questionable before comes now back to the fore; sentimentality triumphs over insight. With a view to the commercial attractiveness of poverty as a titular selling point of this melodrama, Mrs Fairweather's line "we have learned the value of poverty" acquires a double meaning: the theatrical community both on and off stage, it is suggested, has learned a conventional lesson about true values that are never material ones, but at the same time, this melodrama has demonstrated that poverty sells, that poverty is of commercial value for the mass-oriented producers of theatre. The illogical final point made by Mrs Fairweather that the grateful blessings of the poor should be taken as tributes either to themselves or to the play would be eclipsed by the audience's applause. Tableau and curtain.

In George Robert Sims's *The Lights o' London* (1881), Harold Armytage, the son of a rich country squire, and Bess Marks, the daughter of the Armytages' faithful lodge keeper, eloped some years ago to London and have now come back to Armytage Hall for the first time. Harold, who wants to talk to his father once more, has been rejected and disinherited by him as a consequence of the evil machinations of Clifford Armytage, Harold's villainous scheming cousin. Clifford and Seth Preene, a dubious character 'from the north', frame the innocent Harold for a crime so that Clifford will inherit the family fortune instead of Harold. Seth aids Clifford because he hopes that his daughter Hetty – a naive country girl who roundly declares "I hate poor people" (110)[4] – will then marry Clifford and become a rich lady. Harold is convicted and sentenced to gaol, but he escapes to seek Bess and is helped by the Jarvises, a travelling acting family just getting by, who resemble the Crummles family in Dickens's *Nicholas Nickleby*. Returning to London with the Jarvises, Harold is reunited with Bess, who has been earning her living as a lowly seamstress. Meanwhile, Seth visits his daughter Hetty in London; to his horror, she has become Clifford's mis-

---

4 All page numbers refer to Michael Booth's 1995 edition of *The Lights o' London*.

tress, not his wife. After Harold has rescued Seth from drowning, Seth decides to confess his crime so that Harold will receive his inheritance and Clifford will get the punishment he deserves.

The melodrama begins with the slightly unusual situation of both the hero and the heroine having already been reduced to poverty because the hero has been alienated from his father by his evil rival and banned from his happy country home. Harold's state of desperate poverty has been caused partly by his father's rejection, and partly by his falling for the lure of London:

> HAROLD. [...] we must have some respect for appearances. I may be a scamp, but I'm none the less an Armytage, and want of pride was never a family failing of ours, and I think I have inherited my fair share of the article – and – [*breaking down – coming to Marks*] Hang it, Marks, I can't keep it up. The sight of the dear old home is too much for me. [...] I went up to London, and tried, and – and failed.
> MARKS. Failed?
> HAROLD. Yes, like many another fool who fancies when he sees the Lights o' London he's found an Eldorado and only had to crawl back home again as I do now, a broken-down miserable man. (108)

This first mention of "the Lights o' London" not only refers to the play's title, but also to a popular song for which Sims had written the lyrics. "The Lights of London Town" had been published in the previous year. The following stanzas underline the referentiality of Harold's titular phrase:

> The way was long and weary,
> And gallantly they strode,
> A country lad and lassie,
> Along the heavy road!
>
> The night was dark and stormy,
> But blythe of heart were they,
> For shining in the distance
> The Lights of London lay. [...]
>
> They sought their native village,
> Heart-broken from the fray,
> Yet smiling still behind them
> The Lights of London lay.
>
> Oh! cruel lamps of London,
> If tears your lights could drown,
> Your victims' eyes would weep them,
> Oh! lights of London town. (Sims and Diehl 1880)

The alliterative and metonymic "Lights of London" are responsible for Harold's unspecified failure in the big city. Harold, who meets the melodramatic key qualification of having his heart in the right place, bears only negligible blame for his poverty, and he can thus remain largely intact as the hero. While it conventionally condemns the sins of the metropolis and praises the virtues of an ordered life in the country, the play caters to the audience's interest in everything Londonish. George Robert Sims specialized in London writing, and he created his own intertextual web around the metropolis. As Richard Higgins (2006) explicates, Sims specialized, in many of his writings, in rendering the *über*-city London intelligible – or at least in creating the impression of intelligibility – for his readers and theatre audiences:

> Sims was interested in giving his audience what they wanted. Responding to *The Idler*'s questions in 1897 about the middlebrow nature of his work, Sims asked, 'Mercenary? And who works for art's sake?' [...] What his audience most wanted was London. In plays, novels, and prose collections, such as *Lights o' London* (1881), *The Gay City* (1881), *Horrible London* (1889), *In London Town* (1899), *In London's Heart* (1900), *Living London* (1902), and *The Mysteries of Modern London* (1906), Sims returns again and again to this popular and very lucrative subject. [...] a good part of his work's popularity is due to his ability to render London legible for a middle class hungry for the assurance of legibility he provided. In particular, Sims uses melodrama to impose coherence on contemporary urban conditions. By creating the illusion that audiences were transported into the midst of urban destitution, melodrama collapses the distance between audience and the city's spectacle while simultaneously ensuring that spectators could travel back to the refuge of their West End and suburban homes. Social investigators and authors such as Sims utilized melodrama to reveal and expose the poverty that was unsettling to middle-class urbanites[;] at the same time they could sentimentalize a mostly East End underclass into figures of helpless victimization and paralysis.

Sims helped contemporary armchair travellers discover the unknown country of the poor that existed within the labyrinthine city. Like many others at the time, he would "turn to the models and prescriptions of imperialist discourse" (Tetzeli von Rosador 1997, 139) to get the poor under the control of his rhetoric and his ideological patterns. He did so for instance in his (pseudo-)travelogue *How the Poor Live*, published eight years after *The Lights o' London:*

> In these pages I propose to record the result of a journey into a region which lies at our own doors – into a dark continent that is within easy walking distance of the General Post Office. This continent will, I hope, be found as interesting as any of those newly-explored lands which engage the attention of the Royal Geographic Society [...]. (1889, 1; also Tetzeli von Rosador 1997, 139).

As with the impostures and other strategies mentioned above, poverty in *The Lights o' London* is a matter of social enactment, a play with appearances, similar to acting – the performative dimension of poverty is once again highlighted in the theatre. The actor family of the Jarvises, warm-hearted histrionic enthusiasts, become the centre of the play about poor appearances, from their first meeting with the distressed hero who has just escaped from prison:

> HAROLD. [*raising himself*] Oh, help me get to London, to find my wife, who's dying! I am an innocent man!
> MRS JARVIS. All the convicks is as escapes. Leastways in all the dramas as I ever played in. [...] There's a splendid ghost's costume complete in the corner, only don't get a walkin' about or you'll frighten Jim. (127)

The innocent prisoner is a staple convention of melodrama; Harold cannot hope to convince the Jarvises of his honesty – and yet he does convince them because this is a melodrama that both exhibits its generic conventions and follows them. Having him change his costume to that of a ghost, the play also points to Harold's ghostlike 'absent presence' at this point. Additionally, the acting business of the Jarvises provides metadramatic opportunities. Harold, already an actor in a convict's costume, dresses up as a ghost (with the prestige of *Hamlet* attached to it) and becomes an actor within the dramatic fiction. In London, the Jarvises save Harold from the police who are coming to search for him. They turn the situation into a rehearsal of a play with a convict in it, and Mr Jarvis changes clothes with Harold. As Mrs Jarvis says in the play: "Yes, we're rehearsing a drama for our next tour. It's hard lines as poor folks as gets their living by performing should be took up for what they're acting" (141). She argues that the poor who live from their acting – in this case, criminals – must not be mistaken for the roles they enact. At the same time, it is clear to the audience that Mrs Jarvis is only acting the outraged actress – they are not rehearsing a play, and the prisoner's clothes Mr Jarvis has put on are Harold's. Being accepted as one of the (deserving) poor is here turned into a question of good acting and the right costume. Mr Jarvis is rewarded for his performance as a convict by being arrested.

The Lights o' London offers one character who is meant to be taken as 'genuinely poor'. This minor character is, again in keeping with the melodrama formula, crucial for the unravelling of the villain's evil machinations. The character is listed in the *dramatis personae* as "Philosopher Jack", and on stage he is always addressed as Jack – it seems that he cannot even afford a surname. Right from his first appearance, he is clearly marked as having his own morals, which are not the ones officially promoted by the play:

> JACK. [*reading notices at the police station*] Escaped, a convict – desertion of the wife and family. Well, I can understand a man running away from his wife and blooming kids, but he must be a discontented cove as would run away from a nice warm prison where he gets all his meals regular and plenty of nice light innocent amusement chucked in for nothing.

[DETECTIVE] CUTTS. You've never been in prison, Jack?
JACK. No, I never had the luck to do nothing wus than be poor, and they don't punish a cove with board and lodging for that crime in this country. [...]
Fools goes to the workhouse, rogues goes to prison. Why, cause every man as goes to the workhouse is a fool for not being a rogue. (129)

Emanating subversive humour, Jack easily rejects the family ideology considered well nigh sacred by respectable society, and he regrets, in an almost Wildean turn, that he is only poor, but not criminal, as being the latter would procure him a place in "a nice warm prison". The middle-class prejudice that poverty and criminality are almost the same thing is simultaneously addressed and ironically discarded. Jack argues that being a criminal has its rewards while being merely poor has none. Like the Jarvises, the cynical Jack provides the comic relief that is needed to counterbalance the serious and moralizing main plot. Apart from these lines, Jack has only very little to say in the play; he finds a necklace that was in the possession of the Armytage family and overhears the villain implicating himself – once more, a minor poor character is instrumental for the happy ending. Jack's thoughts about the relationship between poverty and crime and the way the state produces one through the other are, unsurprisingly, ignored for the rest of the play. When the villain has been arrested, Harold Armytage is restored as the rightful heir of his father's estate. Jack is not even on stage to hear Harold proclaim the days of poverty a thing of the past: "[We are a]ll the happier, perhaps, for the trials we have passed through" (170).

4 Conclusion

The above, highly selective readings of the presentations and re-presentations of the poor in melodramas substantiate the claim that the cultural archaeology of nineteenth-century poverty has to include the melodrama as the most popular dramatic genre of the century. The multi-faceted public discourse on poverty acknowledged a performative aspect of poverty. This aspect was considered to be problematic, for instance in separating the deserving from the non-deserving poor (a highly problematic distinction in itself), but it was also richly exploited, for instance on the contemporary stage. The poor as they were written and acted in the melodramas of the time had as much and as little to do with the everyday reality of the audience as all other parts of the performance. At a time when society as a whole was trying to understand the new forms of poverty it was confronted with, the popular stage was one more experimental space to do this. Melodrama acted out many versions of poverty and the poor, from a tranquillizing sentimentality and fairy-tale endings to a breathtaking, if mostly only episodic, audacity which could not have been vented outside the theatre.

The ending of Tom Robertson's *Caste* of 1867 may serve as a concluding illustration of this audacity. At the time of its first production, *Caste* signified, after the London production of Robertson's *Society* (1865), a turn in the melodrama towards a much more pronounced stage realism that was later famously praised by George Bernard Shaw. In the final scene of *Caste*, the hero, Captain George D'Alroy, can, after overcoming many obstacles and in particular the fierce resistance of his mother (the Marquise), finally marry the poor dancer Esther Eccles – the chasm between the different castes can be bridged. There remains only one major problem: Eccles, Esther's father, is a poor drunkard who will never be tolerated by the D'Alroy family, but makes his stage presence felt and threatens to spoil the final tableau. George's officer friend, Captain Hawtree, comes up with a solution to the problem that puts on show more cynical pragmatism than any happy ending would be able to take:

[CAPTAIN HAWTREE] [*aside to* GEORGE]. I think I can abate this nuisance – at least I can remove it.
Rises and crosses C., *to* ECCLES, *who has got round to* R. *side of table, leaning on it. He taps* ECCLES *with his stick, first on* R. *shoulder, then on* L., *and finally sharply on* R. ECCLES *turns round and falls on point of stick* – HAWTREE *steadying him.* GEORGE *crosses behind, to* MARQUISE, *who has gone to cradle* – *puts his arm round* ESTHER *and takes her to mantelpiece.*
HAW. Mr. Eccles, don't you think that, with your talent for liquor, if you had an allowance of about two pounds a week, and went to Jersey, where spirits are cheap, that you could drink yourself to death in a year?
ECCLES. I think I could – I'm sure I'll try. [*Goes up,* L. *of table, steadying himself by it, and sits in chair by fire, with the bottle of gin.* HAWTREE *standing by fire.*] (Robertson n. d. [1867], 144–145)

Works Cited

Boot, Michael R. "Introduction." *The Lights o' London and Other Victorian Plays.* Ed. Michael R. Booth. Oxford: Oxford University Press, 1995. ix–xxvi.
—. *English Melodrama.* London: Herbert Jenkins, 1965.
Boucicault, Dion. *The Poor of New York: A Drama in Five Acts.* New York and London: Samuel French, 1857.
Diedrich, Maria. *Aufschrei der Frauen – Diskurs der Männer: Der frühviktorianische Industrieroman.* Stuttgart: Franz Steiner, 1992.
Dion Boucicault Collections. "*The Streets of London/The Poor of New York.*" *University of Kent* 2012. http://www.kent.ac.uk/library/specialcollections/theatre/boucicault/plays/streets.html (1 October 2013).

Disraeli, Benjamin. *Sybil or The Two Nations*. Ed. Thom Braun. Harmondsworth: Penguin, 1980.

Frenk, Joachim. *'Myriads of Fantastic Forms': Formen und Funktionen des Phantastischen in englischen Sozialmärchen des 19. Jahrhunderts*. Münsteraner Monographien zur Englischen Literatur 20. Frankfurt am Main: Lang, 1998.

Hadley, Elaine. *Melodramatic Tactics: Theatricalized Dissent in the English Marketplace, 1800–1885*. Stanford, CA: Stanford University Press, 1995.

Hays, Michael, and Anastasia Nikolopoulou, eds. *Melodrama: The Cultural Emergence of a Genre*. Basingstoke: Macmillan, 1999.

Higgins, Richard. "London on Stage: The Urban Melodrama of George Sims." *Literary London: Interdisciplinary Studies in the Representation of London*. March 2006. http://www.literarylondon.org/london-journal/march2006/higgins.html (1 October 2013).

Himmelfarb, Gertrude. *The Idea of Poverty: England in the Early Industrial Age*. London: Faber and Faber, 1984.

Jerrold, Douglas William. *The Rent-Day: The Modern Standard Drama. A Collection of the Most Popular Acting Plays*. Vol. IV. New York: William Taylor and Co., 1847. 1–48.

Krug, Christian. "Melodrama, Politics and Popular Culture: Douglas Jerrold's *The Rent Day* (1832)." *That's the Way to Do It: British Popular Cultures in the Nineteenth Century*. Ed. Joachim Frenk. Saarbrücken: Saarland University Press, 2014.

——. *Das Eigene im Fremden: Orientalismen im englischen Melodrama 1790–1840*. Trier: WVT, 2001.

Mayer, David, "Encountering Melodrama." *The Cambridge Companion to Victorian and Edwardian Theatre*. Ed. Kerry Powell. Cambridge: Cambridge University Press, 2004. 145–163.

Nicoll, Allardyce. *British Drama: An Historical Survey from the Beginnings to the Present Time*. 4th Edition. London: Harrap, 1947.

Rippl, Gabriele. "Victorian Melodrama: Thomas Holcroft's *A Tale of Mystery* and Douglas William Jerrold's *The Rent Day*." *A History of British Drama: Genres – Developments – Interpretations*. Eds. Sibylle Baumbach, Birgit Neumann and Ansgar Nünning. Trier: WVT, 2011. 207–222.

Robertson, T. W. Caste: *An Original Comedy in Three Acts*. London and New York: Samuel French, n. d. [1867].

Schmidt, Johann N. *Ästhetik des Melodramas: Studien zu einem Genre des populären Theaters im England des 19. Jahrhunderts*. Heidelberg: Winter, 1986.

Sims, George Robert. *The Lights o' London: A New and Original Drama in Five Acts [1881]*. *The Lights o' London and Other Victorian Plays*. Ed. Michael R. Booth. Oxford: Oxford University Press, 1995. 103–170.

——. *How the Poor Live*. London: Chatto & Windus, 1889.

Sims, George Robert [lyrics], and Louis Diehl [music]. *The Lights of London Town*. London: Boosey and Co., 1880.

Tetzeli von Rosador, Kurt. "Victorian Theories of Melodrama." *Anglia* 95 (1977): 87–114.

——. "Into Darkest England: Discovering the Victorian Urban Poor." *Journal for the Study of British Cultures* 4.1/2 (1997): 129–144.

Thomson, Peter. *The Cambridge Introduction to English Theatre, 1660–1900*. Cambridge: Cambridge University Press, 2006.

Wilson, A. N. *The Victorians*. London: Arrow Books, 2003.

Frédéric Regard

The Sexual Exploitation of the Poor in W. T. Stead's 'New Journalism': Humanity, Democracy and the Tabloid Press

1 Introduction

The Maiden Tribute of Modern Babylon was a series of articles written by William Thomas Stead, published in July 1885 by the *Pall Mall Gazette*. They formed an extraordinarily controversial report on what was then termed "the white slave trade", i.e. forced child prostitution. With provoking subheadings such as "The Violation of Virgins", "Virgins Willing and Unwilling" or "Strapping Girls Down", *The Maiden Tribute* threw the Victorians into a state of what the sociologists of the 1970s would call a "moral panic" (Cohen 1971, 39). Indeed, only within a few weeks after the publication of Stead's report, Parliament was forced to pass the Criminal Law Amendment Act (14 August 1885), which raised the age of consent for girls from thirteen to sixteen. Still, despite – or perhaps because of? – the enormous success of his report, Stead was accused by the rest of the press of "peddling pornography" and of unlawful investigative methods for which he served three months in prison (Baylen 2010). What he was reproached with was his unquestionably ambiguous behaviour in the notorious Eliza Armstrong case – "Lily" in *The Maiden Tribute:* in order to prove the existence of an international traffic in young girls for wealthy débauchés, Stead had bought the child from her impoverished mother using the services of a former prostitute, Rebecca Jarrett, who before the Old Bailey on 30 October 1885 gave evidence that she had indeed procured the girl for £5 (Mulpetre 2012). According to Stead, the ease and rapidity with which he had been able to purchase Eliza simply proved the extreme vulnerability of any poor English girl. Despite the technical violation of the law in obtaining material for his revelations, the agitation Stead caused was lauded by many social reformers, including Cardinal Manning (Baylen 1963), and by most feminist groups, prominent among them Josephine Butler's crusaders against the Contagious Diseases Acts, which were seen as an official encouragement for the sexual exploitation of the poor (Walkowitz 1992).

If Stead is remembered today, however, it is less for the social and political uproar that he created than for his invention of what rapidly came to be called the 'New Journalism', the ancestor of both muckraking journalism and of its serious counterpart, investigative journalism. Convinced that a new political force was emerging – which would lead to what he called "government by journalism" (Stead 1886) – Stead was certainly not ready, however, to print anything which could help raise sales as has sometimes been claimed (Robinson 2012). Joseph Baylen (2010) neatly wraps up what his major achievements consisted in:

> Stead quickly moved to increase the circulation and influence of the paper [the *Pall Mall Gazette*] by endeavouring to make it 'the great tribune of the poor', the conscience of the wealthy, and especially 'a centre of live power' in Britain and its overseas empire. By such journalistic innovations as bold headlines, pictorial illustrations, special interviews, provocative leading articles, attractive drama criticism, perceptive book reviews by such writers as William Archer, Bernard Shaw, George Meredith, and Oscar Wilde, and special 'extra editions', the *Pall Mall Gazette* was made a force to be reckoned with in British politics.

If Stead's ambition was to turn his paper into "the great tribune of the poor", it was first and foremost in the hope of putting an end to the extreme vulnerability of the young girls who were daily offered for consumption on a sex market which had imported into the private sphere the worst aspects of class exploitation, with the tacit complicity of the Establishment. The outrages he denounced were felt to be moral, social and political scandals – a term I shall use to signify not simply "the disruptive publicity of transgression" (Adut 2005, 214), but, more precisely, the furore caused by the revelation of a breach of trust between the powerful rich and the powerless poor, with the sudden exposure of a collusion of interests and of a large measure of hypocrisy on the part of the upper classes. Such scandals had to be revealed to the public for the protection of the defenceless, the improvement of British society and more generally the progress of humanity.

What is nevertheless quite true – and this explains why this 'New Journalism' was also the birth certificate of the late twentieth-century tabloid press – is that once Stead had identified one such scandal, he was ready to exploit its most 'sensationalist' aspects. Sensationalism was not something that was inherent in the facts themselves; the scandal was indeed produced, or rather fashioned and staged through a number of stylistic and rhetorical devices. As a matter of fact, Stead's report on juvenile prostitution included so much fictionalization and narrativization that his work soon became a source of inspiration for most European erotic writers (Praz 1951, 421). Such fictional recuperation of Stead's narrative should not come as a surprise. William Cohen (1996) has argued that a significant number of novels in Victorian England – notably the novels of Charles Dickens, George Eliot and Anthony Trollope – had already contrived to make sex into a scandal, a notion Cohen uses to mean a cocktail of deviant behaviour and concealment. But Stead's 'New Journalism' produced much greater sex scandals than those caused by such novelists, not only in bringing out the as yet ignored social and political aspects of late nineteenth-century sexual practices, but also, precisely, in blurring the limits between fact and fiction, or between testimony and literature. In some measure, it was inevitable that Stead should be brought to court, officially for abduction. More fundamentally, his conception of investigative journalism did accommodate the possibility of using simulacra, dissimulation, perhaps even lie and perjury, to expose outrageous behaviours, thus flouting the sacred principle according to which the testimonial should remain irreducible to the fictional in every aspect of social life (Derrida 2000, 29). But at the same time, Stead's reports were certainly not pure fiction: their ambition was to explore the dark corners of Victorian culture, to expose the inward lust of outward respectability, if necessary by *creating* the conditions of the exposure. What caused the nation's unease, therefore, may to a certain extent be attributed to Stead's genius as a writer: he was not content simply with presenting facts by reporting on them; he chose rather to *re-present* them, seeking through such representation to transform hard, indisputable facts into *news events*.

Stead sought less to distort facts, to manipulate public opinion, than to dramatize the poor's precariousness in order to lend visibility and audibility to that portion of the British population to whom the pimps, procuresses, wealthy débauchés, but also the Government itself, were prone to deny the status of full-fledged citizens, or even human beings. This chapter argues that if Stead was indeed the first muckraker of the modern press, it was primarily because his revelations did shatter a national consensus verging on national blindness. It is this innovative narrativization of precariousness which will lead me to suggest that the origins of the tabloid press were in fact related to issues of humanization and democratization, a view radically opposed to Ronald Pearsall's when he writes that Stead's innovations were "the death knell of responsible journalism" (1969, 373). I claim on the contrary that what was originally at stake in muckraking journalism was an ethics of writing, implying a redefinition of the journalist's moral duty, as well as of his social or political role, when confronted with the scandals he exposed – and contributed to producing through what I will describe as a new poetics of politics.

2 Myth, Commodification and "Bare Life"

As was made clear from the start by their very title, Stead's articles sought to interweave social or realist description and mythological or biblical allusion. *The Maiden Tribute* opens on a reminder of the Greek myth of the labyrinth and the

Minotaur, a monster to whom a sacrifice of virgins had to be made every nine years as a tribute of Athens to her conqueror, Crete. Stead compares this offering of virgins with the destroying of poor girls that takes place in contemporary London, which as a consequence deserves to be called the "Modern Babylon" (after the biblical capital of idols and perversity):[1]

> This very night in London, and every night, year in and year out, not seven maidens only, but many times seven, selected almost by chance as those who in an Athenian market place drew lots as to which should be flung into the Cretan labyrinth, will be offered up as the Maiden Tribute of Modern Babylon. (116–117)[2]

This mythological and biblical dimension of the modern white slave trade is underlined again when Stead reports the existence of a 'London Minotaur'. This striking metaphor is used to refer to a gentleman whose name Stead is very careful not to disclose, but of whom he affirms that his "quantum of virgins from his procuresses is three per fortnight" (181). The narrative's intense metaphorization of contemporaneous urban life is nevertheless predicated on circumstantial eye-witness evidence, so that Stead's articles do lend themselves eventually to being read as intensely realistic, quasi detective investigations, solidly supported by first-hand knowledge acquired in the field, and carefully rearranged into "classifications" – thereby ostensibly using methods borrowed from the techniques of modern police investigation (Thomas 2000). For example, Stead's description of what he calls the "London Inferno" culminates with a list of the various forms of "sexual criminality", presented in a pseudo scientific layout:

> And that crime of the most ruthless and abominable description is constantly and systematically practised in London without let or hindrance, I am in a position to prove from my own personal knowledge – a knowledge purchased at a cost of which I prefer not to speak. Those crimes may be roughly classified as follows:–
>
> I.   The sale and purchase and violation of children.
> II.   The procuration of virgins.
> III.   The entrapping and ruin of women.
> IV.   The international slave trade in girls.
> V.   Atrocities, brutalities and unnatural crimes. (119)

The result of Stead's strategy – this queer combination of realism and mythology – might seem to be a downplaying of the importance of context – of late nine-

---

1 Isaiah, 23:17; Apocalypse, 17:5.
2 All page numbers for Stead's *The Maiden Tribute* refer to the 2003 edition.

teenth-century urban poverty – in the sexual exploitation of young girls: it is the status of all female Londoners which is perceived to have become precarious, but this modern vulnerability seems at the same time to be in line with an immemorial sacrificial tradition. Stead's strategy is in fact much more complex as it is consistently subtended by a critique of the power relationships induced by a specific economic system, which he also perceives to be inevitably gendered. Stead does not simply assert that one sex is by definition more vulnerable than another, that girls are by nature likely to be hurt, wounded or humiliated by men's violent sexual practices. What matters for him is not that the relations of the sexes are now regulated "by the higgling of the market and the liberty of private contract" (118); it is rather that no fraction of the female population seems to be protected from the risk of *commodification*, i.e. the risk of being transformed into what he constantly calls "goods" or "parcels" (125–126), marketable objects to be used at their convenience by the criminals of the superior classes.

What he also seems to suggest is that the organization of Britain as a modern, sovereign state may have paradoxically implied the perpetuation of ancient, barbarous practices, now taking the form of a commodification of poor girls. In an era when childhood and girlhood in particular was "idealized and idolized" as a development stage "as yet unmired by the sullying forces of society" (Robson 2001, 3–4), Stead revealed to his contemporaries that no English girl was in fact granted either ontological or statutary protection against sexual exploitation, that the State itself could not guarantee their safety: not only the Government but the whole of British society had been organized so that all poor girls could be used as marketable bodies. The Contagious Diseases Acts, by registering the healthy girls and locking away the unhealthy ones, had even transformed poor girls, according to Josephine Butler, into "bits of numbered, inspected, and ticketed human flesh, flung by Government into the public market" (2003 [1870], 126). The threat of commodification is not particularized, therefore; it is *universalized*, bearing on the very impossibility of the protection of that portion of the British population to whom the basic dignity of being considered human beings was denied. Any poor girl could indeed be turned into a "bit of flesh" immolated on the altar of male desire, with the complicity of the British juridical system. What Stead suddenly perceived, in other words, was what Giorgio Agamben would later identify as the blind spot of all liberal democracies, namely: the persistence of the *homo sacer* institution of archaic Roman law. The lost girls whose fates he describes are made to embody what Agamben calls "bare life", that part of the political subject's existence excluded from the juridical order instituted by the sovereign power, the very thing that was excluded at the moment of juridical institution, and that yet "finds itself in the most intimate relation with sovereignty" (1998, 66–67). Stead's stroke of genius consisted in gendering "bare life", in feminizing, so to speak, the exception on which British sovereignty was grounded: for him the modern state's power rested on the assumption that poor girls should play the role of *homo sacer*, be turned into those inhabitants of the city who could not be sacrificed according to divine law but who might be killed without their killing being considered murder according to the laws of the city.

3 Ways of Seeing

The procedure Stead adopts in order to reclaim such lives from oblivion or mercantile indifference is always the same. It consists in lending his ears to the as yet untold stories of those British non-citizens who have been forced to experience "bare life" and whose voices have been suppressed by the hegemonic, official narrative of Britain's linear and progressive march to ever more humane, democratic civilization. Stead always ends up presenting himself as a first-hand witness who sees things with his own eyes, hears things with his own ears, venturing like an explorer of uncharted territories into the heart of a *domestic* darkness: "I have been a night prowler for weeks" (209). London – including the West End and its fashionable villas (147–149) – is thus portrayed as an uncanny city, both familiar and unfamiliar, a place thought to be known and charted and yet where a disturbing reality resurfaces as the stumbling block that prevents one from walking safely through its streets. Such stories often seem to reach the journalist almost by chance, in the form of vague rumours which the journalist turned detective decides to verify by himself: "There is nothing like inquiry on the spot", he declares (131). And what so far had been anonymous or second-hand narrative is turned into hard facts the very moment the events are reported through the amateur detective's first-hand narrative: "I can personally vouch for the absolute accuracy of every fact in the narrative", Stead is proud to assert, the use of the first-person singular functioning as a token of verifiable accuracy (136). Stead not only confirms the veracity of the crimes, he also takes this opportunity to provide his readers with figures and statistics, and also to furnish gruesome details as to the tortures inflicted on the girls or as to the purchase prices fetched by "the goods" (125–126), inviting his fascinated audience to follow him on what does indeed strongly resemble a voyeuristic, pornographic tour of the world's capital city.

Still, *The Maiden Tribute* may perhaps be best described as the narrative of a realist exploration of a labyrinthine, mythologized reality, characterized as a consequence by a central, ethical and hermeneutic tension between two aesthetics, two views of life and existence, two economies of self and other, and in fact two ways of reading. The articles contemplate an approach of London which organizes itself underground, which 'encrypts' itself, seeking both to conceal its crimes and to efface its traces, and whose mythic dimension is due to its collapsing of night and day, respectability and monstrosity, civilization and barbarity, justice and murder, sacredness and precariousness. This is the world of the wealthy, protected débauchés, who in the West-End villas install "underground, padded rooms for the purpose of stifling the cries of tortured victims of lust and brutality" (133). Another approach of the same city sketches itself, however, which seeks on the contrary to bring back to the surface the dark, secret life of the nation, and whose realistic dimension is due precisely to the narrator's insistence on scientifically listing various forms of sexual criminality. The 'new journalist' thus defines himself as a detective whose very presence in the heart of darkness, as a realist observer and moral witness, reestablishes a demarcation line between good and evil, and reaffirms the principle of the intangible sacredness of *all* life. The journalist's values, projected into the heart of the mythic "Inferno", form thus the thread of the narrative, the only way to escape from the complex maze of the labyrinth. Like Theseus, the 'new journalist' advances to face the hidden, hideous monster of civilization, playing out his thread.

4 A Parallel Society

Stead's report is also studded with vivid and eloquent evidence of how various characters involved in the traffic in girls account for their own experiences. Such personal attestations come in support of Stead's assertions, in direct speech most of the time, either in the form of autobiographical monologues or in that of interviews conducted by the journalist himself. For example, Stead records "the confessions of a brothel keeper" who tells him about the techniques used to replenish a stock of girls, the prices fetched by children of twelve or thirteen, the various clients of houses of ill-fame, etc. (125–126). Stead also offers his reader a first-hand relation of an escape by one of the girls:

> Within the last month I made the acquaintance of a girl of seventeen, who escaped at the eleventh hour from just such a trap. I interviewed her, as I have interviewed many others, but her story is so striking an illustration of the kind of work that is going on all around us that it is worth while giving it just as she gave it to me, merely premising that I have been able, by independent inquiries at Shoreham and Pimlico, to verify the complete accuracy of her statement:–
>
> My name is A—; I am seventeen years old. [...] (140)

This accumulation of personal testimonies is of course meant to lend Stead's narrative its credibility. *The Maiden Tribute* establishes itself not as a fictional construction of precariousness but as a collection of facts supported by diversified testimonies. What is thus gradually suggested as the narrative unfolds is that the institutionalization of "bare life" rests on the existence of a secret, underground sociological network, which the reporter discloses by effacing himself, allowing the others to speak out. The indirect effect produced by such an accumulation of stories told from different perspectives by direct witnesses – victims, police officers, brothel keepers, procuresses, pimps, certificators of virginity, etc. – is that the reader is made to perceive each character as being embedded within a web of interconnections, a vast capitalist machinery: "There is in full operation among us a system of which the violation of virgins is one of the ordinary incidents" (121). The "system" is also described as having international ramifications: "London [...] is the greatest market of human flesh in the whole world", Stead writes, with girls imported from the rest of Britain, but also from Poland, France or Belgium "for the purpose of being ruined" (217). The catering for the vices of the rich to the detriment of the poor is even presented as a "systematized business", with the brothel-keepers organized into "firms" (149, 158).

What Stead uncovers, in other words, is the existence of a parallel society, made up not of marginals and outlaws, but of a diversity of professions working in strict compliance with the economic regulations of the market, as well as with the laws voted in Parliament. One of Stead's subparts, entitled "The Procuress Learned in the Law", relates the story of a procuress who knows the law better than the journalist himself, and whose favourite pastime is to read in the papers "all the cases in the courts which relate to this subject" (154). Taking as his target "the scandalous immorality of having a severe law for the weak and a lax law for the strong", Stead is not content to denounce "loopholes in English legal and administrative procedure" (Gorham 1978, 359), but contends provocatively that "an alliance is struck up between the brothel keeper and the constable" (Stead 2003, 210, 206). No social field, no economic sector seems to have been left untouched by the development of this parallel society: country girls, nurse-girls, shop-girls, servants, governesses, cooks and of course children may all be caught up in the "system", lured into the "Babylonian maze" (176). Any poor English girl may fall prey to procuresses disguised as nice ladies working for theatres, employment agencies, servants' registries or governess agencies (215). The London described by Stead is presented as "a strange inverted world", the world of business and politics having been put in the service of the infamous trade: "it was the same, yet not the same, as the world of business and the world of politics" (120). Ruin and death can therefore happen to any girl, anywhere, at any time, in a city where female precariousness has become the norm: where the sexual exploitation of children has been made legal, where women's lives have been made "bare", and where every respectable home may have been turned into a Gothic castle for the satisfaction of the rich and powerful's sexual wants.

5 The Moral Duty of Publicity

As Stead's reportage was published in the form of four successive installments between 6 and 10 July 1885, the readers of the paper were afforded with the possibility of reacting to their publication. Quite a number of the "Letters of Protest" which were sent to the editor – and included *The Maiden Tribute* – accused Stead of voyeurism and pornography (200 – 203). To which Stead responded by arguing that the 'New Journalism' was strictly motivated by the duty to protect the poor and innocent against the vices of the rich and powerful. His stance was eminently both ethical and political: the underprivileged needed to be protected, and they also needed to be allowed to speak out. The newspaper was precisely the medium through which those whose lives had not been deemed worthy of the nation's protection, those who traditionally remained silent and invisible, could find a tribune, come forward and challenge the national consensus. The 'New Journalism' was therefore the symptom of a new, rising democratic urge: "The hour of democracy has struck", Stead writes, adding that what he has learnt is "strong enough to wreck the Throne" (117). Stead's fundamental idea was that silence and invisibility were part of the system of institutionalized female precariousness. By exposing the scandal, penetrating into the padded rooms of the upper classes, threatening to give names to the justice of his country, the reporter-detective suggests that Britain is in fact composed of two nations, the visible and the invisible, the audible and the inaudible, and that his duty as a 'new journalist' lies in representing those precisely who have been denied the right of representation, namely the girls of the working classes, who may be best defined therefore as that forgotten category of the British people which has been deprived of a voice and a visibility of their own: the 'new journalist's' duty is to challenge what Stead calls "the conspiracy of silence" (186).

Stead's indictment of the upper classes' criminal practises is thus turned by the same token into a vindication of the 'New Journalism' that he is inventing. Implying that the role of the press should be both political and ethical, he argues that his reportage may be thought to be immoral – voyeuristic or pornographic – only by those of his readers who would in fact be content to maintain the status quo and prolong the conspiracy of silence. The reporter's prophetic mission, sanctioned by God, is on the contrary "to declare trumpet-tongued over sea and land the whole infernal truth in the ears of a startled world" (186). To the law of padded rooms, the 'new journalist', the greatest prophet of modern times, opposes therefore the moral duty of what he calls "publicity": "The one safeguard is publicity, publicity, publicity! And all who attempt to silence the voice of warning must share the guilt of those upon one small portion of whose crimes it is our proud privilege to have turned a little of the wholesome light of day" (228). The metaphor of journalistic light being shed upon the Gothic darkness of a world turned upside down only confirms that fiction and testimony parasite each other in Stead's new journalism. What is perhaps more interesting here is Stead's suggestion that the precariousness of the life of certain categories of the population does not exist until it is acknowledged to exist, and is in fact *made* to exist through publicity. What is at stake is the very recognition of precariousness, which *The Maiden Tribute* asserts is not possible before it has been recognized and brought to public notice by the newspaper article, in the terms adopted by the journalist's report. Publicity consists in making public the reality of the precariousness of the female poor, a precariousness which would otherwise have remained not so much ignored as *nonexistent*. To take up Judith Butler's argument, some lives need to become worthy of public mourning and made into "grievable lives" in order for the victims to be identified as suffering human beings (Butler 2004, 20).

Publicity it is, therefore, that makes precariousness into a true scandal: the evidence of such a collusion between private and political interests should have been kept underground, made inaudible and invisible, but it is suddenly brought back to visibility and audibility, foregrounded on the stage of representation, thus 'poetically' disrupting the tranquillity of 'policed' society, i. e. of established order (Rancière and Panagia 2000, 115–116). To that extent, 'New Journalism' is indeed 'democratic', as Rancière would no doubt argue, insofar as it lends a voice and a face to precisely those who have been denied the possibility of self-representation, and who are now invited to express themselves through a medium – the newspaper article – which at long last *represents* them, both in the aesthetic and in the political senses of the term. The newspaper article does not simply record precariousness, capturing raw facts as a basic photograph would, but reports *on* it, thus redescribing or re-presenting it, for the dual purpose of securing the credibility of the revelation and of making the suffering effectively intolerable, or "grievable", to Stead's readership. Reportage literature thus seeks to modify the cartography of sensibility through what can only be a poetic operation. What is at stake is indeed nothing less than the production of empathy between the precarious lives invited to express themselves through the newspaper article and the secure lives of the readers of the paper invited to reconsider the world which they thought was safe and stable, nicely distributed between good and evil.

6 Empathy, or the Time of Precariousness

Indeed, Stead's reportage lends a multiplicity of voices and faces to female precariousness, thus precipitating what Jacques Rancière (2004) would call a thoroughly subversive "redistribution of the sensible". If "the police", as Rancière puts it, is this form of authority which partitions the sensible into various regimes and therefore delimits forms of inclusion and exclusion, then the 'New Journalism' does redefine the conditions of possibility of recognizable existence, if only through what it is possible to apprehend through the senses. The poor girls whose fates are described are all made singularly identifiable, which is a way of expressing a *dissensus* or "disagreement" with the police by securing a form of visibility and audibility to those Rancière calls the *sans-part*, i.e. those who are not entitled to take part in official history, who are made invisible and inaudible through the usual, consensual distribution of the sensible.

What is of particular significance in this respect is Stead's technique of building up his argument through a succession of interviews, insisting not only on the possibility, but also on the necessity, of such renewed face-to-face communication. Stead is quite obviously conscious of this new feature in his journalistic practice, and of its potential impact. What is so painful about his explorations of underground London, he tells us, is "to have to see the victims face to face, to see their tears and hear their sobs" (86). What is implied is that the knowledge of life made bare, of the utter vulnerability of poor girls in particular, is not enough in itself to create the *reality* of precariousness. What constitutes the news event is not the established fact of the inhuman treatment reserved to poor girls; it is the sudden realization, in the course of this painful interview, that the victims' cries have been muffled, that their tears have remained unseen, their sobs unheard, and that the pain expressed in the present is but a superficial indication of the traumatic experience suffered in the past. This is what an experienced police officer can only confirm to the journalist: "what avails screaming in a quiet bedroom? Remember, the utmost limit of howling or excessively violent screaming [...] is only two minutes" (123). The "procuress learned in the law" tells the reporter exactly the same thing: "The time for screaming is not long. As soon as it is over the girl sees it is no use howling. [...] I have never known one case of interference in the four years I have been in the business" (157).

In the face-to-face interviews between the journalist and the abused girls, the tears and sobs are finally admitted into reality, but only as belated, attenuated reiterations of the initial traumatic experience. The tears and sobs of the poor girls are no longer due to the violence inflicted on them, but to the sudden memory of that violence, provoked by the questions of the reporter. In other words, the screaming and the howling are always already things of the past when the journalist records the victims' testimonies. This is certainly not to diminish the impact of Stead's report. On the contrary, the screaming and howling *must* have been unheeded, must have been left without any exterior interference, to offer the interview its full justification and significance: paradoxically, the prayers of the victims must have been left unanswered to reach their maximum effectiveness. The injustice of the poor girls' fate becomes *felt* injustice precisely because of this belatedness: to the horror of sexual abuse is now added the remorse of not having been there, of having closed one's eyes and ears to the crime while it was being committed.

What I call the temporal and enunciative structure of precariousness implies therefore that there should be at least two agencies – three if one includes the reader –, one who calls for help, for interference, who prays for exterior help; and one who not only acknowledges the sufferings of the other but who belatedly answers her call for help, substituting himself for all the other indifferent characters, to listen at long last to the victim's prayers. Such prayers are no longer for immediate help, of course, but for compassionate ears and eyes. The structure of precariousness supposes the awareness that the face-to-face meeting recorded in the newspaper article comes too late, that the news event produced by the revelation of the scandal includes in fact a certain degree of mourning – mourning the irretrievable, mourning the loss of innocence, mourning also the absence of those who are no longer alive to bear witness, along with the journalist's traumatized interlocutors, the survivors of the nightmare.

Like all reportage literature, Stead's narrative is thus Janus-faced, looking in two temporal directions at the same time, torn between its mourning for lost opportunities and its longing for reparation, between the painful realization of a past injustice and the feverish demand of a justice to come. Precariousness, the *OED* (2013) explains, is a prayer for help (*precor* in Latin), a prayer for the good will, the benevolent presence of the other; which means that it is not a cry for mercy, the cry of the vulnerable victim begging her torturer to spare her honour or her life. It is always already too late to prevent precariousness, which commands therefore that the future should be redefined. This tension between emotional remembrance and ethical exigency accounts indeed for the narrative structure of the *Maiden Tribute* which is interspersed with scenes of encounter between a former victim whose cries have been unheeded and the journalist-detective who records an interview which is both necessary and futile, allowing the girl to speak at long last, to make herself heard, while calling attention to the ghost-like presence of her former suffering self and of so many other similar anonymous victims.

The enunciative structure of precariousness implies therefore that the two interlocutors should also be two suffering agencies, perhaps even two suffering bodies: the formerly tortured but still weeping victim, and the grieving, emotionally disturbed journalist. The anonymous victim of the traffic in women is suddenly seen and heard as an imploring face and a sobbing body; the cool, scientific investigator is revealed to himself as a pained conscience and a co-suffering being. This sudden mutual redefinition of victim and detective-journalist is also what transforms facts into events, constituting such encounters as what might be called epiphanies of humanity, moments of revelation of a shared, empathic humanity, between reporter, victim and reader. Due to the temporal structure of the acknowledgement of precariousness, the melodramatic representation of the girls' distress does not, however, trigger an engagement with Stead's characters whereby absolute identification between victim and journalist – or reader – precludes any self-other differentiation (Coplan 2004, 148). Both journalist – no longer the social explorer doing his "inquiry on the spot", but the moral, armchair agency of the writing reporter – and reader are invited to become deeply involved in the poor little victims' experiences without relinquishing their separate identities: the rhetorical and narrative strategies of *The Maiden Tribute* induce them both to simulate the poor girls' experiences, to feel *for* the victims, but at the same time to maintain their own separate identities. This is due mainly to the belatedness of the acknowledgement of the victims' grievability, but also to the ethical exigency that is ignited by the scandalous revelation of past – and ongoing – abuse.

7 Humanity and the Ongoingness of Inhumanity

In one of her most recent essays, Hélène Cixous argues that what constitutes our humanity is in fact our cowardice: "we prefer not to see [...] what *makes man*." She immediately adds, however, that those she calls "the knights of humanity" are precisely those who have seen "the cowardice of those who do not want to see the cruel face of humanity" (2011, 279–280). Humanity is thus also defined as what survives both "bare life" and cowardice, what accrues to inhumanity, so to speak, when humanity has been denied to an invisible, inaudible fraction of the population as well as to the various hypocritical, selfish or indifferent British citizens who chose to close their ears and eyes to the fate of so many sacrifical victims.

Stead was one such "knight of humanity", a seer of blindness, one might say. Reporting on the fate of all those unmourned, ungrieved, lost girls, was indeed seeing humanity at its worst in the face, while ensuring at the same time that a good humanity, a lucid humanity to come, would eventually take place after all, when it was perhaps least expected, in the eleventh hour, Stead would have said, "in the extreme end" (*à la dernière extrémité*) as Cixous puts it. All it took was for a lone wanderer to make time to meet the scum of the earth, take down her story "from her own lips" (Stead 2003, 217) and precipitate the reader's recognition of the existence of a grievable life and awareness of the unavoidability of empathic engagement. Adopting the "melodramatic tactics" (Hadley 1995) which had already worked wonders in the history of British political dissent, Stead certainly used the dramatization of the poor little victims' tears and sobs to break the spell of cowardice and indifference: emotion and grief would bridge the gap between observer and observed, subject and object, man and girl, rich and poor, pen and parcel, reader and witness, in such a way, however, that simulation and identification would maintain the necessary, ethical play of differentiation and open the way for a future humanity to express itself. Too late, always already too late, but not irremediably so, the prophet, the seer, the 'new journalist' seems to whisper.

Of course, the tense mostly used by the narrator of *The Maiden Tribute*, as is the case of most narratives of exploration or investigation, is the past. But Stead constantly manages to abolish the temporal and spatial distance implied by the use of the preterit by employing two particular techniques. The first, as we have seen, consists in interrupting his narrative with interviews during which the law of reported, indirect speech prevalent in the rest of the narrative is suspended, and the two interlocutors – the journalist and a procuress, the journalist and a police officer, the journalist and a young victim – are made to speak directly, therefore in the present tense. For example, when Stead interviews the "procuress learned in the law", she is reported to declare: "our business is in maiden heads, not in maids. [...] Our gentlemen want maids, not damaged articles" (155). The second technique consists in constantly giving the impression that the reporter has "but skimmed the surface of the subject" (186), that sexual criminality is in fact more widespread than is suggested by the accumulation of testimonies, that precariousness and vulnerability are in fact endless.

What I suggest is one of the major characteristics of reportage literature, therefore, is that the journalist does not investigate into past criminal cases as a detective would; reportage is mostly an indication of what is currently *going on*, ceaselessly, even as the reader is discovering the cases disclosed in the articles. This is also what constitutes the scandal: its ongoingness. For example, once Stead has recorded the story of Marguerite de S., a French girl whose terrible life in the hands of one "M. B---, 33, T--- street, Lambeth, London" (218) is told by herself, he concludes: "This man is still at work" (220). Only one page further, about the foreign traffic between Belgium and Britain, Stead notes:

"Only last week a sample lot of three colis, or parcels, left the region of Leicester Square for Belgium. Two of them are now in Antwerp, one in Brussels. A much larger consignment is expected shortly" (221). As the journalist reports what he has just learnt – *The Maiden Tribute* was originally read as a series of articles, which surely added to this feeling of an ongoing threat – the criminal practices continue, as if speech were both helpful and helpless, a very temporary glimmer of light in an eternity of darkness, a fragile present of the enunciation drowned by the unceasing, but still unheard screams and howls of the victims.

This narrative strategy is meant to prompt the readers to act, to replace reading with political action. And it did work as we now know, since Parliament was forced to modify British law. But the more enduring effect of such a strategy teaches us something else about precariousness: exposing the scandal of precarious lives is a procedure that is never quite completed. Stead's narrative makes revelations while at the same time suggesting that the impact of such publicity can only be temporary, that precariousness is unrelenting, vulnerability continuous. The present of the exposure abolishes therefore neither the past nor the future. That is profoundly why precarious lives are always somewhat interchangeable and can never be stabilized by their narrativization. They are floating lives, whose identities can never be arrested, whose fates can never be fixed. Stead's narrative of investigation ensures that the girls are turned into a crowd of ghosts, whose sudden, temporary coming to visibility and audibility only acts as a disturbing trace of the other side of reality, its dark, hellish, but also restless side. The tortured girls are retrieved from past oblivion, only the better to haunt the present as well as the future: representation is meant to prevent time from closing in on the unfortunate victims. The extremely repetitive structure of Stead's narrative finds here its ultimate justification: the purpose of the reportage is not to construct a story, with a beginning, a middle and an end, leading for example from quest, to discovery and happy reintegration; it is rather to precipitate narrativity into an endless crisis, whereby British civilization and culture are made to split at the seams to reveal the permanent inhumanity that constitutes its foundation.

Stead's exploration of the dark side of the capitalist system owes its enduring fascination to precisely this handling of horror: the narrative simultaneously brings into light the repressed material and rejects it into obscurity, raises it to publicity and confines it again to padded rooms, exposes the scandal of a collusion between the lawful and the lawless and allows it to sink back into impunity. Stead offers a striking metaphor for his narrative's doing – and undoing. He invites his readers to think of themselves as the spectators of a shipwreck and compares his action to "throwing a rope into the abyss" (217). What the metaphor suggests is that the narrative thread itself should be construed as some such rope, repeatedly thrown into the darkness of the abyss, affording a limited number of poor souls to manifest their presence to the straining eyes of the rescuers, no second opportunity being afforded to the multitude of the other drowning characters. Their ghosts will therefore come back to haunt the present of the readers, to re-present themselves in representation, not only to invalidate the theory of a safe England, but also to forbid the illusion of a better, humane future. It is therefore the lives of the readers themselves which are thus made precarious. The late nineteenth-century Theseus does not eventually reach the centre of the maze to kill the monster; nor does he return to his ship and set sail for home. His place is on the beach where he has fastened his thread, which he is condemned to throw back into the abyss, eternally. The late twentieth-century tabloid press is still stranded on the same beach. Only the nature of the news event has changed.

Works Cited

Adut, Ari. "A Theory of Scandal: Victorians, Homosexuality, and the Fall of Oscar Wilde." *American Journal of Sociology* 111.1 (July 2005): 213–248.

Agamben, Giorgio. *Homo Sacer: Sovereign Power and Bare Life*. Trans. Daniel Heller-Roazen. Stanford, CA: Stanford University Press, 1998.

Baylen, Joseph O. "Stead, William Thomas (1849–1912)." *Oxford Dictionary of National Biography*. Online edition. http://www.oxforddnb.com/view/article/36258?docPos=3. Oxford: Oxford University Press, 2010 (7 January 2012).

——. "Cardinal Manning and W. T. Stead: Notes of an Unpublished Interview." *The Catholic Historical Review* 48.4 (January 1963): 498–507.

Butler, Josephine. "The Moral Reclaimability of Prostitutes" [1870]. *Josephine Butler and the Prostitution Campaigns: Diseases of the Body Politic*. Vol. 1: *The Moral Reclaimability of Prostitutes*. Eds. Jane Jordan and Ingrid Sharp. London and New York: Routledge, 2003. 121–127.

Butler, Judith. *Precarious Life: The Powers of Mourning and Violence*. London and New York: Verso, 2004.

Cixous, Hélène. "Volleys of Humanity." *Volleys of Humanity*. Ed. Eric Prenowitz. Trans. Peggy Kamuf. Edinburgh: Edinburgh University Press, 2011. 264–284.

Cohen, Stanley, ed. *Images of Deviance*. Harmondsworth: Penguin, 1971.

Cohen, William. *Sex Scandals: The Private Parts of Victorian Fiction*. Durham, NC: Duke University Press, 1996.

Coplan, Amy. "Empathic Engagement with Narrative Fictions." *The Journal of Aesthetics and Art Criticism* 62.2 [Special Issue: Art, Mind, and Cognitive Science] (2004): 141–152.

Derrida, Jacques. *Demeure: Fiction and Testimony* (1998). Trans. Elizabeth Rottenberg. Stanford, CA: Stanford University Press, 2000.

Gorham, Deborah. "The 'Maiden Tribute of Modern Babylon' Re-Examined: Child Prostitution and the Idea of Childhood in Late-Victorian England." *Victorian Studies* 21.3 (1978): 353–379.

Hadley, Elaine. *Melodramatic Tactics: Theatricalized Dissent in the English Marketplace, 1800–1885*. Stanford, CA: Stanford University Press, 1995.

Mulpetre, Owen. "W. T. Stead & the Eliza Armstrong Case." *The W. T. Stead Resource Site* 2012. http://www.attackingthedevil.co.uk/pmg/tribute/armstrong/ (5 June 2013).

OED. "precarious, adj." Etymology. *The Oxford English Dictionary*. Online Edition 2013. http://www.oed.com/view/Entry/149548?redirectedFrom=precarious#eid (20 November 2013).

Pearsall, Ronald. *The Worm in the Bud: The World of Victorian Sexuality*. London: Weidenfeld and Nicolson, 1969.

Praz, Mario. *The Romantic Agony*. Trans. Angus Davidson. 2nd ed. Oxford: Oxford University Press, 1951 [1950].

Rancière, Jacques. *The Politics of Aesthetics: The Distribution of the Sensible*. Trans. and introd. Gabriel Rockhill. London and New York: Continuum, 2004.

Rancière, Jacques, and Davide Panagia. "Dissenting Words: A Conversation with Jacques Rancière." *Diacritics* 30.2 (2000): 113–126.

Robinson, W. Sydney. *Muckraker: The Scandalous Life and Times of W. T. Stead*. London: The Robson Press, 2012.

Robson, Catherine. *Men in Wonderland: The Lost Girlhood of the Victorian Gentleman*. Princeton, NJ: Princeton University Press, 2001.

Stead, William Thomas. "The Maiden Tribute of Modern Babylon" [*The Pall Mall Gazette*, 6, 7, 8, 10 July 1885]. *Josephine Butler and the Prostitution Campaigns: Diseases of the Body Politic*. Vol. 4: *Child Prostitution and the Age of Consent*. Eds. Jane Jordan and Ingrid Sharp. London and New York: Routledge, 2003. 115–234.

——. "Government by Journalism." *The Contemporary Review* 49 (May 1886): 653–674.

Thomas, Ronald R. *Detective Fiction and the Rise of Forensic Science*. Cambridge: Cambridge University Press, 2000.

Walkowitz, Judith. *City of Dreadful Delight: Narratives of Sexual Danger in Late-Victorian London*. Chicago, IL: University of Chicago Press, 1992.

Marina Remy Abrunhosa
"The Amateur Casuals": Immersion among the Poor from James Greenwood to George Orwell

I

As Peter Keating remarked in his seminal anthology of social exploration, "the long tradition to which Orwell [...] belongs, is less often remembered" (1976, 16). Indeed, despite a growing scholarly interest in the different forms reportage was to take in parallel to the expansion of journalism in the nineteenth and twentieth centuries, when one thinks of examples of influential reportage, one is still more likely to quote Orwell's documentaries of the 1930s rather than lesser-known Victorian examples of undercover immersion such as James Greenwood's "A Night in a Workhouse" (1866). And yet, such texts played a crucial role in shaping and defining investigative immersion reporting.

George Orwell's first published book, *Down and Out in Paris and London* (1933) stands out as one of the most important English works on poverty, precariousness and destitution of the twentieth century, to the point that some contemporary readers give him credit for having initiated the method of immersion reporting. Along with other early works such as *The Road to Wigan Pier* (1937), *Down and Out* undoubtedly helped turn Orwell into a model and a myth, "the most famous of twentieth-century social explorers" (Keating 1976, 16). Together with *Homage to Catalonia* (1938), *Down and Out* and *The Road to Wigan Pier* constitute indeed crucial instances of twentieth-century reportage literature, which have had a potent and durable influence on several generations of journalists and undercover reporters across the continents, from John Howard Griffin's 1961 book *Black Like Me* or Günter Wallraff's enquiries into homelessness and marginalization (*Ganz Unten*, 1985; *Aus der Schönen Neuen Welt*, 2012) to Florence Aubenas's immersion into the lives of those assigned to precarious employments (*Le Quai de Ouistreham*, 2010).

Still, as several historians of reportage have shown, the tradition of undercover reporting emerged in fact during the second half of the nineteenth century, to be later refashioned by numerous lesser-known writers and journalists such as Nellie Bly (*Ten Days in a Mad-House*, 1887) or Mary Higgs (*Glimpses into the Abyss*, 1906), before it was eventually taken up by reporters such as Jack London and George Orwell. The Victorian era witnessed the multiplication of reports on the living conditions of the destitute. The vast expansion of industries and cities, with their corollary increase in poverty, overcrowding and precarious work, made it all the more necessary and urgent to bear witness to that reality, and even to participate in it, be it directly or indirectly. Such concerns would lead, with a narrowing of focus, to the immersion into the central institution of the workhouse, which had been generalized by the highly controversial Poor Law Amendment Act of 1834. The expansion of reportage – like the social novel's parallel rise – was also enabled by serialization, newspapers soon providing another privileged space for figuring the poor. To a certain extent, Victorian reportage literature may be said to have developed from the hybridization between the spheres of the novel and the newspaper article, at a time when the growth in paper production and circulation opened up forums for discussing the Poor Law and voicing the growing demands for social reform, especially in the wake of prominent scandals such as the Andover workhouse scandal of 1846 and the Huddersfield scandal of 1848 (Fowler 2008, 7, 50).

Amidst this diversity of writings on the workhouse which at first mainly took the shape of parliamentary enquiries and accounts of visits to the workhouse[1] – a memorable one being Charles Dickens's "A Walk in a Workhouse" (1850) published in *Household Words* – another way of writing about the workhouse appeared literally "overnight" according to Seth Koven (2004, 26), and was to play a crucial part in the tradition that has been passed on to us. James Greenwood's 1866 series of articles entitled "A Night in a Workhouse" can indeed be said to have initiated the "vogue" of immersion (Keating 1976, 16). A social explorer, journalist and prolific writer, Greenwood published his articles in the *Pall Mall Gazette* on 12, 13 and 15 January 1866. It was James's brother, Frederick Greenwood – the first editor of the *Gazette* – who had made the suggestion that James go undercover to write this report (Keating 1976, 16).

As noted by James Grant a few years later, the articles became "a newspaper sensation, such as has seldom been known" (1871–1872, 118). As Greenwood "made his slum 'dives' and himself into news" (Koven 2004, 82), immersion became inextricably linked with both sensationalism and investigation, initiating not only the trend but also the very techniques of undercover immersion reporting in general and into the workhouse in particular. London, Orwell and many

---

1 Workhouse writing was also shaped through a steady stream of anonymous or collective ballads, biographies of workhouse paupers, workers or visitors, poems and plays. Peter Higginbotham, the author of several books on workhouse life and the creator of a website devoted to the history of the workhouse (www.workhouses.org.uk), has compiled a useful series of literary, journalistic and artistic works referring to the workhouse in the nineteenth and twentieth centuries (Higginbotham 2013).

others would follow in Greenwood's footsteps, "with the older tradition of personal exploration blending into the newer techniques of sociological analysis" (Keating 1976, 10). As Keating also explains, it inaugurated not so much a new subject as a particular "frame of mind":

> Above all, it is a frame of mind that is offered here, a way of looking at and describing society that undergoes frequent change yet is continuous in both its attitudes and the nature of its concerns. (1976, 9)

To see "how the poor live", or how "the other half" fares (and how often, in the workhouse, they die) – as George Robert Sims (1883) or Jacob A. Riis (1890) put it – became the mission of reportage literature. In the wake of the literature of exploration, reportage literature became interested in what might be called "the others within": those who were confined within the closed space of the workhouse, locked inside; those also who were within the city but out on the streets, marginalized, locked, so to speak, outside.

II

Inviting their readers to reconsider who was worthy of representation and figuration, reporters contributed to a redefinition of the status of the marginalized, of those whose lives, in a seemingly paradoxical fashion, had to be written down to become more pressingly real. Through their first-hand, incognito enquiries, reporters distanced themselves from a genealogy of writers and journalists who did not write on location. One had to immerse oneself in the workhouse, so as to see, if only for a night, what happened behind closed doors to the workhouse inmates and the vagrants in the casual ward sections. Inevitably, reportage literature then started to question the institution and organization of the workhouse, this central space for marginalized populations which should indeed be listed among Foucault's "heterotopias of deviation" – those other spaces where those considered abnormal could be isolated from the rest of society (Foucault 1986, 25; Marie-Laverrou 2012, 44–45).

Tracing the lineage from James Greenwood to George Orwell will enable me to analyze the ways in which both writers chose to expose the day-to-day living conditions of the most precarious amongst the precarious, the 'casuals', i.e. those among the poorest who were constantly forced to move from one ward to another. Throughout *Down and Out*, Orwell denounces the absurdity of a system which reinforced the invisibility of the tramps, unjustly punished when they presented themselves in the same ward too often: "they have to keep moving, for you may not enter any one spike [...] more than once in a month, on pain of being confined for a week" (1999, 145). Through this transformation of destitution into the condition of the 'casual', who came to be seen as dependent on the will of another, precariousness became inextricably linked with an economic system increasingly relying on a casualized workforce (Stedman Jones 1983) – a system which had already started to be denounced by Henry Mayhew in the 1840s and 1850s. Because of this constant displacement of the poorest, enquiry was rendered even more difficult, and behind Greenwood's and Orwell's texts lay the ambition to find out, both as observers/witnesses *and* as participants, the unofficial version of things and what it was like to stay in a casual ward, and be, albeit temporarily and imperfectly, amongst the downtrodden.

In terms of their reception and influence, Greenwood's articles "ha[d] a lasting impact on how contemporaries perceived and represented the poorest of the poor" (Koven 2004, 27). They initiated a reflection on the workhouse and the casual wards manifest both in the wish for "reform" (Koven 2004, 27) and in the way they prompted many to emulate Greenwood's enquiry (Koven 2004, 47– 49). This led Peter Keating (1976, 3) to adopt "A Night" as "a starting point" for his anthology, which contributed to a growing interest within academia for "A Night" as a seminal text (Koven 2004, 27). As both Keating and Koven recognize, despite its being a pioneer work of immersion and an overnight sensation, "A Night" built on earlier traditions and was undoubtedly influenced by the works of those who "had remained sympathetic outsiders and observers of life among the poor" (Koven 2004, 26) – Defoe, Cobbett (Keating 1976, 9), Mayhew (Keating 1976, 9; Koven 2004, 26) and Dickens (Koven 2004, 26), amongst others – and whose works still continue to influence contemporary misery representations (Korte 2012, 76).

It is then important both to underscore the novelty of undercover journalism and to recall that the tradition of social exploration it is grounded in partly stems from a generation of writers and journalists who, influenced namely by Dickens, had already sought to write about the world – so near and yet so far – of deprived urban areas such as the East End or Southern London. Through the development of the Condition-of-England novel, the social and urban realist novel (which would lead to the multiplication of slum narratives in the later half of the century) had already occupied the terrain of destitution, while novelistic accounts of the workhouse in *Oliver Twist* (1837– 1839) and journalistic depictions of "A Walk in a Workhouse" had trodden the grounds of precariousness and state provision and provided an already complex – and at times divergent – view of the workhouse, workhouse inmates and lives. Journalistic accounts like "A Walk" and "A Night" were also very much inspired by a long tradition of "urban flanerie" which would lead to "slumming" (Koven 2004, 3, 74) – the visit of poverty-stricken areas – and to "tramping" (Freeman 2001, 99), a tradition London and Orwell would become closely associated with in the following century.

III

A few years after Greenwood's death in 1927, but nearly seventy years after Greenwood's immersion into the workhouse, Orwell drew on and renewed this tradition of personal experience and social exploration with the publication of *Down and Out in Paris and London* in 1933. Orwell focused his attention on the plight of the underdog, of those who continued to frequent the London workhouses and, within those workhouses, the specific place devoted to the casual poor. This reality is imprinted both in the title of Orwell's first published essay on the question, "The Spike" (1931) – the slang word for the casual ward – and in Greenwood's publication of "A Night", written under the pseudonym of "The Amateur Casual". Jack London also named his own chapter on the workhouse "The Spike" (Chapter IX) in *The People of the Abyss* (1903). But when Orwell's "The Spike", initially published in the *Adelphi* under the author's real name, Eric Blair, was reworked and expanded into chapter XXVII of *Down and Out*, "Orwell literally became Orwell" (Koven 2004, 81). This reworking of material, place and form (from not only previous accounts of workhouse stays such as those provided by Jack London and earlier predecessors, but also from earlier and shorter texts Orwell had himself written) manifests a renewed interest in experimenting with forms and questioning the best ways in which to tell untold, precarious lives.

Amongst Orwell's own self-acknowledged predecessors is indeed Jack London (Koven 2004, 82), whose steps he closely retraced through the East End, and whose influence is not only visible in the places observed but also in the method and style employed, even if certain aspects in their prose and outlook differ (Dow 2002). By not being content with "simply examining and writing about the lives of the poor but [in] becoming, temporarily one of them" (Keating 1976, 16), Orwell relied on a method initiated by several others before him, inevitably inserting himself within a certain tradition, and both stepping into and away from the shoes of his predecessors, others who, like him, had momentarily tried to step into the shoes of others further still. Notwithstanding his constant defiance and mistrust of ready-made categories, it may be argued that Orwell chose this mode of writing for its openness and potential for hybridity and variety in tone and style, as well as for the multiplicity of perspectives on different forms of precariousness it might allow. And yet, despite at times uncanny similarities between Orwell's and London's reportage, on the one hand, and Orwell and some of his Victorian predecessors, on the other, there is no trace of a direct reference in Orwell or London to Greenwood. It appears therefore that "both writers paid indirect – and presumably unintended – homage to Greenwood" (Koven 2004, 80, 82) and to their undercover predecessors. One may then establish connections between the two immersive experiences and writings – Orwellian and Victorian – without erasing their specificities, their particular contexts and, at times, distinct purposes, postures and outlooks.

In spite of the kinship between Greenwood's articles and Orwell's reportage in the methods and objects of study, these works present major differences in their views, and their particular contexts should certainly not be occulted. Greenwood's articles are in many ways revelatory of the context of political reform and debate surrounding the Poor Law. He even addresses the Poor Law Board through a series of questions and goes as far as to offer its members his assistance (53–54).[2] He also seeks to provide an alternative to the abstraction of statistics and the aridity of Poor Law reports by Poor Law Boards, Royal Commissions and others. It is true that his articles are still imbued with Victorian morals, which they nonetheless subvert to a certain extent.

Much had changed when Orwell's book was published, after the First World War and during the Great Depression. Profound changes had also affected British society. Yet, both texts illustrate the pervasiveness of the workhouse structure in English society in the wake of the Poor Law Amendment Act of 1834. As Simon Fowler explains, in spite of certain material improvements and important social and legal changes, "many of the casual wards described in 1929 by George Orwell in *Down and Out in Paris and London*, had clearly not changed much in sixty or more years" (2008, 57). The Poor Law was to be abolished only in 1929–1930, nearly a hundred years after its implementation, but in fact many workhouses continued to exist under other names, so that one had to wait for the advent of the Welfare State in 1948 to see the complete suspension of the Poor Laws. It is then striking – and surprising to those who saw the workhouse as an exclusive fixture of the Victorian Era – to note how little seems to have changed overall between the time Greenwood penetrated the Lambeth workhouse in 1866 and that when Orwell stayed in several workhouses at the end of the 1920s (gathered in the book under the fictional name of "Romton"). The pervasiveness of these realities accounts, to be sure, for some of the disquieting similarities between the two works.

---

2 All page numbers for Greenwood refer to the 1976 reprint of "A Night in a Workhouse" in Keating's anthology.

IV

Both Greenwood and Orwell masked their (shabby) gentility so as to try and enter undetected the world of the poor. Unlike the poverty of those they shared a ward with, the poverty of both Orwell and Victorian gentlemen-reporters was induced and temporary. Unlike Orwell, Greenwood did not on his own decide to spend a night in a workhouse; it was his brother, whom James refers to as "Mr Editor" (52), who had the idea to ask his brother to go undercover in order to try and get a scoop that would benefit the *Gazette*. James was at first reluctant to fulfil his brother's request, even if, after his "fourteen weary hours" in the workhouse (52), he went on other enquiries on prostitution, human-baiting or homeless children, recounted in *The True History of a Little Ragamuffin* (1866), *The Seven Curses of London* (1869) and *The Wilds of London* (1874), continuously showing, in the wake of journalists like Mayhew, a keen interest in working-class culture, language and social problems.

Orwell's several months spent in Paris and London trying out precarious jobs – hop-picking in Kent, living with miners in the North – recall this gradual process of learning through living the lives of others and similarly call for a questioning of the place of the "invisib[les]" (Orwell 1968a [1939], 391) in literature, be it in "Marrakech" (1939), in "The Spike" (1931), in *Down and Out* or in *Burmese Days* (1934). These experiences also give birth to hybrid writings, associating the modes of literary reportage, investigative journalism and the essay, through which emerges, however, a distinctively Orwellian voice. Indeed, the book form of *Down and Out* and *The Road to Wigan Pier* enables the writer to focus on multiple encounters with memorable characters, such as Paddy or Bozo, who are made to recount their own stories. Greenwood's articles were first published in instalments in the *Pall Mall Gazette*, later reprinted in the *Times* and then as a pamphlet, which explains why they eventually reached a wide audience and even prompted broadsides to be written about them (Keating 1976, 16–17). "A Night" provoked a great variety of responses, from the general public, from the poor themselves, from other journalists and newspapers, but also from entertainers and even from government officials (Koven 2004, 49, 51). Both Greenwood and Daddy, the workhouse pauper in charge of the ward, were hailed as "heroes" (Koven 2004, 63) and "'Daddy' [even] became a minor celebrity on the music hall stage" (Fowler 2008, 94).

When reading side by side the pages devoted to the casual ward in *Down and Out* and in "The Spike", on the one hand, and Greenwood's "A Night in a Workhouse" on the other, one remarks a number of echoes concerning the reality of the workhouse, compared to prisons by both writers. For Orwell, even smells become "prisonish" (146), as he wrote in *Down and Out*.[3] Both authors note the squalor, the boredom, the "passages" leading to the ward, and the memorable ritual of the bath both had to go through on entering the workhouse, famously described as a "weak mutton broth" by Greenwood (36). Reading Greenwood and Orwell side by side and establishing connections between the Victorian and modern varieties of the genre makes patent the ways in which the fragility of the positioning of the observers and the precariousness of the observed interrelate in the body of the texts, which precariously place themselves at the crossroads between literature and journalism.

Greenwood reveals in his opening lines the othering process the reporter must go through in order to enter the ward, to present himself as other, as "a sly and ruffianly figure, marked with every sign of squalor" (34). This self-othering is reinforced by the move from third to first-person narration, with the belated revelation that "[t]his mysterious figure was that of the present writer" (34). Both Greenwood and Orwell dwell on their new clothes and on the fear of being uncovered as frauds. Interestingly, both present themselves as artists: Greenwood claims to be "[a]n engraver [...] to account for the look of [his] hands" (35) – which was not quite a lie, since Greenwood knew the trade (Tomkins 2010) –, and Orwell poses "as [a] 'painter'", which he believes to be a half-truth, since we have all, he writes, "painted water-colours" (1999, 145). Both Orwell and Greenwood thus portray the observer as being both an outsider and an insider, but Greenwood insists more on his position as an outsider, explicitly stating his aims at the beginning and end of his text – which Orwell also does occasionally – and reminding the reader of the reading and writing processes.

Phrases addressing the reader such as "you should remember" or "as I said before, and cannot help saying again" abound in Greenwood's text (37). Reminding one of the artificiality and constructedness of the account of the experience, such utterances point to the temporality of the text itself, to that of the act of reading and even to the presence of the author, to his posterity, and his intended readers. Greenwood also stresses that he is a gentleman, brought and picked up by carriage, greatly relieved finally to "escape" from the ward (36, 40, 52). The irony of calling the other casuals "gentlemen" (42, 45, 51) further contributes to reinforcing the narrator's status (Koven 2004, 42). Orwell, on the other hand, in spite of his awareness of the difficulty – if not, at times, the impossibility – of becoming other, tries to erase his own gentility, and desire for closeness is shown in the recurrent use of the pronoun 'we'.

---

3 All page numbers for Orwell's texts refer to the editions cited in the bibliography.

What is at stake for both writers is the production of a valid though fragile identity, supposed to enable the observer to enter the world of the underdog with the distance which makes the telling of the story possible, while achieving a closeness without which the encounter of and the coexistence with the outcast would simply not be viable. The questions both Greenwood and Orwell ask about bedding and schedules betray their ignorance of the world they pretend to be part of, a limitation in their knowledge which both writers readily confess to the reader. A reversal in roles is displayed when the observers are guided through long passages which materialize their separation from the outside world and their former identities. What is at work in such texts is the re-figuration of the image of the know-all reporter, who now projects an uncertain image of himself, caught in an unstable posture, simultaneously powerful and vulnerable. The professional self seeks to 'otherize' itself, but also makes sure he does not become quite an other and remains indeed an "amateur". The reporter's excentricity is thus balanced by his implicit desire to return to the centre from which he derives his legitimacy (Koven 2004, 49).

Nowhere is this better shown than in the memorable bath scenes in both texts. The immersion, the will to abide by the ward's rules in order to bring the depths to the surface, becomes a literal submersion, which can be seen as a degradation, but also as some sort of lay "baptism" (Koven 2004, 40), water suggesting the porosity of the frontiers between self and other, inside and outside. The ritual of the bath can also be seen as a test on the enquirer's limits, a proof of his 'courage'. Greenwood writes he plunged into the bath "[w]ith a fortitude for which [he] hope[s] some day to be rewarded" (36), revealing both a desire of closeness and understanding, and a fear of contamination (Koven 2004, 40). This fear is also patent in the insistence on the diseases of the casuals. Orwell's observer momentarily "panic[s]" about having caught the smallpox from his bedmate (1999, 149) and Greenwood writes memorably about the different types of coughs he hears in the ward.

V

Indeed, both Greenwood and Orwell copiously deal with the corporeality of poverty, the bodily ravages of destitution, observed with mixed disgust and empathy. So as to force us not only to read about but also to see, smell and hear what usually remains hidden or ignored, both Greenwood and Orwell seek to awaken their readers' senses, favouring the lexical field of sight and smell in Orwell epitomized in the "subfaecal stench of the spike" (1999, 149), and the lexical field of hearing in Greenwood (43). Interestingly, Greenwood even lends coughing the power to irritate not the observer but silence itself: "the silence was more and more irritated by the sound of coughing" (45). References to noises and sounds abound, with terms such as "flapping", "rustling", "pattering" (43, 45, 47), which describe in detail which noises trouble the night in a workhouse, as if the unseen were suddenly made somewhat too audible, too materially present. Orwell too, seeks to make the invisible palpable and perceptible, in keeping with his famous principle: "[t]o see what is in front of one's nose needs a constant struggle" (1968c, 125).

Such formulations suggest that the reporter's gaze is faced with a reality which resists representation. And indeed, the translation of the observer's perception of things into intelligible language becomes a crucial question, as is shown by both Greenwood's and Orwell's insistence on the difficulty of conveying reality: "[n]o language with which I am acquainted is capable of conveying an adequate conception of the spectacle I then encountered" (37), Greenwood writes, before coming to the conclusion that the "detail of [the] horrors" witnessed should be deliberately omitted (54). The observer's perspective becomes a problematic issue, as is made clear in the very beginning of "A Night", where numerous phrases raise the problem of the reliability and credibility of personal testimony (34). In Orwell's "The Spike", one finds sentences conveying similar thoughts: "[n]o one can imagine, unless one has seen such a thing, what pot-bellied, degenerate curs we looked" (39), a passage taken up again in *Down and Out* (148).

Such notations force the readers to revisit their preconceptions, in parallel with the observer himself. Indeed, the texts play with and counter certain set ideas on the poor and how the poor live. Both writers lay the stress for instance on their surprise in finding the "passages all so scrupulously clean" (Greenwood 1976, 35), or "unwillingly clean" (Orwell 1999, 145). Greenwood in particular stresses the clash between reality and his expectations (34). His account is always to be read against the background of his "worst apprehensions" (36) or of his "most serious misgivings" (35). Orwell for his part questions ingrained and internalized beliefs taught from an early age, for instance that according to which "*the lower classes smell*" (1989, 119), a statement which implies a belief in the moral squalor of the working classes, insidiously "divid[ing] [us] from our fellows by our sense of smell" (121). Both Orwell and Greenwood insist on the vulnerable bodies and faces of the poor, on their "physical rottenness" (Orwell 1999, 149). Their proximity to death is constantly underlined and their bodies are described as "carcase[s]" (Greenwood 1976, 43) or as "corpse[s]" (Orwell 1968b, 39; Greenwood 1976, 38).

Both authors also meditate the effects of promiscuity, such as homosexuality, amongst the casuals, a dimension Koven (2004, 44) minutely analyzes in his queering reading of "A Night", focusing on the ambiguous figure of an "androgynous" fifteen year-old boy, Kay, who awakens in Greenwood mingled feelings of desire, admiration, disgust and pity. Greenwood's technique consists in saying enough to "excite" his reader's attention, but not enough to overstep the limits set by Victorian moral codes (Koven 2004, 46). In other words, Greenwood both titillates and represses his readers, destabilizing them, challenging their norms, placing them also in a precarious position. Throughout his narrative, Greenwood insists on the moral degradation of certain paupers, due to the negative effects of mixing the vagrants – not only the sick and the young, but also the indecent and the decent (Koven 2004, 42) – but the use of a vocabulary which connotes opposed values, oscillating between pain, suffering and pleasure, humanity and dehumanization, introduces trouble into his representation of precarity. Greenwood's techniques of double entendre, preterition, understatement, mixed with hyperbolic statements, theatricality and at times a sensationalist approach bordering on voyeurism may, however, seem to jar with certain bouts of empathy for the human suffering he witnesses. Such contradictions are in fact the symptom of an eminently complex reality, the puzzling dimension of which must be rendered through linguistic or rhetorical subtleties journalism is not usually associated with (Freeman 2001, 112). Ambivalence is definitely a *textual* effect.

Greenwood dwells mostly on the sufferings of the men he sees as deserving but also stresses the compassion he feels for the fifteen year-old Kay, noting that his situation was "almost enough to make a man cry" (46). His description then seems to waver between the shattering acceptance of a new reality and the reassuring power of cliché. The narrator's portrait of Kay is still tainted by the concept of "vice" (46), and throughout his text Greenwood relies on the Victorian dissociation between deserving and undeserving poor, pitting the two categories against each other when he describes the near riot which opposes the ruffians of the ward to the decent casuals, or stresses the laziness of some casuals during work-time at the ward. Orwell rather emphasizes the decency of most casuals, focusing on the causes that have led them to their present condition. His texts are more concerned with sensation, insisting on the various forms of feeling poverty, on the *perceptions* of life on the edge, which leads him to refuse the stigmatization of poverty and to challenge the idea that precarity is a condition one chooses, enjoys or even deserves. For instance, he explains about his friend Paddy the Tramp, in the chapter following the depiction of the ward, that "[i]t was malnutrition and not any native vice that had destroyed his manhood" (1999, 154). Orwell's text evinces a will to go beyond disgust as it challenges the idea that the poor intrinsically smell, or as it seeks to understand homosexuality in the wards, for instance when the narrator engages in a conversation with his sleep partner after the latter has made "homosexual attempts upon [him]" (1999, 148).

Greenwood's attention to the stories of others appears in the dialogues he overhears, although that is also where the lingering of stereotype is most apparent, with the omnipresence of words connoting moral judgement. This is particularly notable when he reports the offensiveness and obscenity of the casuals' language, described as a "bestial chorus" (45). The result of such strategies is that the poor are almost turned into alien creatures. According to Judith Walkowitz, "[t]he literature of urban exploration also emulated the privileged gaze of anthropology in constituting the poor as a race apart, outside the national community" (1992, 19). This "[o]rientaliz[ation]" and "[r]acialization of the tramp" (Koven 2004, 60) is encapsulated in some analogies – "just as the brutes do in those books of African travel" (Greenwood 1976, 46) –, or, also in Greenwood, in the choice of certain adjectives like "horrible", repeated in a crescendo to describe the tales he overhears (45). Subjected to an "[i]mperialist rhetoric" (Walkowitz 1992, 18), to the language of colonial exploration (Koven 2004, 60–61), to an alienating gaze akin to that of "ethnographers in a domestic setting" (Freeman 2001, 113), the other within runs the risk of becoming the other without. Greenwood's overt "theatrical[ity]" (Koven 2004, 26), together with his tendency to a certain "sensationalism" (Koven 2004, 75), may lead him to incarcerate the casuals back into a system of binary, ontological opposites.

VI

Yet, what binds Orwell and Greenwood together is their common will to write about a world of deprivation and squalor which is also at times a world of solidarity and humanity. Surprisingly enough, for all the rigidity of the workhouse system, there appears to be room for some freedom in it, as is suggested by Greenwood when he reports the games and songs through which the casuals try not only to kill time away and stave off boredom, but also to become part of a group, that of the habitués of the ward, contrasting with the habitual precariousness of those condemned to move from one ward to the next. Still, although he insists on the hospitality of Daddy, Greenwood's persona appears to be more worried about surviving the night than engaging in real encounters and conversations with the other. Orwell's narrator in *Down and Out*, on the other hand, insists that when leaving the ward, he "had a mate now" (149), in the person of Paddy, with whom he will continue his travels in the following chapter. What is asserted is the indeterminacy of the encounter with the other, of the sharing of the present of the other, the preservation of a certain humanity, the reassertion of a fundamental solidarity, which may take the form of tips exchanged about other wards, or of cigarette ends offered to the newcomer. Even if poverty leaves little room for thought and conversation – "emptiness of belly leaves no speculation in [the casuals'] souls", as Orwell writes in "The Spike" (39) – this potential for humane solidarity is preserved. This is shown in the ending of "The Spike" (as well as in chapter XXXV of *Down and Out*), where a "friendly" fellow tramp gives the narrator a few cigarette ends to repay him for the gesture of having offered him some when he had none (43).

Such alternation between the best and the worst potential of humanity, which testifies to a desire to avoid representing univocal realities, is also evinced whenever it comes to dealing with the "obscene", both in Greenwood and Orwell. Greenwood (38, 42, 51) often uses the adjective "obscene" to describe the behaviour of the ruffians who steal, playfully punch and swear. Orwell refers to the "dull obscenities" uttered by the casuals in "The Spike" (39) but also to moments when obscene brutality and contempt prevail, be it in the figure of the Tramp Major, the contemptuous waitress serving the vagrants a meal after their night in the ward, or in the "rather superior tramp" (41) who dismisses his fellow tramps as "scum" (41–42). The obscenity of the system is denounced in Orwell's description of bags of food being discarded in the workhouse by casuals on the brink of starvation – which also stresses the differences between the workhouse and the casual ward (41). In both Orwell and Greenwood the dehumanizing process to which the poor are subjected is suggested mostly through a lexical field connoting animalization and references to promiscuity and nakedness.

However, although the two writers heavily insist on the animalization of the poor, the phenomenon is treated very differently. In *Down and Out*, it is the porter who is described as a "ruffian" (145), and the animalization of the poor seems to be inflicted on them, from above, as the porter is said to "treat [them] like cattle" and "herd [...] [them] all into the passage" (146). As for Greenwood (36), he insists on the poor being stripped and put in workhouse clothes, before they are eventually given a number for their bundle of clothes – "No. 34 you are", says Daddy – but the narrator also praises Daddy's thoughtfulness.

There are, however, moments of respite, of beauty even, especially in the description of the streets outside the ward. Orwell opens and closes "The Spike" with a description of chestnut trees, seeming to close his down-to-earth enquiry on purely aesthetic considerations: "the blossom covered the chestnut trees like great wax candles" (43). Such passages are in fact meant to draw the reader's attention to a style which can be realistic to stress the squalor of life, while using unexpected similes which express the complexity of the author's perception of things. Greenwood's articles also display a richness of style visible in his use of irony (Koven 2004, 42), or in his description of Kay in a finely-shaded and highly ambivalent portrait (Koven 2004, 44). In different yet relatable ways, such finely written passages illustrate both humanity's admirable struggle for survival and the difficulty of retaining one's humanity in conditions of precarity, contrasting moments of obscenity and ugliness with evidence of decency and beauty.

Yet, the conclusions they reach or the explanations they provide at times greatly differ. What emerges in Orwell is the way abjection and dejection may still become a site of formation for the superior idea of humanity: for him, bringing the literally 'ob-scene' back onto the scene of representation and thus lending it a newfound dignity is the higher duty of journalism. Despite his wish to denounce inhuman living conditions and notwithstanding the modernity of his endeavour, Greenwood continues to rely on the traditional tropes of the exploration of the abyss, the exoticization of the other, making ample use of melodrama techniques, biblical imagery and the rhetoric of the London inferno. *Down and Out*, on the contrary, shows how telling the lives of others may lead both the self and his others – the casuals – to become open to reconfiguration and be spoken by more than one voice. Although the complexity of reportage literature is not directly proportional to its length (or publication date), it remains true that the book form of *Down and Out* and *The People of the Abyss* allowed greater attention to be paid to the causes of poverty, and the focus on multiple encounters with memorable characters invited to tell their own stories is indicative of a new communicational ethics, which nevertheless can be found at a budding stage in their slum and workhouse-exploring predecessors.

VII

One may wonder finally whether the marginality these texts deal with can be at least in part related to their relative marginalization in literary history and in the literary canon. The question raised is that of "[the] links between social and literary marginality, or the ways in which literature encounters [...] social history" (Forest and Szkilnik 2005, 15). John C. Hartsock (2000, 7) deplores the "homeless [ness of literary journalism] in library science", its thematic or too general classification, its problematic treatment in both literary and journalism studies. As Raymond Williams puts it, the conventional division between genres points to the problem of social relations and social divisions: "[Orwell] saw the division as it actually presented itself to him as something more than a formal problem. He saw it, correctly, as a problem of social relationships" (1984, 42). Williams concludes: "the problem of social relationship is, then, a problem of form"

(1984, 43). Even if immersive reportage is not the exclusive terrain of marginal and precarious lives and spaces, there appears to be an original proximity between the two that may have led in part both to the validation and to a certain marginalization of reportage literature.

Such texts can be seen as "more than the sum of their critical parts" (Hartsock 2000, 12), as more therefore than journalism giving itself to be read *as* literature. They require that their readers go beyond both a predominantly factual understanding of the events narrated and a literary analysis of the tale. For as John Rodden reminds us about Orwell, "the plain style can mask a submerged complexity" (1989, 24). This comment may indeed be applied to reportage literature in general and to immersion literature in particular, in both its Victorian and modern strains.

Quite obviously, the question of the genre's denomination remains in today's academia an open one. Referring to such texts as belonging to 'literary *journalism*' amounts to insisting on their original affiliation with journalism, while stressing a certain degree of literary mastery concerning in particular "narrativization", which, as Hayden White (1980, 8) reminds us, is indeed constitutive of any form of narration, therefore indissociable from both journalism and literature. Referring to such texts as 'reportage *literature*' obviously puts the emphasis on the literariness of such texts, while also recalling the original links with journalism. But what is also suggested by the same token is some sort of ontological kinship between reportage and literature, which clearly emphasizes the importance of the writing process in the representation of precarious lives.

A crucial aspect of these immersions is the uncertain perspective from which they are written. I argue that such indecision is characteristic, precisely, of the genre, that the reportage writer's stance is never secured, characterized on the contrary by its precariousness. Despite their notable differences, Greenwood's and Orwell's texts read side by side expose primarily the precariousness involved in narrating the stories of those who seem to escape any kind of fixity. At the end of *Down and Out*, Orwell compares his book to a "travel diary" (215). Such texts may perhaps be better defined as travelling narratives, by which I mean: narratives that travel both through society's frontiers and between genres, defying formal categorization. As Seth Koven reminds us, "London and Orwell, like Greenwood, were perpetually crossing borders" (2004, 81). Their minute descriptions of room sizes, their insistence on figures, their scrupulous information on food, bedding, routine work, are evidence of their striving for a certain degree of objectivity, which nevertheless coexists with the use of symbolism, dialogue, memorable figures, a novelistic eye for detail, personal commentary and bouts of what Frédéric Regard calls "subjective emotion", which he sees as being at the heart of Orwell's eminently ethical conception of style (1994, 25). These writings are of course never blunt recordings of reality; they are inevitably literary constructs whose literariness has received only limited recognition so far. This is due mainly to the fact that they purport to fulfil different, sometimes contradictory purposes, such as seeing and knowing, recording and reporting, feeling and fact-gathering, observing and empathizing, exposing and reforming. Immersion literature is also a way of rethinking self and other, of redefining the ethics of intersubjective relationships.

By looking at those who are relegated to the margins of society's sphere of representation, such authors confer upon precarious lives a certain visibility, however imperfect or limited. By bringing the other to the forefront, they therefore point to a certain politicity of literature, prompting a reflection on who speaks in the common space, calling thus for what Jacques Rancière calls another "distribution of the sensible": that which "determines the ability or inability to take charge of what is common to the community [...] [and] defines what is visible or not in a common space" (2004, 12–13). By pointing to such possible refigurations of the poor, literary reporters unhinge the fixed notions of social class and generic status. This is perhaps the constitutive paradox of such literature: it turns precariousness and the instability of the writer's posture into something positive. Bound by not so rigid a sequencing or emplotting, at the crossroads between genres, such texts strive on precarious margins. They seek to go both beyond abstraction, which is without any doubt the greatest challenge to traditional forms of representation, and beyond precarity, further interrelating their precarious ethics and aesthetics, somewhere between journalism and literature.

Works Cited

Dickens, Charles. *Oliver Twist, or The Parish Boy's Progress* [1837–1839]. Ed. Philip Horne. London and New York: Penguin Books, 2003.
——. "A Walk in a Workhouse." *Household Words* 1.9 (25 May 1850): 204–207.
Dow, William. "Down and Out in London and Orwell." *Symbiosis: A Journal of Anglo-American Literary Relations* 6.1 (2002): 69–94.
Forest, Philippe, and Michelle Szkilnik, eds. *Théorie des marges littéraires*. Nantes: Editions Cécile Defaut, 2005.
Foucault, Michel. "Des espaces autres" [1967]. *Architecture, Mouvement, Continuité* 5 (1984): 46–49. ["Of Other Spaces." Trans. Jay Miskowiec. *Diacritics* 16.1 (1986): 22–27].
Fowler, Simon. *Workhouse: The People, the Places, the Life Behind Doors*. Kew: National Archives, 2008 [2007].
Freeman, Mark. "'Journeys into Poverty Kingdom': Complete Participation and the British Vagrant, 1866–1914." *History Workshop Journal* 52 (2001): 99–121.
Grant, James. *The Newspaper Press: Its Origins, Its Progress and Present Position*. Vol. 2. London: Tinsley Brothers, 1871–1872.

Greenwood, James. "A Night in a Workhouse" [1866]. *Into Unknown England, 1866–1913: Selections from the Social Explorers*. Ed. Peter Keating. Manchester: Manchester University Press, 1976. 33–54.

Hartsock, John. C. *A History of American Literary Journalism: The Emergence of a Modern Narrative Form*. Amherst: University of Massachusetts Press, 2000.

Higginbotham, Peter. "Workhouse Literature & Arts." *The Workhouse* 2013. http://www.workhouses.org.uk/lit/index.shtml (22 May 2013).

Keating, Peter John, ed. *Into Unknown England, 1866–1913: Selections from the Social Explorers*. Manchester: Manchester University Press, 1976.

Korte, Barbara. "Dealing with Deprivation: Figurations of Poverty on the Contemporary British Book Market." *Anglia: Zeitschrift für englische Philologie* 130.1 (2012): 75–94.

Koven, Seth. *Slumming: Sexual and Social Politics in Victorian London*. Princeton, NJ: Princeton University Press, 2004.

Marie-Laverrou, Florence. "Les chemineaux dans *Dans la dèche à Paris et à Londres*, de George Orwell." *Le Vagabond en Occident: sur la route, dans la rue, XXe & XXIe siècles*. Vol. 2. Eds. Francis Desvois and Morag J. Munro-Landi. Paris: L'Harmattan, 2012. 43–58.

Orwell, George. *Down and Out in Paris and London*. Harmondsworth: Penguin Books, 1999 [1933].

——. *The Road to Wigan Pier*. Harmondsworth: Penguin Books, in association with Secker & Warburg, 1989 [1937].

——. "Marrakech" [1939]. *The Collected Essays, Journalism and Letters of George Orwell*. Vol. 1: *An Age Like This 1920–40*. Eds. Sonia Orwell and Ian Angus. London: Secker & Warburg, 1968a. 390–392.

——. "The Spike" [1931]. *The Collected Essays, Journalism and Letters of George Orwell*. Vol. 1: *An Age Like This 1920–40*. Eds. Sonia Orwell and Ian Angus. London: Secker & Warburg, 1968b. 36–43.

——. "In Front of Your Nose" [1946]. *The Collected Essays, Journalism and Letters of George Orwell*. Vol: 4. *In Front of Your Nose 1945–1950*. Eds. Sonia Orwell and Ian Angus. London: Secker & Warburg, 1968c. 122–125.

Rancière, Jacques. *Le Partage du sensible, esthétique et politique*. Paris: La Fabrique, 2000. [*The Politics of Aesthetics: The Distribution of the Sensible*. Trans. Gabriel Rockhill. London: Continuum, 2004].

Regard, Frédéric. *1984 de George Orwell*. Paris: Gallimard, 1994.

Riis, Jacob August. *How the Other Half Lives: Studies among the Tenements of New York*. New York: C. Scribner, 1890.

Rodden, John. *The Politics of Literary Reputation: The Making and Claiming of 'St George' Orwell*. Oxford: Oxford University Press, 1989.

Sims, George Robert. *How the Poor Live*. London: Chatto & Windus, 1883.

Stedman Jones, Gareth. *Languages of Class, Studies in English Working Class History, 1832–1982*. Cambridge: Cambridge University Press, 1983.

Tomkins, Alannah. "Greenwood, James William (bap. 1835, d. 1927)." *Oxford Dictionary of National Biography*. Online edition. http://www.oxforddnb.com/view/article/41224. Oxford: Oxford University Press, 2010. (22 May 2013).

Walkowitz, Judith R. *City of Dreadful Delight: Narratives of Sexual Danger in Late-Victorian London*. Chicago, IL: University of Chicago Press, 1992.

White, Hayden. "The Value of Narrativity in the Representation of Reality." *Critical Inquiry* 7.1 (1980): 5–27.

Williams, Raymond. *Orwell*. London: Flamingo, 1984 [1971].

Marie-Luise Egbert

Flann O'Brien's *The Poor Mouth* and the Deconstruction of Stereotypes about Irish Poverty

1 Introduction: Ireland, Poverty and Agency

There are few European countries as closely associated with poverty as Ireland. Even if the rise of the Celtic Tiger in the last decade of the twentieth century brought her a brief period of great affluence, Ireland historically evokes images of utter material deprivation affecting large portions of the population. That association goes back in part to the Great Famine of 1845 to 1852, when the potato blight had caused a dramatic failure in home-grown food crops. Combining with political inaction in the face of predictable disaster, the Famine led to mass-emigration and the death of many of those who remained in the country. While the Famine was for many Irish a trauma that went into the formation of their collective identity, deprivation had already marked the life of many Irish for several centuries. Ever since the Anglo-Norman invasion in the twelfth century, Ireland had effectively been controlled by England, but systematic colonization and exploitation began in the sixteenth century under Elizabeth I and was intensified by her successor James I, who installed Scottish and English Protestant settlers in Ulster. By the eighteenth century, the descendants of these British settlers were known as the Protestant Ascendancy, a group of landowning people who made up only some ten per cent of the population of Ireland but who effectively constituted the ruling class.

The devastating economic and social effects of this imbalance of a wealthy Protestant elite in a predominantly Catholic country were memorably satirized by Jonathan Swift, himself an Irishman, in his *A Modest Proposal for Preventing the Children of Poor People in Ireland from Being a Burden to Their Parents or Country, and for Making Them Beneficial to the Public* (1729). In that pamphlet, he satirically suggested that poor Irish families should sell their infants as food to the wealthy Anglo-Irish, thereby reducing the number of mouths to be fed and providing money for those who remained. Swift's famous satire is just one of many literary responses to the conflict between the Irish and the English and the hardships suffered by the poor in Ireland. Thus, in her novel *The Absentee* (1812) Maria Edgeworth (herself Anglo-Irish) indicts the practice of absentee landowners who wasted the income earned from their Irish estates to live an easy life as part of London's fashionable society. Both in *A Portrait of the Artist as a Young Man* (1916) and *Ulysses* (1922), James Joyce offers glimpses of what it meant to be an aspiring but destitute poet in the period leading up to Ireland's independence (Great Britain granted Ireland the status of a Commonwealth country in 1922, named The Irish Free State). Political liberty notwithstanding, Ireland remained among the least economically thriving countries of Europe well into the second half of the twentieth century. Among twentieth-century representations of poverty in Ireland, none has probably been as influential as Frank McCourt's *Angela's Ashes* (1996), a memoir of a childhood and adolescence among the Irish working-class poor. The phenomenal success of the best-selling novel as well as its filmic adaptation by Alan Parker (1998) did much to shape or reinforce popular self- as well as other-images of Irish people as suffering from adverse social and economic conditions and also bearing the brunt of the excruciating authority of the Catholic Church.

Literary representations of poverty such as those mentioned above deserve special attention insofar as, differing from social statistics or economic enquiry, they focus on the lived experience of the material as well as socio-cultural deprivation involved in being poor. In the case of Ireland, literary texts can throw a light on the background to the particularly close associative nexus of being Irish and being poor. Indeed, that nexus can hardly be considered outside the context of Ireland's having been for so long the object of colonial domination and exploitation. In this respect, Ireland resembles many so-called developing countries whose poverty is largely a legacy of colonization.

Like colonization, poverty raises urgent ethical questions. These include issues such as social and distributive justice and the responsibility that those who have plenty may have towards those in need. Another, perhaps less obvious, ethical issue is the question of who should (be allowed to) articulate the experience of poverty, hence, who should have the agency to speak. As used in historical and postcolonial studies, agency is "the free capacity people have to do things for themselves", and apart from action as such, agency includes "a subject's ability to think for themselves and tell stories about their own actions which are not given to them by other people" (Wilson 2008, 245).

As dependent subjects and as people who are largely excluded from social communication and interaction, the poor are in a position of inferiority and marginalization in comparison with the affluent members of society. And by analogy with other marginalized groups like immigrants or individuals whose religious or sexual orientation is deviant by the standards of the social majority, a claim can be made for the poor to have the right to articulate their experience themselves. Freedom of opinion and expression is a universal human right (Declaration of Human Rights, Art. 19), and this right can be instrumental in empowering poor people to change their situation for the better if it triggers political action. However, it is a fact that the marginal and subjugated frequently are *not* able to speak for themselves. This may be because they simply lack the material means to make their story known to the rest of society (e. g. access to media), or because interested parties appropriate their stories for political purposes so that, while attention is drawn to their plight, the agency to speak about it and to change it actually lies with others.[1]

The issue of agency is particularly relevant in the realm of literary representations of poverty. Where stories of poverty are told by writers themselves unaffected by poverty, this may continue the marginalization of poor people in the area of representation since the agency to tell is then assumed by others. It must be made plain here that this is not the same as subscribing to an essentialist notion according to which only someone who is or was once poor can create a fictional account of being poor which is 'authentic'. Indeed, it is part of the nature of imaginative literature that first-hand experience is not a prerequisite for verisimilitude.[2]

It is in an ideological and political sense that the issue of agency in telling the lives of poor people is relevant to Flann O'Brien's *The Poor Mouth*, the fictional representation of poverty that will be studied in what follows. Since the characters in the tale are Irish peasants, their lives are doubly precarious: they are poor people placed on the lowest ranks of Irish society, and, as part of that society, are colonial subjects suffering from the (effects of) exploitation of Ireland by the British.

---

1 The latter point is made by Gayatri Chakravorty Spivak in her seminal essay "Can the Subaltern Speak?" (1988, 308). Spivak contends that the impossibility for subalterns to speak has got to do with the fact that subaltern subjects are construed by western intellectuals as part of a homogenous group, their individuality and heterogeneity as subjects not being sufficiently recognized (1988, 285).

2 For a stimulating discussion of the implications of a writer's own social position and an experience of poverty or lack thereof, see Salamon, who engages with William T. Vollmann's *Poor People* (2007), a collection of interviews with poor people from around the world. Slightly overstating the point Vollmann makes in the introduction to his book (2010, 169–170), Salamon summarizes it as follows: "He tells us that writing on poverty cannot be done successfully by people who are themselves poor" and claims that Vollmann suggests that "the poor are the least able narrators of their own poverty"). One does not have to subscribe to Salamon's polemical summary of Vollmann's point to note that the correlation he suggests is indeed problematic. Salamon (2010, 170–176) goes on to evaluate Vollmann's and Orwell's aesthetics of description in writing about poverty.

2 Original, Translation, and Audiences

Both in terms of his subjects and his style, Flann O'Brien[3] has been placed in a line of tradition with his fellow countryman James Joyce, but whereas Joyce represents literary modernism, O'Brien is mostly characterized as a proto-postmodernist, a reputation based primarily on his novel *At Swim-Two-Birds* (1939). And like Joyce, whose *Ulysses* has been celebrated annually on Bloomsday (16 June) ever since 1954, O'Brien has meanwhile received his own day of commemoration – the first Mylesday in honour of him was celebrated on All Fools' Day in 2011 in Dublin. The designation 'Mylesday' derives from one of his pseudonyms: between 1940 and 1966, O'Brien was writing a column for *The Irish Times*[4] under the pen name of Myles na gCopaleen.[5] He had adopted the name from Victorian

---

3 He was born as Brian Ó Nualláin (anglicized as Brian O'Nolan), and Flann O'Brien is only one of the various pen names of this writer and journalist. While he took on the name of Flann O'Brien for his English-language fiction when he had begun to work as secretary to a government minister (writing under his real name would have conflicted with his professional position), his choice of several different authorial personae also bespeaks a certain playfulness about identity (Wimfre 2007, 277). Following widespread practice, he will henceforward be referred to here as Flann O'Brien.

4 Entitled the *Cruiskeen Lawn* (Irish 'Cruiscín Lán', 'the little brimming jug', Day 2011, 32), that column appeared on a daily to thrice-weekly basis over a period of 26 years. This journalistic work is especially interesting because of O'Brien's position as "a Gaelic cuckoo in an Anglo-Irish nest of the *Irish Times*" (Wheatley 2011, 15). While he began writing the column in Gaelic, he later also produced English-language contributions and after 1943 moved away from Gaelic altogether (Taaffe 2008, 91, 98). The reasons behind this may have been his increasingly anti-nationalist position and the lack of a modern tradition of Irish writing with which O'Brien could have engaged (Taaffe 2008, 117). Long deemed secondary to O'Brien's literary achievement, the column has recently drawn increased critical attention. For instance, Day (2011), who demonstrates that the existing five different editions with selections from the column convey an inadequate picture of it since they fail to reproduce his plays on words (misread by editors as errors and therefore normalized). What is also lost is the materiality of the newspaper column: O'Brien habitually played with the graphic shape of his text, for instance by having arrows inserted pointing to neighbouring columns, and these things are not preserved in the selections. Day (2011, 48) points at the online version of *The Irish Times* now available as a more suitable copy text and further suggests the creation of a fully annotated online version of *Cruiskeen Lawn*, which should prove even more useful for scholars.

5 Critics have underscored the significance of this name: Kiberd considers it in connection with O'Brien's metafictional experiments, stating that his use of a fictional character's name for a pseudonym to be in keeping with O'Brien's "democratic programme mapped out for the modern novel in *At Swim-Two-Birds* (1939), according to which each character should be allowed 'a private life, self-determination and a decent standard of living'" (1995, 498).

playwright Dion Boucicault,[6] in whose melodrama *The Colleen Bawn* (1860) the character is the type of the Stage Irishman. It is also under the name of Myles na gCopaleen that O'Brien published *An Béal Bocht* (1941), the Gaelic original of *The Poor Mouth* (1973).

An Béal Bocht is a scathing satire directed primarily against the romanticizing of Irish peasant life in the western coastal regions for which O'Brien held responsible the Irish Revivalists and the guardians of culture of the early decades of the Irish Republic.[7] Its being written in Gaelic meant that the book could be read only by a comparatively small group of people, and it effectively barred access to most of those whom it attacked: its targets were predominantly of Anglo-Irish extraction and did not know Gaelic at all, or at least not well enough to read the text. The book was so successful with its Gaelic-speaking readers – both common readers and critics (Taaffe 2008, 109–110) – that a second edition was soon printed.[8] O'Brien himself rejected suggestions for an English translation on the grounds that most of its impact was based on features of the Gaelic language, and that these would not survive the process (Taaffe 2008, 110). However, that rejection may also have expressed a wish to reclaim the language from those who were its self-proclaimed guardians. In the end, an English translation (prepared by Patrick C. Power) did appear, but not before 1973, seven years after the author's death. In the preface to his translation, Power writes: "It is time that this book, which should have acted as a cauterisation of the wounds inflicted on Gaelic Ireland by its official friends, might do its work in the second official language of Ireland. That it may do so, is the translator's wish and hope" (1996, 6).

For the reader not versed in Gaelic, there are real drawbacks in this case since some of the humour of the original arises from differences in idiomatic usage and slang between the two languages. O'Brien also integrates transliterations of English words into the Gaelic text, such as *axplinayshin* for 'explanation' (translator's note in O'Brien 1996, 125). These features of the Gaelic original create a kind of humour fully appreciated only by someone knowing both languages. This is one important tool of O'Brien's satire, as it places in a superior posi-

---

6 On Boucicault's treatment of poverty, see Joachim Frenk's chapter in the present volume.
7 The complexity of the satirical thrust has frequently been studied. It is particularly well captured by Taaffe (2008, 103–104).
8 According to Ó Conaire (1973, 138), it was appreciated both for its prose style and for the ridicule it poured upon the genre of the Gaelacht autobiography (on this, see below). But there were also some rather negative reactions to the text, reproaching the writer for his inadequate Gaelic which mixed several regional dialects (Taaffe 2008, 110). It is likely also that some of the native Gaelic speakers of the western seaboard were offended by the far from flattering portrayal of them as ignorant people sharing their houses with pigs (Wimfre 2007, 280–282).

tion those who are bilingual (Booker 1995, 76–77). Another important element which is at least obscured in translation is the parody of the literary styles and elements of plot of various Irish writers that is a recurrent feature of the book (Power 1996, 6; Farnon 1997, *passim*).

The English translation, on the other hand, opened up a much enlarged readership for this fascinating book. Indeed, *The Poor Mouth* is a hilariously funny text well worth reading both for its sheer humour and for the stereotypes about life in the west of Ireland which it deconstructs. 'Stereotype' is used here in the sense of a "preconceived and oversimplified idea of the characteristics which typify a person, situation, etc" (*OED* 2013a, def. 3b). It contrasts with 'image', which also is a representation of the characteristics of a thing or person, but has neutral or even positive connotations (*OED* 2013b, def. 5b). Crucial among the stereotypes evoked in the novel is that of poor peasants living in proximity to nature, and wresting their living from the soil. These people's poverty appears as picturesque rather than a cause for concern.

The Poor Mouth is the literal rendering of the original title *An Béal Bocht*. That Gaelic expression has its analogue in the Irish English phrase *to put on the poor mouth*, meaning "making a pretence of being poor or in bad circumstances in order to gain advantage for oneself from creditors or prospective creditors" (Power 1996, 5). And the tale is indeed one of exaggeration and excess. The characters are not just poor, but poor to the extreme, living in abject circumstances and literally sharing their houses with their cows and their beds with their pigs. Since the narrator evaluates these preposterously reduced circumstances as desirable and affirms poverty as a mark of authenticity for his community, the satirical vein of the text is plain.[9]

Even if poverty and suffering are part of the account of the peasants' life, *The Poor Mouth* does not primarily articulate the reality of poor lives on behalf of a suffering community. Rather, it deconstructs existing literary and other discursive representations of life in the Gaelic-speaking west of Ireland. O'Brien's satire suggests that there are vested interests behind those representations. Hence, studying *The Pour Mouth* is rewarding inasmuch as the text draws attention to misrepresentations of poverty and to the ideological underpinnings behind them. These misrepresentations have crucially to do with who articulates the facts of poverty, and for what purposes. It should be noted though that, even if the text clearly replaces previously dominant conceptualizations, *The Poor*

---

9 The nature of O'Brien's satire is explored by Booker, who reads *The Poor Mouth* with the help of Bakhtin's definition of Menippean satire. Elements of this type of satire are the degrading of the Other as thoroughly base, a dialogical mixing of voices (in this case, several different styles) and features of the carnivalesque (Booker 1995, 1).

Mouth is not a case of self-articulation to replace other-representation: O'Brien was proficient in Gaelic and knew parts of the Gaeltacht quite well,[10] but as a Dublin-based civil servant and the son of a customs officer, he was himself from an urban middle-class background and did not share the experience of poverty.

In what follows, the targets addressed in O'Brien's satire will be identified. The emphasis is placed on the power relationships between those represented in the stereotypes and those blamed for furthering them. In the process, *The Poor Mouth* is revealed as a case of the abrogation as well as appropriation of the language of the oppressor, both of them typical stages of development in postcolonial societies. Hence, issues of articulation and agency turn out to be of utmost importance in this representation of poor lives. However, to explicate the satirical thrust of *The Poor Mouth*, the background to the stereotypes attacked in the book is first provided.

3 Refigured Images of Irishness: Poverty as Authenticity

Taken by itself, the image of Irish peasants undermined in O'Brien's text is a rather positive one with which it is difficult to take exception as such. According to this concept, Irish peasants typically lead a simple life dominated by the rhythms of nature but in which the farmers and their families can become the victims of failed harvests and of exploitation by their landlords. Nonetheless, it is a life not yet spoiled by civilization and therefore somehow 'authentic' and 'genuine'. These notions are the basic elements of an auto-image of Irishness that was current around the turn of the twentieth century. It forms a contrast with the mid-nineteenth-century concept of the Stage Irishman, the Paddy figure so popular in music-hall drama and English weekly papers (Hirsch 1991, 1119). This figure was a buffoon whose chief features were his struggling with the English language and his perennial drunkenness. As Hirsch contends, this rather benign mid-century image changed significantly around the end of the nineteenth century and the beginning of the twentieth, when the Famine had driven many Irish to England, where they led poor lives in urban slums, and when the nationalist movement was beginning to form and violent agrarian revolts were occurring in Ireland. In the wake of these developments the comical

---

10 He regularly spent time in the areas of Cloughaneely and Gweedore, Co. Donegal (Gallagher 1983, 233).

figure of the Irish peasant was replaced by that of an uncivilized, savage, even sub-human creature as portrayed in contemporary English cartoons (e.g. in *The Times* and *Punch*, Kinealy 2006, 20). That image suited well with the ideology of British superiority over the Irish as their colonial subjects. However, the refigured English notion of the Irishman received its counterpart in the above-mentioned Irish auto-image:

> The dehumanization of the Irish in English periodicals (and on the stage) was fiercely challenged by the alternative tradition in Irish newspapers of portraying the peasant as a noble, honest, victimized farmer. No dramatization or portrayal of Irish peasant life could ever be wholly free of the looming shadow and presence of the English colonizer. (Hirsch 1991, 1119)

That Irish peasant was conceived of as part of an ancient tradition, a tradition which was rather the revivalists' own projection than historical fact, hence amounting to an invented tradition (Hobsbawm 1993, 1). The assumption of a peasant tradition was instrumental in the creation of a distinct Irish national identity to set Ireland off from her long-time oppressor (Hirsch 1991, 1120 – 1121), and it was functionalized for the purposes of cultural nationalism.

Similarly, Anglo-Irish literature of the period drew its claim to authentic Irishness from a putative line of continuity with the literature and culture of some hazy Gaelic past with which the Irish peasants were still in touch (Hirsch 1991, 1121), a link also claimed and exploited by the Gaelic League (founded in 1893), among whose members were Douglas Hyde and Patrick Pearse. The League campaigned for the use and preservation of Gaelic as part of an Irish national identity. After centuries of British political and cultural domination, only a minority of people at the time still spoke Gaelic as their mother tongue.[11] The Gaelic League endeavoured to preserve and promote the language by various means, including the teaching of Gaelic, the publication of Gaelic texts and the organization of language competitions. This linguistic preservation work was another element in the struggle for an independent nation. The language situation in Ire-

---

11 It is interesting to note here O'Brien's own special position regarding language: while the family spoke Irish at home and Gaelic was hence O'Brien's first language, neither the mother nor the father were themselves native speakers but had acquired Gaelic as adults. The father, Michael O'Nolan, was for some time an active member of the Gaelic League. An uncle of O'Brien's held the Chair of Irish at Maynooth (Ó Conaire 1973, 127). Hence, as Taaffe (2008, 93) states, O'Brien was brought up in a household dominated by the ideology of the Gaelic revival, but the language was not supported by a community of speakers outside the family. This artificial situation has a parallel in the strange outcomes of the language ideology indicted in *The Poor Mouth*.

land of the second half of the nineteenth century helps to explain how the close association between the west of Ireland and poverty could turn into a stereotype:

> Because of the importance of Irish to cultural nationalism, and the impoverishment of remaining vestigial communities of Irish speakers, what counted as authentic literature in Irish overwhelmingly concerned the harsh, 'traditional' life of the western, coastal poor, seen as unself-conscious, heroic and doomed. (McKibben 2003, 96)[12]

It is important to note in this context that the Anglo-Irish writers and other intellectuals who promoted ideas of a romantic life of the peasants were themselves doubly removed from the population in the countryside: they were part of an urban elite and mostly Protestant while the rural population was Catholic. This divide between them made it easier for the Anglo-Irish Revivalists to virtually mystify Irish peasants and to draw of them a romantic image that eschewed the exacting realities actually characterising the changing rural communities (Hirsch 1991, 1122; Gallagher 1983, 238).[13] The reproach that they were far removed from any experience of life in the west could certainly be made to some of the literary representatives of Irish Revivalism like J. M. Synge, W. B. Yeats and Lady Gregory.[14] Writing in English, these playwrights had created images of an essential Irishness of the west of Ireland where Gaelic had survived

---

12 Offering a "gendered, postcolonial reading of *The Poor Mouth*", McKibben contends that Irish was not only symbolic of a long cultural tradition but that the Irish language itself symbolized manliness: "The Irish language [...] became a talisman of the lost manly virtues of independence and fidelity, as well as much-needed proof of national distinctiveness in an increasingly anglophone and anglophilic society. Such idealised formulations in turn strongly impacted those who fought for independence, in part to recover that vitiated national manhood" (2003, 96, see also 99–100). McKibben's claim of a postcolonial critique in *The Poor Mouth* is rejected by Neil Murphy (2005, 28) on the – not quite cogent – grounds that O'Brien wrote much of his fiction and journalism in English and therefore could not be questioning the linguistic hegemony of the English-speaking oppressor. He believes O'Brien to be more generally undermining the validity of any grand narrative.

13 For a detailed account of the evolution of stereotypes of 'the Irish peasant' see Hirsch, part of whose essay is summarized in this paragraph. In the second part of his text, Hirsch studies Yeats, Synge, Joyce, O'Brien and Kavanagh for their "successive literary refigurations of the peasant" (1991, 1127).

14 O'Brien holds the likes of these poets and dramatists responsible for furthering or perpetuating the romanticized notion of Irish peasant life in the remote Gaeltacht. He was particularly critical of Synge, who seems to have served as the model for the Gaeligores in *The Poor Mouth*, since, like them, he was reproached by O'Brien with being ignorant of the language of the Gaels at the same time as professing an earnest interest in it (Gallagher 1983, 237). Taaffe (2008, 104) states that O'Brien berated Synge for creating an image of Irish peasants that was taken by many as an authentic portrayal of these people.

(e.g. Synge in *Riders to the Sea*, 1903, and *The Playboy of the Western World*, 1907).[15]

The romanticized notions of peasant life were indeed re-affirmed in the Gaeltacht autobiographies. Especially popular in the 1920s and 1930s, these life stories of and by simple people from the region celebrated their patience and everyday heroism in the face of adversity, characteristics which had also been promoted by the Revivalists. The first of a whole series of texts in this genre was Tomás Ó Criomhthian *An tOileánach* (published by An Gúm in 1929; translated into English by Robin Flowers as *The Islandman*). Other well-known titles were *Peig*, by Peig Sayers (1936) and Séamas Ó Grianna's *Caisleáin Óir* (1924).[16] These autobiographies had become rather conventionalized and predictable by the time O'Brien was writing and could therefore become the object of his parody. However, he was not so much poking fun at the genre as such but criticized its appropriation by the Irish Free State as a means to promote claims towards an essential Irishness (Wheatley 2011, 14).[17]

It is this continued mystification of Irish peasant life and the conventionalized portrayal of the Irish rural population, begun by the intellectuals of the Revival and the Gaelic League and then continued by Gaelic autobiographers themselves, which O'Brien's comic tale attacks.

---

15 After the formation of the Irish Free State, the cultural preservation work was continued by official bodies founded for that purpose. In 1926, for instance, the state-subsidized publishing house An Gúm was established for the printing of Gaelic-language literature, and in 1927, the Folklore of Ireland Society was founded. These institutions were instrumental in inspiring the writing of autobiographies of Gaeltacht life (Farnon 1997, 89–90).

16 While Ó Grianna was from Ulster, Sayers and Ó Criomhthian are two of many autobiographers from the area of Corca Duibhne, a place name whose phonology resembles Corkadoragha (Farnon 1997, 90), the fictional village that is the setting of *The Poor Mouth*. The area "occup[ies] a peninsula located between Dingle and Tralee and including also the Blasket Islands" (Farnon 1997, 90). Farnon goes on to state that the Gaelic autobiographies became very fashionable not because of any great literary merit but because they were very favourably reviewed in Gaelic journals and magazines.

17 Even so, the textual features of the Gaeltacht autobiographies deserve critical attention, since, as Richard T. Murphy (2011, 72–73) argues, O'Brien's parody concentrates on the genre's conventions to reveal that the idealized notions of Irishness propagated through that genre were first and foremost a textual construction rather than being based on any observation of the reality of Gaeltacht life.

4 The True Irish Fate of Being Poor

Usually designated as a 'short novel', the *The Poor Mouth* is the fictional auto-biography of one Bonaparte O'Coonassa,[18] who begins his account on the sad note of his impending death and motivates the telling by his wish to preserve the memory of his life and the village of Corkadoragha for posterity, since, as he claims here for the first time, the likes of him and his fellow villagers "will not be there again".[19] Bonaparte states about his own birth:

> I was born in the middle of the night in the end of the house.[20] My father never expected me because he was a quiet fellow and did not understand very accurately the ways of life. My little bald skull so astounded him that he almost departed from this life the moment I entered it [...]. The people said that my mother was not expecting me either and it is a fact that the whisper went around that I was not born of my mother at all but of another woman. All that, nevertheless, is only the neighbours' talk and cannot be checked now because the neighbours are all dead and their likes will not be there again. (13)[21]

Thus are introduced Bonaparte and his family, a set of simple-minded people, as ignorant of procreation as of almost every other fact of life, who never cease to wonder at the miracles that the world has in store for them. One source of amazement for Bonaparte is the squalor of his family's house. This, like every-thing else, is put down to the Gaelic fate and therefore meekly accepted:

> We lived in a small, lime-white, unhealthy house, situated in a corner of the glen on the right-hand side as you go eastwards along the road. Doubtless, neither my father nor any of his people before him built the house and placed it there; it is not known whether it was god, demon or person who first raised the half-rotten, rough walls. [...] It has always been the destiny of the true Gaels (if the books be credible) to live in a small, lime-white house in the corner of the glen as you go eastwards along the road and that must be the explanation that when I reached this life there was no good habitation for me but the re-

---

18 The protagonist's name must certainly be taken in an ironic sense since he shares nothing of the heroism of his famous namesake. On the choice of personal names in *The Poor Mouth*, see Ó Háinle (2007).

19 This phrase becomes a leitmotif in the story and is already indicative of the parodic nature of the text as it is built on an analogy with "Our likes will never be again" used by Ó Criomhthian in his *An tOileánach* – even if it crops up there no more than once, and only in the conclusion at that (R. T. Murphy 2011, 71).

20 The original Gaelic of this, *tóin an tighe*, is an instance of the linguistic ambiguity so often exploited by O'Brien. *Tóin* also means 'a person's backside' (Farnon 1997, 95; translator's note in O'Brien 1996, 125).

21 This and all further references are to the reprint of the 1973 edition of *The Poor Mouth* listed in the Works Cited.

verse in all truth. [...] Yes! people were in bad circumstances when I was young and he who had stock and cattle possessed little room at night in his own house. Alas! it was always thus. I often heard the Old-Grey-Fellow speak of the hardship and misery of life in former times. (16–18)

The passage breathes the fatalism with which Bonaparte's story is imbued. The stupidity and inertia of the inhabitants of the village – where there is a circular return of the suffering of one generation in the next since all fail to take their lives into their own hands – is certainly a source of mirth. Everything is as it ever was, from the rain which falls every night in Corkadoragha and always leaves the inhabitants drenched to the bone to Bonaparte's reliving the experience of his father. Like him, Bonaparte is thrown into prison for a deed he never committed just because he lacks English and cannot follow the legal procedures.[22] In keeping with the nature of satire, there is of course a residue of truth in this grotesquely overdone depiction of squalor and suffering. The details given evoke a reality only too well known to, or remembered by, many Irish (Gallagher 1983, 232–233, 236). Even so, O'Brien is clearly criticizing the attitude of people who accept their misery as God-given and unchangeable and who thereby, as it were, become victims of misfortune and exploitation by their own fault (Booker 1995, 74; Kiberd 1995, 503).

5 The Oppressor's Language: Appropriation and Abrogation

The satire centres on some of the excesses of the period of cultural nationalism, and there is only little criticism of the English (Wimfre 2007, 278). Even so, the text criticizes the effects of the English language policy in Ireland, but the actual agents here are the Irish teachers who diligently follow the rules stipulated by the English, i.e. the monolingual English-language policy for Irish schools[23] and the systematic anglicizing of personal names (Ó Háinle 2007, 211). It is in this context that Bonaparte is able to turn the English-only policy to his family's

---

22 The constant conversations about the weather and Bonaparte's tendency to exaggeration are themselves examples of preconceived notions of Irishness that O'Brien satirizes (N. Murphy 24–25). On further aspects of contemporary Irish society and the folkloristic and literary themes which are taken up in the original text, see Ó Conaire (1973, 130–135) and especially Farnon (1997).

23 In 1831, a Board of Education in Ireland was set up by the British government. From then on, all teaching in Irish schools had to be done in English (Kinealy 2006, 9).

financial advantage. But the fight against material poverty in this case is less important than that against the linguistic impoverishment and oppression that results from colonial domination.

The English language policy and its effects on the local population emerge in a passage in which Bonaparte tells of his first day at school (Ch. 3). When the schoolmaster addresses him in English and asks him his name, Bonaparte is bewildered as he does not understand the language. Another pupil translates the question into Gaelic, and he then answers by giving his full name as: "Bonaparte, son of Michelangelo, son of Peter, son of Owen, son of Thomas's Sarah, granddaughter of John's Mary, granddaughter of James, son of Dermot..." (30).[24] In response, the teacher gives him a savage stroke on the head with an oar and tells him that his name is "Jams O'Donnell". In the same brutal fashion, the other pupils are also renamed on their first day at school, all of them receiving the same name. Back home, Bonaparte wants to know of his mother why it is that they all become Jams O'Donnells at school. He learns from her that this is in keeping with established practice:

> 'Don't you understand that it's Gaels that live in this side of the country and that they can't escape from fate? It was always said and written that every Gaelic youngster is hit on his first school day because he doesn't understand English and the foreign form of his name and that no one has any respect for him because he's Gaelic to the marrow. There's no other business going on in school that day but punishment and revenge and the same fooling about *Jams O'Donnell*. Alas! I don't think that there'll ever be any good settlement for the Gaels but only hardship for them always'. (31–34)

Under the circumstances, Bonaparte decides that this was his first and last day of schooling. Set against the backdrop of his general patience in suffering, this decision amounts to an act of resistance. Here and elsewhere, the postcolonial resonances of O'Brien's tale are strong.[25] Writing some twenty years after Irish independence, he takes issue with English as a tool of colonial oppression and the unwillingness of the dominant British to concede any individuality to the Irish, whom they turn into their inferior, non-human Others as they even deny them individual personal names (Booker 1995, 73).

---

24 In the original, this corresponds to one of the long genitive constructions which can be formed in Gaelic and sound less awkward than this English construction (translator's note in O'Brien 1996, 126).

25 Booker considers Beckett and Joyce as Irish writers who were susceptible to the "colonial echoes inherent in English" (1995, 68) and reacted to it in their works. But while they do so in their English-language texts, O'Brien actually uses Gaelic as an alternative literary language (Booker 1995, 69).

However, Bonaparte later embraces his English name when that is in his interest. To promote the use of English, every Irish child who can give evidence that they know the language will receive two pounds of money as a reward.[26] The resourceful grandfather manages to increase the number of heads that will earn them two pounds each: the family dress up their sow's many piglets in human clothes. When the English inspector comes to count the English speakers, he turns out to be half blind. Not wanting to enter the family's house because of the appalling smell that emanates from it, he takes the piglets' squealing for the children's inarticulate pronunciation of English. Thus, the family make use of English expectations concerning the Gaels' use of English to play a trick on him. More significantly, Bonaparte's brutal re-christening now has its rewards. When the inspector asks for his name, Bonaparte this time promptly answers "Jams O'Donnell, sor" (37–38), and this is sufficient for the inspector as proof that he speaks English. But there is an additional twist to the passage inasmuch as the apparent mispronunciation of the form of address *sor* is homophonous with the Gaelic word for 'louse' (translator's note in O'Brien 1996, 126). Hence, the deferential form of address is at the same time a term of abuse.[27] In this way, the family actively subvert the project of the promotion of the English language, turning it to their own advantage. As Booker puts it: "the Gaels manage a dexterously double-voiced use of language that rings of submissiveness to the ear of the oppressor but that is in fact highly subversive" (1995, 77).[28]

Here and elsewhere, the tale shows typical processes of postcolonial reactions to the dominance of the language of the colonial oppressor. The most overt instance of such a reaction is the very choice of Gaelic for the text itself,

---

26 It should be noted that the episode can at the same time be read as critical of the promotion of the use of *Irish* in post-independence Ireland since the practice of a financial reward for speaking the right language parallels the two pounds which were offered as an incentive to use Irish at home, a grant introduced in 1933 by the Irish Minister of Education, Thomas Derrig (Taaffe 2008, 104, note 61).

27 According to Farnon, a similar ambiguity arises from the name of the poorest of the people of Corkadoragha, Sitric Ó Sánasa. Because he is so extraordinarily poor, the Gaeligores consider him the most Gaelic of Gaels. But this essential Gaelicness is undermined in his very name since, by a process of metathesis, Ó Sánasa becomes Ó Sasana, which is the Gaelic word for England (Farnon 1997, 102).

28 Contrasting with what is maintained here, Richard T. Murphy believes that there is "not the voice of the subaltern speaking back to the obscuring and distorting discourse of outsiders, since the novel resists the very claims of authorship (even his pen name, Myles na gCopaleen, is lifted from Boucicault's stage-Irish 'shaghraun') required to mount such a reality-based critique" (2011, 80). That the use of an alias and a non-realist mode of writing should rule out such a critique is far from plausible – it is the very nature of satire to provide space for social and political critique.

which undermines that dominance. But that language choice is significant also with respect to existing images of poor Irish peasants. As Kiberd contends, O'Brien's granting the Irish their own tongue helps to overcome the essentialist image of Irishness represented in the Stage Irishman with his restricted command and mispronunciation of English:

> In the character of Myles na gCopaleen, O'Nolan rescues the buffoon from the Victorian state and makes him articulate. The feckless clown who had once stuttered in broken English is now permitted to speak in his native language, and so he is shown not as the English wish to visualise him, but as he sees himself.[29] The eclipsing 'g', which had been omitted from the final word of his name in *The Colleen Bawn*, is now restored, so Myles na Coppaleen may resume the fuller status of Myles na gCopaleen. (Kiberd 1995, 497–498)

The rejection of the dominant language corresponds to the abrogation of language, a typical phenomenon in postcolonial societies when the claim to superiority of that language is called into question (Ashcroft et al. 1989, 38). When, as here, English is no longer granted the position of the prestigious standard, reproaches of inarticulate pronunciation are also invalidated.

The ambiguity between English *Sir* and the vernacular word *sor* occurring in a diglossic situation can be considered a case of appropriation (Ashcroft et al. 1989, 38): knowing a mere couple of words of the language, Bonaparte appropriates English to gain an advantage over the inspector. He earns the family some money and makes a language joke at the inspector's expense. With the exception of this particular episode, involving an inspector who is actually English himself (37), the persons from whom Gaelic is reclaimed are the "dominant (English-speaking) elements of Irish society [who are] the ones in command of the various languages of power; they are the ones in charge of definition and classification" (Booker 1995, 70–71). Hence, these Anglo-Irish occupy a position very similar to that formerly held by the English colonial rulers, and O'Brien openly criticizes them for this.

6 Linguistic and Cultural Essentialism Debunked

Contrasting with the indictment of English-language policies, the veneration and celebration of Gaelic becomes an object of satire in its turn. This emerges in the

---

29 As argued above, even though its narrator is a poor person from the west, the text does not in fact convey an auto-image of Irish peasants but rather O'Brien's outsider's view of them, and one which is satirical at that.

episode of the Gaelic feis ('festival') that is celebrated in Corkadoragha. For more than ten years, the narrator explains, there have been gentlemen coming to the village to do linguistic field work. They are known to the local population as Gaeligores, specialists of the language who encourage its use (N. Murphy 2005, 24). When these specialists flock to Corkadoragha in great numbers on the day of the feis, the inhabitants marvel at their folkloristic attire and the fancy honorary names that they have adopted ("The Running Knight", "The Dative Case", "John of the Glen"; 52–53). The village people themselves have neither such dress nor such names: they are shamed to recognize that they lack these features of true Gaelicness.

The major event of the feis is a language competition. The president of the Gaeligores has promised a prize for him who is "most in earnest about Gaelic" (58). What is meant by being in earnest about it becomes clear from the president's own opening oration:

> Gaels! he said, it delights my Gaelic heart to be here today speaking Gaelic with you at this Gaelic feis in the centre of the Gaeltacht. May I state that I am a Gael. I'm Gaelic from the crown of my head to the soles of my feet – Gaelic front and back, above and below. Likewise, you are all truly Gaelic. We are all Gaelic Gaels of Gaelic lineage. He who is Gaelic, will be Gaelic evermore. I myself have spoken not a word except Gaelic since the day I was born – just like you – and every sentence I've ever uttered has been on the subject of Gaelic. If we're truly Gaelic, we must constantly discuss the question of the Gaelic revival and the question of Gaelicism. There is no use in having Gaelic, if we converse in it on non-Gaelic topics. He who speaks Gaelic but fails to discuss the language question is not truly Gaelic in his heart; such conduct is of no use to Gaelicism because he only jeers at Gaelic and reviles the Gaels. There is nothing in this life so nice and so Gaelic as truly true Gaelic Gaels who speak in true Gaelic Gaelic about the truly Gaelic language. (54–55)

With its tautological word repetitions and the claim that the Gaelic language should only ever be used for meta-linguistic reflection, the speech conveys a sense of empty essentialism. In this episode, O'Brien's targets are the self-proclaimed keepers of the Holy Grail of things Gaelic, among them the members of the Gaelic League. O'Brien is criticizing the language revival as a circular, self-reflexive activity, a mere end in itself. In his journalistic work, he reproached the revivalists with idealizing the language and its speakers and stated that, rather than help them or the nation as a whole, this idealizing served to confirm their economic backwardness and consequent destitution.[30]

---

30 In her illuminating chapter on "Irish Myles: *Cruiskeen Lawn* and *An Béal Bocht*", Taaffe (2008, 91–125, esp. 114–125) traces the links and contradictions between O'Brien's fiction and his column and other non-fiction concerning the language issue, drawing attention to several 'precursor stories' to *An Béal Bocht* (also set in Corkadoragha) published in *Cruiskeen Lawn*.

That the above-mentioned link between the west of Ireland and poverty had indeed been cemented by the time O'Brien was writing and that he is poking fun at this bizarre valorization of destitution is borne out by a passage which thematizes squalor as "an essential indicator of cultural authenticity" (R. T. Murphy 2011, 73). It occurs in connection with the Gaeligores, whose visits to the village are becoming less frequent – a troubling fact for Bonaparte and his grandfather, who are worried they may have lost their true Gaelicness:

> When [the Gaeligores] had been coming to us for about ten years or thereabouts, we noticed that their number among us was diminishing and that those who remained faithful to us were lodging in Galway and in Rannafast while making day-trips to Corkadoragha. Of course, they carried away much of our good Gaelic when they departed from us each night but they left few pennies as recompense to the paupers who waited for them and had kept the Gaelic tongue alive for such as them a thousand years. People found this difficult to understand; it had always been said that accuracy of Gaelic (as well as holiness of spirit) grew in proportion to one's lack of worldly goods and since we had the choicest poverty and calamity, we did not understand why the scholars were interested in any half-awkward, perverse Gaelic which was audible in other parts. (49)

The grandfather suspects that their village has become unattractive to the linguists because the money the scholars brought helped to reduce their poverty and hence made the place less authentically Gaelic and the language less genuine. But he then learns the true reason: the scholars begin to come less frequently to Corkadoragha when they find the "tempest of the countryside [...] too tempestuous", "the putridity of the countryside [...] too putrid", "the poverty of the countryside [...] too poor" (50). They are tired of those essential qualities for which they had once admired the Gaels of Corkadoragha because spending time there means that they themselves are exposed to these unpleasant realities. In the logic of the book, where meek acceptance of unpleasant circumstances is the rule, the Gaeligores' unwillingness to share the discomforts of poverty is good proof that they are not Gaels themselves.

7 Representation and Agency Revisited

The Poor Mouth effectively deconstructs the myth that poverty – which sadly marked the lives of many in the western coastal regions – was an essential part of Irish identity and should therefore be embraced as a sign of authenticity. In formulating a correlation between poverty and Gaelic authenticity through his narrator, O'Brien reveals the perversity of romanticizing the poor.

Even though O'Brien is parodying the autobiographies, he is not *primarily* putting the blame on the writers' self-representation. The real culprits appear to be the Anglo-Irish preservers of Gaelic culture and language, some of whom had created literary allo-representations of poverty. Their representations were based on the gaze of people unaffected by the poverty that they saw and not always sufficiently versed in the Gaelic language or culture to understand the reality of those lives. Functionalized as they were in the struggle for Irish independence and in defining a national identity in the first decades after independence, these discursive constructions of Irish peasants in the Gaeltacht served ideological and political purposes.

Since the figurations of Irishness in question still had currency when the Gaeltacht autobiographers were writing their life stories, they could build their own representations on them and hope to find a readership familiar with these stereotypes and responsive to autobiographical accounts that confirmed them from the perspective of insiders. While these writers' images were hence derivative rather than original, O'Brien is certainly also criticizing the Gaeltacht writers – who had the agency to tell their lives themselves – for adopting and perpetuating them. Hence, the book makes it quite plain that these self-representations of poor lives are no more disinterested accounts than the allo-representations created by some of the Anglo-Irish Revivalists. Neither kind of representation is inherently superior or ethically more acceptable, nor does either of them have a greater claim to authenticity over the other.

In the satirical mode that he is using, O'Brien himself has created yet another allo-representation of poverty. However, his thoroughly entertaining story brings to the fore the double plight of a community trying to overcome colonial oppression and suffering from poverty. O'Brien opens up a space for these subjects to subvert the power relations that are built on language and thus to become agents who begin to direct the course of their own lives.

Works Cited

Ashcroft, Bill, Gareth Griffiths, and Helen Tiffin. *The Empire Writes Back: Theory and Practice in Post-Colonial Literatures.* New York, London: Routledge, 1989.

Booker, M. Keith. *Flann O'Brien, Bakhtin, and Menippean Satire.* Syracuse, NY: Syracuse University Press, 1995.

Brüns, Elke. "Einleitung: Plädoyer für einen *social turn* in der Literaturwissenschaft." *Ökonomien der Armut: Soziale Verhältnisse in der Literatur.* Ed. Elke Brüns. München: Fink, 2008. 7–19.

Day, Jon. "Cuttings from *Cruiskeen Lawn*: Bibliographical Issues in the Republication of Myles na gCopaleen's Journalism." *'Is it about a bicycle?': Flann O'Brien in the Twenty-First Century.* Ed. Jennika Baines. Dublin: Four Courts, 2011. 32–48.

Farnon, Jane. "Motifs of Gaelic Lore and Literature in *An Béal Bocht.*" *Conjuring Complexities: Essays on Flann O'Brien.* Eds. Anne Clune and Tess Hurson. Belfast: The Institute of Irish Studies, The Queen's University Belfast, 1997. 89–109.

Gallagher, Monique. "*The Poor Mouth*: Flann O'Brien and the Gaeltacht." *Studies: An Irish Quarterly Review* 71/72 (Autumn 1983): 231–241.

Hirsch, Edward. "The Imaginary Irish Peasant." *PMLA* 106.5 (1991): 1116–1133.

Hobsbawm, Eric. "Introduction: Inventing Traditions." *The Invention of Tradition.* Eds. Eric Hobsbawm and Terence Ranger. Cambridge: Cambridge University Press, 1993. 1–14.

Kiberd, Declan. *Inventing Ireland.* London: Cape, 1995.

Kinealy, Christine. "The Stricken Land: The Great Hunger in Ireland." *Hungry Words: Images of Famine in the Irish Canon.* Eds. George Cusack and Sarah Goss. Dublin: Irish Academic Press, 2006. 7–28.

McKibben, Sarah. "*The Poor Mouth*: A Parody of (Post) Colonial Irish Manhood." *Research in African Literatures* 34.4 (2003): 96–114.

Murphy, Neil. "Flann O'Brien." *Review of Contemporary Fiction* 25.3 (Fall 2005): 7–41.

Murphy, Richard T. "'A root of the new sprout?': Flann O'Brien, Minor Literature and the Modern Gaelic Canon." *'Is it about a bicycle?': Flann O'Brien in the Twenty-First Century.* Ed. Jennika Baines. Dublin: Four Courts, 2011. 67–82.

na gCopaleen, Myles. *An Béal Bocht.* Dublin: National Press, 1941.

O'Brien, Flann. *The Poor Mouth: A Bad Story about the Hard Life.* Transl. Patrick C. Power, ill. Ralph Steadman. Normal, IL: Dalkey Archive, 1996 [1973].

Ó Conaire, Breandán. "Flann O'Brien, *An Béal Bocht* and Other Irish Matters." *Irish University Review* 3.2 (1973): 121–140.

OED. "Stereotype, n." Def. 3b. *The Oxford English Dictionary.* Online Edition 2013a. http://www.oed.com/view/Entry/189956?rskey=97XNm4&result=1#eid (4 November 2013).

OED. "Image, n." Def. 5b. *The Oxford English Dictionary.* Online Edition 2013b. http://www.oed.com/view/Entry/91618?rskey=DCCy0d&result=1#eid (4 November 2013).

Ó Háinle, Cathal. "Personal Names in *An Béal Bocht.*" *Proceedings of the Eighth Symposium of Societas Celtologica Nordica.* Eds. Jan Erik Rekdal and Ailbhe Ó Corráin. Stockholm: Uppsala University Library, 2007. 209–221.

Power, Patrick C. "Translator's Preface." *The Poor Mouth: A Bad Story about the Hard Life.* Flann O'Brien. Transl. Patrick C. Power, ill. Ralph Steadman. Normal, IL: Dalkey Archive, 1996 [1973]. 5–6.

Salamon, Gayle. "Here Are the Dogs: Poverty in Theory." *differences: a Journal of Feminist Cultural Studies* 21.1 (2010): 169–177.

Spivak, Gayatri Chakravorty. "Can the Subaltern Speak?". *Marxism and the Interpretation of Culture.* Eds. Cary Nelson and Lawrence Grossberg. Urbana: The University of Illinois Press, 1988. 271–313.

Taaffe, Carol. *Ireland Through the Looking Glass: Flann O'Brien, Myles na gCopaleen and Irish Cultural Debate.* Cork: Cork University Press, 2008.

Vollmann, William T. *Poor People.* New York: Ecco, 2007.

Wheatley, David. "A Day of His Own. 100 Years on: Time to Find the Right Place for Flann O'Brien." *The Times Literary Supplement* 30 September 2011: 14–15.

Wilson, Jon E. "Agency, Narrative, and Resistance." *The British Empire: Themes and Perspectives*. Ed. Sarah Stockwell. Oxford: Blackwell, 2008. 245–268.

Wimfre, Iwan. "*An Béal Bocht:* A Critique of Irish Nationalism, Irish-Language Literature and the People of the Gaeltacht?". *Proceedings of the Eighth Symposium of Societas Celtologica Nordica*. Eds. Jan Erik Rekdal and Ailbhe Ó Corráin. Stockholm: Uppsala University Library, 2007. 275–284.

Eveline Kilian
Frames of Recognition under Global Capitalism: Eastern European Migrants in British Fiction

1 Introduction

Narratives of migration in British literature have mostly emerged from a postcolonial context. The issues of racism, of cultural identity, home and belonging they raised as well as the transformation of Britain into a multi-ethnic and pluricultural society were for a long time almost exclusively tied to Britain's colonial past and its aftermath. Eastern European migration to Britain, despite its long history, has only resurfaced more perceptibly in British literature and criticism in recent years (Korte 2010), in the wake of the various upheavals and developments in Europe over the past decades. Geopolitical changes like the end of the Cold War and the disintegration of the former Soviet Union as well as the expansion of the European Union in 2004, have brought economic migrants from the new member states, particularly from Poland and Lithuania, to Britain to join the already well-established migrant groups from Southern and Eastern Europe (Burrell 2006, 4–5). As a result of the various ethnic conflicts on the Balkans, Britain, like other European countries, has seen an influx of refugees notably from the former Yugoslavia and from Romania. These migrants are often precarious subjects, in economic terms and, in the case of asylum-seekers or victims of human trafficking, with respect to their legal status. By now British literature has undertaken a number of explorations of the migrants' struggle to survive and create a new life for themselves, and of the impact these developments have had on British society, some of them in a humorous (e.g. Marina Lewycka's *A Short History of Tractors in Ukrainian*, 2005, and *Two Caravans*, 2007), others in a more serious vein (e.g. Monica Ali's *In the Kitchen*, 2009).

Literary and cultural theory, too, has responded to these new developments by merging postcolonial with globalization studies and by extending the scope of the postcolonial to embrace transcultural and transnational perspectives more adequate to deal with contexts and networks largely determined by transnational agents, capital and markets, and a global flow of technology, knowledge, culture and information (Loomba et al. 2005, 2). This is mostly effected by foregrounding the natural link between these two areas, i.e. the "inescapable global dimension" (Childs and Williams 1997, 21) of postcolonialism. Childs and Williams, for example, describe postcolonialism as a phase of imperialism which expresses itself in "the globalizing of capitalism" (1997, 21), others point out historical connections and structural affinities between "empires and the neo-imperial structures of global inequality" (Loomba et al. 2005, 4; Ashcroft et al. 2000, 112).

In the following I will take a closer look at two contemporary literary texts focusing on migrants from Eastern Europe faced with post-1989, global capitalism and ethnic conflict: Rose Tremain's *The Road Home* (2007) and Kate Clanchy's *Antigona and Me* (2008). Despite their common subject, they crucially differ both in their narrative technique and the kind of protagonist they portray. Whereas *The Road Home* features a male economic migrant from one of the new EU member states and, broadly speaking, follows the pattern of a *Bildungsroman*, Clanchy's text is a first-person narrative based on the author's encounter with a young female Kosovan refugee. Clanchy portrays the asylum seeker's life as it emerges from their numerous conversations but filters it through her own perspective. I will explore the diverging ideological groundings of these two texts against the backdrop of a renewed critical interest in an ethics of recognition and its political consequences for a society's treatment of minorities and precarious subjects. This ties in with some of the issues foregrounded in theories of globalization, but my main point of reference will be Judith Butler's concept of recognition, which she developed in the context of her gender theory and which gained new poignancy when she turned her attention to the international conflicts of the late twentieth and early twenty-first centuries and probed the ethical implications of Western responses to these conflicts. In her collection of essays *Precarious Life* (2004), Butler presents several pieces that were written after 9/11, particularly in response to the US's handling of the attacks and the subsequent heightening of nationalist discourse. In *Frames of War* (2009) she continues these investigations into questions of violence, racism, immigration policies and human rights around the US-led military interventions in Iraq and Afghanistan and their representation in the media.

It is these ethical concerns that I am particularly interested in. Although the literary texts in question do not refer to the same political crises as Butler's essays, the epistemological value of her approach lies in the interdependencies it reveals between individual subject positions, intersubjective interaction, discursive structures and political power differentials. This provides a theoretical framework to place questions of identity and alterity, which lie at the heart of the two novels in question, in a wider network of power differentials and political issues of inclusion and exclusion. In literature, this network becomes palpable and accessible in the narrative discourse, predominantly in the structure of the text, its genre, its choice of focalization. Narrative technique is all the more important, because, contrary to postcolonial subjects, the Eastern European migrants' command of English is usually not sufficient to enable them to become the writing subjects of their own stories of migration. Consequently it is mostly British authors who take up this new field of interest, and their literary explorations are inevitably pervaded by their own negotiations of self-positioning and othering. The substantial differences between Tremain's and Clanchy's texts will bring to light the political effects of forms of representation, a problem Butler addressed with respect to media representations of war. In turn, the confrontation of these literary investigations of scenarios of migration with Butler's philosophical inquiries will also be instrumental in demarcating the limitations of Butler's reflections, specifically with respect to her conceptualization of the subject and the human. My discussions of *The Road Home* and *Antigona and Me* will be preceded by an explanation and contextualization of Butler's concepts of recognition and precarious life.

2 Judith Butler's Theory of Recognition

Butler's more recent concerns sparked by the rising level of global conflict can be directly linked to her earlier, gender-based books on subject formation and agency as well as her writings on ethics and recognition.[1] One of her principal tenets in her earlier writings is the discursive constitution of the subject as a gendered subject within the constitutive constraints of the hegemonic gender norm: "Subjected to gender, but subjectivated by gender, the 'I' neither precedes nor follows the process of this gendering, but emerges only within and as the matrix of gender relations themselves" (Butler 1993, 7). This passage not only describes the subject as the product of a specific discourse, but also tackles the question of agency. Butler conceptualizes subject formation along the lines of Michel Foucault (1980) and Teresa de Lauretis (1986) as a paradoxical process of simultaneous subjection and subjectivation.[2] This paradox is precisely the condition of agency (Butler 2004, 3) and places the subject in "an enabling and limiting field of constraint" (Butler 2005, 19). Although the culturally intelligible subject

---

[1] Her interest in the concept of recognition can be traced back to her early Hegelian studies, for example *Subjects of Desire: Hegelian Reflections in Twentieth-Century France* of 1987, the book based on her doctoral dissertation.

[2] Teresa de Lauretis's definition reads as follows: "subject in the two senses of the term: both subject-ed to social constraint and yet subject in the active sense of maker as well as user of culture" (1986, 10).

is produced by a set of norms, it must at the same time negotiate these norms for itself (Butler 2005, 10), and this can also imply developing a critical distance to them.

This is the philosophical horizon Butler repeatedly draws on in her later publications, notably in her theory of recognition, which she unfolds in her Adorno Lectures held in Frankfurt in 2002 (Butler 2005 and 2007). She presents two interlinked perspectives on recognition and subject formation. The first one is derived from Hegel, who posits recognition as a reciprocal act and describes the self's encounter with the other in the struggle for recognition as a movement that irreversibly propels the subject outside itself. In this "ek-static notion of the self" (Butler 2004, 148) the emergence of self-consciousness is always linked to self-loss, a kind of dispossession of the self, which is another term for the decentring of the self:

> [I]f we are to follow *The Phenomenology of the Spirit*, I am invariably transformed by the encounters I undergo; recognition becomes the process by which I become other than what I was and so cease to be able to return to what I was. There is, then, a constitutive loss in the process of recognition, since the 'I' is transformed through the act of recognition. (Butler 2005, 27–28)

Butler's second perspective connects this intersubjective model to a discursive framework and translates it into an encounter between the individual and the norms that regulate their intelligibility as a subject. This is where Butler's model links up with Althusser's notion of interpellation, the act through which ideology constitutes the subject (Althusser 1971, 173–174). Butler sets her concept of performativity and the subject's agency against Althusser's view of interpellation as a unilateral process, however, by stressing the subject's possibility of disobedience and resistance in their appropriation and repetition of the norm (Butler 1993, 122–123; Ferrarese 2011, 761–763; Salaverría 2011, 38).

The interdependence of the two perspectives outlined above is motivated by the fact that as much as the norm itself is impersonal in the sense that it transcends the self, it nevertheless needs to be mobilized on an interpersonal level. So, again paradoxically, individual subjects implement the norm that in turn effects their own dispossession (Butler 2005, 25–26). These norms "decide [...] what will and what will not be a recognizable form of being" (Butler 2005, 22), thereby setting the terms of recognition. Consequently, this regime of truth also provides the reference point for the subject's agency: "it is in relation to this framework that recognition takes place or the norms that govern recognition are challenged and transformed" (Butler 2005, 22). Butler's argument that norms "decide in advance who will and will not become a subject" (2005, 9) remains a powerful one throughout her writing. In *Undoing Gender* (2004), she applies this idea to transgendered individuals, who mark the boundary between culturally intelligible and unintelligible subjects. The gender norm produces a framework of recognition for male and female subjects and makes it difficult or impossible to recognize those who do not fit this binary grid and who are therefore often denied recognition (Butler 2004, 2) and become the victims of humiliation or violence. This, in Butler's view, necessitates a redrawing of the boundary to make the gender norm more inclusive and thus to maximize the conditions for a liveable life (2004, 8). The same principle recurs in *Precarious Life*, although now the focus is no longer on gender but on the recognition of ethnic others in international conflicts. Here Butler reads the huge gap between the nationally recognized grieving of certain victims and the blocking out or derealization of other losses, whose grieving becomes even unthinkable, as an indicator of the specific norms that produce the viability of a subject:

> Some lives are grievable, and others are not; the differential allocation of grievability that decides what kind of subject is and must be grieved, and which kind of subject must not, operates to produce and maintain certain exclusionary conceptions of who is normatively human: what counts as a livable life and a grievable death. (2004, xiv–xv)

In *Giving an Account of Oneself*, Butler makes frequent use of the term *frame* (or framework) as a synonym for the system of norms that governs intelligibility and recognition as in the following example: "the other only appears to me [...] if there is a frame within which I can see and apprehend the other in her separateness and exteriority" (2005, 25). It is foregrounded even more in *Precarious Life* and becomes the central concept in *Frames of War*. The productivity of this term lies in the various connotations it opens up. A frame is something that is easily movable, that can change according to context and situation, something that determines the perspective one is invited to take, and that needs some kind of agent to adjust the frame according to particular (political) goals. In other words, this term highlights the "historically contingent ontology" (Butler 2009, 4) of the normative conditions as well as the power relations that inform the framing.

Furthermore, the term frame refers to modes of visual representation, in Butler's examples specifically the media coverage of the participants in armed conflicts, their visibility or invisibility, and the way they are made to appear through a particular lens. These are the means to produce an "evacuation of the human through the image" (Butler 2004, 146), or, more precisely, through what the chosen frame includes and what it excludes: "This derealization takes place neither inside nor outside the image, but through the very framing by which the image is contained" (Butler 2004, 148). Despite their controlling power and normative force, frames are also fragile and subject to subversion or even reversal, however. This is due to "the iterable structure of the frame" (Butler 2009, 12), i.e. the fact that it needs to be repeatedly mobilized, in order to unfold its effect.[3] This is particularly obvious with respect to war photographs, which are circulated and reproduced in different contexts, thus exposing and sometimes calling into question the rationale of their frame, as was the case with the images of humiliated and tortured prisoners in Abu Ghraib that caused widespread outrage when they were leaked to the public. My readings of *The Road Home* and *Antigona and Me* will make use of these different meanings and connotations of the term frame.

3 From Eastern European Communism to European Community: Rose Tremain's *The Road Home*

The publication of Tremain's *The Road Home* in 2007 was met with predominantly favourable reviews. It won the Orange Broadband Prize for Fiction, and the writer was praised for her imaginative insight and empathy with her protagonist and for her "distinctive literary boldness" (Brownrigg 2007; Marriott 2007). There have also been some more reserved assessments, however, which mainly centre on Tremain's lack of first-hand knowledge of her subject-matter leading to shallow generalizations and unreflected projections (Müller 2008) or, read from a postcolonial perspective, to orientalizing representations of the Eastern European Other (Jaskulski 2010). It is these critical perspectives that my own analysis of the novel will link up with.

Lev, the protagonist of *The Road Home,* is a man in his early forties from an unnamed former Communist country in Eastern Europe, which has only recently joined the European Union. The 2004 expansion of the EU provides the central frame of recognition on which the whole novel hinges. It functions as a dividing line between the old and the new and as a motor of momentous transformations. Despite her partly critical attitude towards the state of British society as well as some of the excesses, inanities and blurred visions of reality displayed by the metropolitan cultural elite, Tremain leaves no doubt as to how these global changes ought to be evaluated. She does so mainly through her description of Lev's home country, which has been run down by inept officials, is on the

---

3 This notion of the iterability of the frame is again modelled on Butler's concept of gender performativity as a repetition of the norm that can be subtly altered through introducing variations into the repeated acts (Butler 1990, 33; Butler 1993, 2, 94–95, 107).

brink of a complete breakdown and beyond any hope of recovery. The novel gives us sporadic snapshots of a governing class oblivious and indifferent to the welfare of their people and of a destitute country rife with unemployment and shortages of pretty much everything, complete with ecological disasters and levels of lethal contamination that might be the reason for the abnormally high number of cases of leukaemia in the area of Lev's home town, the illness which also caused his wife's death.

But EU membership opens up new possibilities, which the novel sets out to explore. It confers a new kind of citizenship that protects the inhabitants of a member state, at least technically, from discrimination and grants them the right to move and reside freely as well as the right to apply for employment in any of the member states.[4] Recognition is thus shown in its material consequences (Fraser 1997). This legal framework enables Lev to go to London as an economic migrant, to take on a job and earn money, which he can send home to support his five-year-old daughter and his mother. Making Lev a legal immigrant who finds it comparatively easy to find a job is important for the shaping of Tremain's plot. Her focus is clearly on Lev's personal growth rather than on the intricacies of immigration policies and their consequences. *The Road Home* has a decidedly retro touch produced by the use of a highly conventionalized genre, the *Bildungsroman* (Crişu 2010) and its focus on individual development, which prevents Tremain from critically reflecting the mechanisms of globalization and leads her to elevate the Western European subject to the status of the universal subject.

Tremain's plot is based on the journey, a staple feature of the Bildungsroman. Lev leaves his home country by coach at the beginning of the novel and returns by plane in the last but one chapter, after having spent about a year and a half in England, working as a kitchen porter in a stylish restaurant in Clerkenwell, as a waiter in a Greek taverna, as a chef in a care home, and, for a brief period, as a vegetable picker in Sussex. The difference in the means of transport already indicates his relative financial success that will enable him to start a new life back home. Lev's learning process is connected to his relationship to time: in order to shape, pursue and finally realize his big dream, he must replace his preoccupation with the past with an unswerving focus on the future, and his lethargy with a strong sense of perseverance (114)[5] and practical intelligence. This is

---

4 Articles 20 and 45 of the "Consolidated Version of the Treaty on the Functioning of the European Union" (2008).

5 All page numbers for Tremain's novel refer to the 2008 edition.

encapsulated in one of Rudi's maxims, who acts as Lev's mentor in his native village: "Only the resourceful will survive" (16).

The turning point comes after several months in London, when Lev learns of the plans to build a dam above Baryn, which will wipe out his village Auror, whose inhabitants will be relocated to newly-built apartments in Baryn. The distress of his family and friends fills him with a strong sense of purpose and responsibility. Given the structural changes that will come to Baryn with the dam, the reservoir and the electric power station, it stands to reason to assume that the derelict and poverty-stricken town might be turned into a centre of prosperity in the near future. Lev is willing to seize this opportunity and devises a plan to open a restaurant in Baryn with the skills he has learnt in the catering business in London, and thus to complete his journey of self-improvement.

The Road Home differs from other narratives of its kind in that its main concern is not the migrant's negotiation of cultural identity in view of settling in the host country, but the development of a perspective for the migrant eventually to contribute to a revitalization of his own country. Lev, who is driven from home by lack of employment, is unable to develop a sustained vision of his life abroad. But when he becomes obsessed by his Big Idea, he can vividly picture a life and a future back home. Structurally this enables Tremain to present a vision of a self-help programme that is built on a fruitful transfer of Western European know-how and attitudes to rebuild Eastern Europe. What it also implies, however, is the replacement of a local with a foreign normative order that must be implemented to generate success and that thus is envisioned as a global frame of recognition.

The building of the dam and the destruction of Auror can be read as a symbolic reenactment of the political upheaval several years before, i.e. the dissolution of the Eastern Bloc and the transition of Lev's country to a post-communist state. Lev functions as the model of a successful survivor, because he is able to find a market niche and create a new life for himself: to replace "Communist food" (275) with good cuisine. His newly developed business spirit provides him with the means to turn the course of history to his own advantage and prosper under the new conditions. Lev's self-stylization as a successful entrepreneur and his rejection of the past become a blueprint for the future of the country as a whole, as it is depicted in *The Road Home*. There is nothing in Lev's country that seems worth preserving: no traditions, no culture, no political ideas; it is a place with "[n]o future" (84). Consequently Lev's final evaluation comes as no surprise: "And he thought [...] that Auror was a place so lonely, so abandoned by time, it was right to drown it, right to force its inhabitants to leave behind their dirt roads, their spirit rags, and join the twenty-first-century world" (344).

It is Tremain's radically asymmetrical conceptualization of Britain and 'Eastern Europe' that presents one of the crucial problems of the novel. It results in an erasure of the Other and its past that leaves a blank space on which the terms of a new order are inscribed, and this new order is an unmitigated version of Western capitalism. The fact that Tremain placed Lev's roots in an unnamed (and unidentifiable) post-Communist state is probably due to her lack of sufficient first-hand knowledge of any of these countries.[6] This lack of local specificity unfortunately makes her narrative prone to stereotypes and, moreover, constitutes an inappropriate generalising gesture (Jaskulski 2010, 35–36). Does this imaginary Eastern European country stand in for all Eastern European countries? Are they all the same, and are they all like that? If we assume that globalization reorganizes the axis between the global and the local (Beck 1997, 30, 54) and initiates a complicated dynamic of de-localization and re-localization (Beck 1997, 86) – what Roland Robertson has called 'glocalisation' (Beck 1997, 90) – then the local side is certainly not fleshed out sufficiently in *The Road Home*. This deficiency produces a rather lopsided picture and has us imagine contemporary Eastern Europe as a *tabula rasa*, as a place that can be reinvented from scratch, using the model of a market economy that has been practiced uninterruptedly in Western Europe for the past three centuries. Against the backdrop of the ethical framework outlined earlier, *The Road Home* displays a remarkable lack of recognition of the Other, who is subjected to a new economic and cultural regime as the only alternative to certain ruin. Tremain's heterodiegetic narrative mirrors this process. Although the narrator seems to give us repeated insights into Lev's thoughts and feelings, there is a clear narrative voice that regulates the cultural intelligibility of the protagonist as a new member of an expanding Europe.

This appropriative gesture is in part obfuscated by Tremain's vision of the Western European as the universal subject as well as her negotiation of cultural difference and sameness. The few situations of exclusion Lev experiences on account of his difference are counterbalanced by an overriding sense of a common human bond that unites most characters in the novel no matter what their background, from Lev's Irish landlord Christy to the successful businessman GK Ashe, and from Ahmed, the owner of an Arab Kebab place, to Lev's compatriot Lydia. The universal humanity they are all part of is epitomized by *the* British cultural icon: Shakespeare. Lydia presents Lev with a copy of *Hamlet*, a play she finds relevant to her and Lev's situation as exiles, with Hamlet being an out-

---

6 This can be inferred from her Acknowledgments: "My grateful thanks to Jack Rosenthal [...] for the introductions to his Polish field-workers, who told me true and invaluable tales from Eastern Europe" (367).

cast and constantly haunted by the past (133). And, indeed, in the moment of Lev's biggest crisis, the play provides invaluable inspiration: when he feels the mounting pressure to come to the rescue of his family and friends in Auror, Hamlet's soliloquy "To be or not to be..." shows him the way "to take arms against a sea of troubles / And by opposing end them" (261). Claiming universal value and applicability for certain cultural texts and scripts, which just happen to be English, contributes to the general tendency of the novel to subsume the Other under the umbrella of the dominant Western European culture. By becoming members of the European Union, the inhabitants of the former Eastern Bloc countries acquire the status of *legal* migrants and this status entitles them to become again beneficiaries of a cultural heritage their Communist leaders spurned. This is yet another way in which *The Road Home* reproduces and enforces hegemonic structures.

Tremain's criticism of some of the excesses of Western capitalism does not fundamentally change this outlook. It only introduces an unresolved ambivalence. In London, Lev encounters a society that is mainly profit-oriented and demands a constantly high level of performance and commitment. In general, there is a tendency for money, consumption and business to obliterate more ethical considerations. Deplorable as this may be, becoming "part of the British economy" (67) and subscribing to its logic enables Lev to get a grip on life again, recover his self-respect and improve life for himself, his family and friends in his home country. These different perspectives are brought together in a stance of ambivalence towards the end of the novel when Lev is on his way to Baryn from the airport and looks

> at the abandoned farms and silent factories, at the deserted coal depots and lumber yards, at the new high-rise flats and the bright, flickering heartbeats of American franchises, at a world slipping and sliding on a precipice between the dark rockface of Communism and the seductive, light-filled void of the liberal market. (337)

Despite this more cautionary note, in *The Road Home* global capitalism remains an inescapable force, an unquestionable given to which Lev has to adapt if he does not want to be left behind. GK Ashe teaches him about competition and the value of maximum ambition: "Why not aim high? You said 'food like they've never had'. If this is an expanding arena of new capitalism, it'll be chocka with restaurants before you can say *beurre noisette*. So, how're you going to make yours the best?" (280). His prediction turns out to be correct, as Lev soon discovers with the rapid changes taking place in Baryn: the old 'Café Boris' is renamed 'Brasserie Baryn', the former music shop next to Lev's restaurant is turned into an art gallery, and an immensely popular American Burger Bar has opened nearby. Such developments illustrate Ulrich Beck's argument that an ever-growing world market will swallow the 'white spots' on the world economic map one by one, and will integrate non-capitalist states and regions successively into a world capitalist system (Beck 1997, 164). In *The Road Home* this absorption into another system marks a new beginning and the regeneration of these regions – at the cost of establishing Western European capitalism as the global frame of recognition.

4 'Our two cultures had made us profoundly different': Kate Clanchy's *Antigona and Me*

Kate Clanchy's narrative handling of her material is radically different from Tremain's in that it displays a much higher degree of ethical self-reflexivity. This has a decisive impact on the form of the text and both elucidates and contextualizes the question of recognition and the philosophical assumptions on which it is based. *Antigona and Me* is the story of a female Kosovan refugee in London. It originated in 2001, in a chance meeting between writer Kate Clanchy and Antigona, the Kosovan refugee living in the neighbourhood with her three children. Clanchy, then mother of a small child, offered Antigona a job as a nanny and a cleaner. In the course of the following years, until 2006 when Antigona's papers were not renewed and she left to live illegally in another European country, Clanchy recorded their numerous conversations in her diary and finally turned them into the book in question, changing the original names and locations, however, to protect her protagonist (Mansfield 2008). The refugee's extraordinary strength and power of will already announce themselves in the name Clanchy gave her, which is reminiscent of Sophocles' heroine Antigone and her daring act of defying the law of the father. In Judith Butler's reading, the figure of Antigone stands for "an alternate legality that haunts the [...] public sphere" (2000, 40), and this connotation certainly also resonates with Clanchy's text.

Antigona and Me relates Antigona's life-story as remembered and told to Kate in retrospect, her struggles with her jobs, with her brothers, her family in Albania and with her teenage daughters during her years in London, as well as the author's reflections on questions of politics and feminism. It does not proceed chronologically but thematically, a form that suits its generic mixture and allows for ample authorial comments on various subjects. In a sense it also mirrors the exuberance of Antigona's story that sometimes seems to take over Kate's life as it forms itself along unstoppable dramatic incidents that occur on a day-to-day basis and that bear the imprint of a sinister past that never seems to loosen its grip. It also pays tribute to Antigona's own irreverence of neat plot-lines, of cause and effect, of development and teleology; a tribute to "an Albanian time frame, where there are tomorrows but very few names of months or years" (179)[7] and in which the proper sequence of events is irrelevant and disregarded. Unlike Tremain's neatly resolved and coherent narrative of Lev's journey, Clanchy's story presents slices of Antigona's life which do not shape themselves into any recognisable pattern and which contain gaps that cannot be filled because traumatic experiences during the war remain unspeakable (172–173).

First of all the problem of recognition becomes an issue on the personal, intersubjective level. Although the relationship between Kate and Antigona grows very close as time goes by and by far transcends that of an employer to her employee, there remains an irreducible difference between the two women that cannot be bridged by any amount of quasi-sisterly devotion and that is rooted in their radically different biographies, as Clanchy explains:

> I have everything I want; I have to strain to think of a birthday gift; I wear clothes 'ironically'; I search out battered armchairs. Antigona comes from a country which has not even begun capitalism, which has nothing but state-run quarries and wrecked collective farms, which has recently been devastated by war. The day I met her, her possessions would fit into a suitcase. (132–133)

This knowledge has a direct impact on the question of recognition. First of all and on the most basic level, it exemplifies the constitutional difference between self and other, as Paul Ricoeur reminds us again – similarly to Judith Butler – in his last study *The Course of Recognition* (2004). He places alterity at the centre of mutual recognition (2005, 321). Irrespective of the success or failure of recognition, the other always remains a stranger, always remains ultimately unfathomable in her/his alterity, and this condition is all the more pronounced in Clanchy's and Antigona's case on account of the fundamental disparity between the two women. Secondly, this fundamental difference raises questions about the representation of the other and its validity. In what way does Clanchy's assumption of narrative authority shape the narrative negotiation of self and other? And how do the different backgrounds and experiences of the two characters influence their respective handling of normative frames?

Although recognition as an intersubjective process always assumes two participants engaging in an equal measure of decentring, we tend to direct our attention to the most obviously precarious subject, i.e. the one who is in danger

---

7 All page numbers for Clanchy's novel refer to the 2009 edition.

of foregoing recognition.[8] In the case of *Antigona and Me* and its specific narrative situation, this brings up a complex issue. Comparing Kate and Antigona, Antigona is quite clearly the more 'precarious' subject, suffering from a lack of recognition in many respects: as a woman in her highly patriarchal native culture, which considers her the property of her husband and other males of the extended family; as a victim of Serb atrocities; and legally, as a refugee dependent on the political will and generosity of Western democracies. Clanchy's text serves as a means to make this condition public, to provide a space for a voice that is otherwise not heard. Antigona cannot write down her own story, not only because she is only gradually learning to speak English, but also because, although she is a gifted storyteller, she has not been given the education to turn her stories into a written text. Clanchy is very much aware of the pitfalls of representing the life of another, of the dangers of appropriating their story, of being politically incorrect, specifically since their difference in status is so obvious. She takes great pains to reflect all these questions, to attribute a high degree of agency to Antigona and to treat her as an 'equal'. In fact, much of her narrative (and, indeed, many of her actions) are driven by the guilt of doing wrong by Antigona, of not taking into account her own privileged position as a white, middle-class Englishwoman. It is precisely the knowledge of their difference that motivates her to adopt the specific narrative stance of the book, to tell "[n]ot Antigona's story as it happened to her, but her story as it happened to me" (5).

Nevertheless, the fact that Clanchy writes in the first person puts her own point of view centre-stage, and while acknowledging Antigona as the 'precarious' subject, inevitably focuses on her *own* involvement in Antigona's fate and what it does to her. This double perspective brings to light two significant aspects: first of all it demonstrates that even the privileged subject is a precarious subject, in fact, that every subject is precarious in the sense that it subjects itself to a process of decentring in the encounter with the other: "It is not that we are born and then later become precarious, but rather that precariousness is coextensive with birth itself" (Butler 2009, 14). At times, Clanchy's text is full of anxiety: the story changes her, exposes her ignorance and prejudices (5), and her constant feeling of guilt betrays a basic insecurity regarding how to position herself with respect to a subject as precarious as Antigona. A subject as fundamentally different from Clanchy as Antigona seems to call into question Clanchy's own frame of normality and her own sense of self in an almost existential

---

8 This is also Judith Butler's perspective, since her focus is on the mechanisms that exclude certain individuals from recognition and on the ways discursive boundaries can be shifted to change the conditions of recognition.

way. Possibly this fear of becoming too decentred themselves might furnish a reason why privileged subjects tend to avoid engaging with precarious others and mobilize mechanisms of ignoring their existence instead. Secondly we are made aware of the fact that the terms Clanchy associates with recognition, specifically a sense of equality between subjects (3, 6), are not necessarily Antigona's. There is, for example, a whole chapter on the exploitation of foreign workers by white middle-class women that enables them to live their feminist goals (Saner 2008). This again bespeaks Clanchy's own feelings of guilt but does not reflect Antigona's point of view for whom her various jobs are a means to secure a living for her family. In a similar way, Antigona laughs at Kate's qualms about turning her story into a book and enthusiastically embraces the project: "'Good. And then a feature film, actually, Mini-series'" (5). She considers the project another means to heighten her chances of survival and of a better life.

These juxtapositions of different evaluations of seemingly crucial situations bring to light that the centrality of recognition as the first and foremost condition of subjectivity so central in Western philosophical thought is itself a prerogative of the privileged. The struggle for recognition takes markedly different forms when physical and economic survival are at stake and produces a very different conceptualization of life. For Clanchy, reared on the heritage of the Enlightenment, recognition first and foremost confers equality, in its feminist version more specifically equality between men and women. Furthermore it implies being recognized as a member of a welfare state that offers security, and as a participant in a social contract that confers rights and duties. All this does not hold for Antigona's life. Her culture does not recognize a woman as an independent subject but as the property of a man. She has no state to rely on, no guaranteed place of residence and no perspective of stability. And yet she is a subject who by sheer will and self-assertion handles various levels of recognition to her advantage – with temporary and context-specific results.

Moving from the personal to the structural level, it becomes clear that Butler's notion of the frame or the norms that bring about the subject in the first place is highly relevant for *Antigona and Me*. In addition to Butler's abstract model, however, the text also demonstrates that there is not one frame but many. Antigona is bound up in a number of interlocking, often contradictory frames that she cannot cast off but that she sometimes uses strategically for her own aims. A prominent point of reference is the unwritten, traditional patriarchal law of the Mountain people she comes from, which she has not fully escaped by coming to England, because there it is represented by her brothers; she herself has internalized part of it and uses it to ostracize her daughters and their 'English' attitudes. Paradoxically, she also adopts the 'English'/Western frame of autonomy and self-determination to carve out a more independent life for herself that quite clearly contradicts her traditional upbringing. These frames are based on different concepts of personhood and individuality. The traditional law of the mountains (the Kanun of Lek) considers women the property of their husbands and refuses to recognize them as autonomous subjects; similarly, Antigona considers her daughters as part of herself and therefore expects their subjection to her views, thereby denying them autonomous subject status as well. At the same time Antigona feels attracted to the idea of the autonomous subject that has governed Western philosophical tradition since the Enlightenment. All these conceptions exist side by side, are observed in certain contexts, challenged and rejected in others.

In the realm of policy, Western Europe carved out a frame to privilege Kosovan refugees, who were legally recognized as refugees and given the right to stay in Britain after NATO's intervention in 1999. They became privileged others, and Antigona makes strategic use of this status when she calls herself a Kosovan refugee rather than an Albanian asylum-seeker, thus immediately triggering people's sympathies. This is a frame also created by the media and by public opinion (Clanchy 2009, 12), which shape and control the knowledge we have about Kosovo and the moral judgments we pass. In order to be recognized as a refugee in a legal sense, Antigona narrates her story to fit the frame of recognition set by the government of the country she appeals to for recognition of her refugee status. Antigona's complex negotiations of available frames of recognition, coupled with the fact that she is eventually forced to leave the country reveal the material effects of recognition (Fraser 1997, 282), its impact on social and economic participation and on the right to stay and live in a particular place.

Antigona's deployment of agency is crucial, because, as Butler notes in *Precarious Life,* those who succeed in representing themselves heighten their "chance of being humanized" (2004, 141). Agency is relative and tied to the existence of multiple frames of recognition. In Butler's monolithic model, the precarious subject's agency is severely curtailed, because it is placed on the margins of the normative order. But seen from Antigona's perspective, this situation enhances her personal agency. Paradoxically, her escape to Britain has loosened the hold of the Kanun of Lek on her life and given her access to other subject positions, which she claims are at her disposal: "There I was like a dog. I borrowed money for bread. Here – I can work. I can do anything. I can choose my life" (21). Exerting agency for Antigona also includes finding ways to circumvent the restrictions imposed on her by the British legal system as an asylum seeker. And yet, the movement between different frames of recognition is not entirely free, because they leave their traces in the subject's memory. Their constant reiteration leaves an imprint on the body and cannot be simply shaken off:

> We take our laws and customs into our bodies [...]. In her head, Antigona believes in a version of the Declaration of Human Rights as explained to her by me, *EastEnders* and her lawyer. In her guts, Antigona believes that love is violent. With her head, she rejects the shame of the Kanun of Lek, but her body feels it. The Kanun is not finished with its work on Antigona just because she has left her husband, crossed the border. (92–93)

In *Antigona and Me*, Clanchy shows the contingency and unpredictability of social practices in action that cannot be grasped by generalizing and abstract assumptions about situations of recognition but need to be understood by a context-specific approach, as Jacinda Swanson has argued, that takes into account the complicated and often contradictory nature of hegemonic formations which "shape different parts of the social world in specific and diverse ways, and thus interpellate and affect individuals differently" (2005, 107).

5 Theoretical and Literary Models: A Conclusion

In comparison, *The Road Home* at first sight presents a more pleasing, because generically conventional and coherent story than the much more untidy and less easily classifiable narrative of *Antigona and Me*. As the analysis has shown, however, the unevenness and unpredictability of Clanchy's text corresponds to the haphazard nature of the protagonist's precarious existence, and, in contrast to Tremain's novel, it is accompanied by a substantial degree of self-reflexivity as to the representability of a subject so very different from the author's own range of experience. *The Road Home* has more than once been praised for its emotional empathy,[9] and Tremain herself takes pride in being able to fathom "the unfamiliar, even the unknowable" in her writing (qtd. in Sceats 2005, 166). This betrays an unquestioning belief in the power of the literary imagination to act as a universal tool of understanding which never even so much as considers the possibility that the imagination itself might be severely limited in its scope by its own situatedness in a specific frame of reference to which it automatically reduces what it perceives. Lev's successful adaptation to Western capitalism is achieved at the expense of the erasure of his home country's past and implies a process of homogenization, which effectively negates the Other's difference or otherness (Hetzel et al. 2011, 7–8). In light of Butler's outline of the mechanisms of recognition, Tremain's claim that Lev, by the end of the book, "is fully human and knowable to us and we are more knowable to ourselves" (qtd. in Crişu 2010, 365) seems an almost ironic instance of misrecogni-

---

9 For example by Kirsty Lang, chair of the Orange Prize's judging panel (qtd. in Singh 2008).

tion and reveals perhaps first and foremost the specific frame of recognition in which Lev is allowed to attain to the status of the human. Clanchy, on the other hand, is very much aware of this danger and uses the gap between self and other to explore the destabilization of the self through the incommensurability of the Other and to probe her own standards of recognition, that is, her own ethical frame of reference (Hetzel 2011, 31). According to Clanchy, the imagination is no adequate tool to bridge that gap completely: "I couldn't pretend to imagine being her, because one of the things she taught me was that our two cultures had made us profoundly, not superficially, different" (5).

Beyond a comparison between Tremain's and Clanchy's approaches to representing migration from Eastern Europe, confronting the literary material with the theoretical framework outlined also proves instructive. A number of scholars have criticized Butler for her high level of abstraction that lacks historical differentiation, especially with respect to the complex mechanisms of contemporary capitalist society (Fraser 1997, 282–284), and is not sufficiently capable of describing the complicated ins and outs of actual lives and their various forms of embeddedness in different communities (McIvor 2012, 421). The intricacies around subjectivity, agency and recognition developed in Clanchy's text support this view. Specifically Antigona's handling of the various and sometimes contradictory forms of recognition she is exposed to or has access to as well as her self-willed use of agency and her attachment to different social environments that help her to cope with and resist oppressive forms of recognition (Allen 2006, 217–218) produces unpredictable effects not accounted for by Butler's monolithic model. McIvor emphasizes the diverse and context-specific nature of situations of recognition when he states that "we are responsive to a plurality of faces, and each of these faces has more than one face" (2012, 421).

Furthermore, the ethical obligation Butler derives from her view of precariousness as a condition of human existence that implies a "fundamental dependency on anonymous others" (2004, xii) as well as her evocation of "egalitarian standards" or "basic egalitarian norms" (2009, 22) makes a universalising claim that remains unsubstantiated. By doing so, she prioritizes a Western tradition of philosophical thinking and evokes a global community that does not really exist. Instead, there are communities with different and often enough incompatible regimes of truth and different understandings of recognition and its terms. If we add the fact that the laws of politics are not always coincidental with the laws of ethics, it becomes clear that Butler's position constitutes less a cogent political rationale than a rational appeal that may or may not be heeded.

Works Cited

Allen, Amy. "Dependency, Subordination, and Recognition: On Judith Butler's Theory of Subjection." *Continental Philosophy Review* 38 (2006): 199–222.

Althusser, Louis. "Ideology and Ideological State Apparatuses: Notes Towards an Investigation" [1969]. *Lenin and Philosophy and Other Essays.* Trans. Ben Brewster. New York: Monthly Review Press, 1971. 127–186.

Ashcroft, Bill, Gareth Griffiths, and Helen Tiffin. *Post-Colonial Studies: The Key Concepts.* London and New York: Routledge, 2000.

Beck, Ulrich. *Was ist Globalisierung? Irrtümer des Globalismus – Antworten auf Globalisierung.* Frankfurt am Main: Suhrkamp, 1997. [*What Is Globalization.* Cambridge: Polity Press, 2000].

Brownrigg, Sylvia. "No Place Like Home." Review of Rose Tremain, *Sacred Country. The Guardian* 9 June 2007. http://www.theguardian.com/books/2007/jun/09/featuresreviews.guardian review21 (12 September 2013).

Burrell, Kathy. *Moving Lives: Narratives of Migration among Europeans in Post-War Britain.* Aldershot: Ashgate, 2006.

Butler, Judith. *Frames of War: When Is Life Grievable?* London and New York: Verso, 2009.

——. *Kritik der ethischen Gewalt.* Trans. Reiner Ansén and Michael Adrian. Frankfurt am Main: Suhrkamp, 2007 [2005]. [English version: *Giving an Account of Oneself,* 2005].

——. *Giving an Account of Oneself.* New York: Fordham University Press, 2005.

——. *Precarious Life: The Powers of Mourning and Violence.* London and New York: Verso, 2004.

——. *Undoing Gender.* New York and London: Routledge, 2004.

——. *Antigone's Claim: Kinship between Life and Death.* New York: Columbia University Press, 2000.

——. *Subjects of Desire: Hegelian Reflections in Twentieth-Century France.* New York: Columbia University Press, 1999 [1987].

——. *Bodies That Matter: On the Discursive Limits of 'Sex'.* New York and London: Routledge, 1993.

——. *Gender Trouble: Feminism and the Subversion of Identity.* New York and London: Routledge, 1990.

Childs, Peter, and R. J. Patrick Williams. *An Introduction to Post-Colonial Theory.* London and New York: Prentice Hall/Harvester Wheatsheaf, 1997.

Clanchy, Kate. *Antigona and Me.* London and New York: Picador, 2009 [2008].

"Consolidated Version of the Treaty on the Functioning of the European Union." *Official Journal of the European Union* C15 (9 May 2008): 47–199. http://eur-lex.europa.eu/LexUriServ/LexUriServ.do?uri=OJ:C:2008:115:0047:0199:EN:PDF; (12 September 2013).

Crişu, Corina. "British Geographies in the Eastern European Mind: Rose Tremain's *The Road Home.*" *Facing the East in the West: Images of Eastern Europe in British Literature, Film and Culture.* Eds. Barbara Korte, Eva Ulrike Pirker, and Sissy Helff. Amsterdam: Rodopi, 2010. 365–379.

Ferrarese, Estelle. "Judith Butler's 'Not Particularly Postmodern Insight' of Recognition." *Philosophy and Social Criticism* 37.7 (2011): 759–773.

Foucault, Michel. "Two Lectures – Lecture Two: 14 January 1976." Trans. Kate Soper.
    Power/Knowledge: Selected Interviews and Other Writings 1972–1977. Ed. Colin Gordon.
    New York: Harvester Wheatsheaf, 1980. 78–108.
Fraser, Nancy. "Heterosexism, Misrecognition, and Capitalism: A Response to Judith Butler."
    Social Text 52.23 (Autumn/Winter 1997): 279–289.
Hetzel, Andreas. "Alterität und Anerkennung: Einleitende Bemerkungen." *Alterität und
    Anerkennung*. Eds. Andreas Hetzel, Dirk Quadflieg, and Heidi Salaverría. Baden-Baden:
    Nomos, 2011. 11–34.
Hetzel, Andreas, Dirk Quadflieg, and Heidi Salaverría. "Vorwort." *Alterität und Anerkennung*.
    Eds. Andreas Hetzel, Dirk Quadflieg, and Heidi Salaverría. Baden-Baden: Nomos, 2011.
    7–10.
Jaskulski, Józef. "Friday Re-educated: Orientalising the Eastern European Other in Rose
    Tremain's *The Road Home*." *Looking at Ourselves: Multiculturalism, Conflict & Belonging*.
    Ed. Katherine Wilson. Oxford: Inter-Disciplinary Press, 2010. 33–42.
Korte, Barbara. "Facing the East of Europe in Its Western Isles: Charting Backgrounds,
    Questions and Perspectives." *Facing the East in the West: Images of Eastern Europe in
    British Literature, Film and Culture*. Eds. Barbara Korte, Eva Ulrike Pirker, and Sissy
    Helff. Amsterdam: Rodopi, 2010. 1–21.
Lauretis, Teresa de. "Feminist Studies/Critical Studies: Issues, Terms, and Contexts." *Feminist
    Studies/Critical Studies*. Ed. Teresa de Lauretis. Basingstoke and London: Macmillan,
    1986. 1–19.
Loomba, Ania et al. "Beyond What? An Introduction." *Postcolonial Studies and Beyond*. Eds.
    Ania Loomba et al. Durham, NC and London: Duke University Press, 2005. 1–38.
Mansfield, Susan. "Survivor in an Alien Land." Interview with Kate Clanchy. *The Scotsman* 5
    July 2008. http://www.scotsman.com/news/survivor-in-an-alien-land-kate-
    clanchy-interview-1-1078872 (6 October 2013).
Marriott, Edward. "Down But Not Out in Latterday London." Review of Rose Tremain, *Sacred
    Country*. *The Observer* 10 June 2007. http://www.theguardian.com/books/2007/jun/10/
    fiction.features1 (12 September 2013).
McIvor, David W. "Bringing Ourselves to Grief: Judith Butler and the Politics of Mourning."
    Political Theory 40.4 (2012): 409–436.
Müller, Sandra. "Book Review: Rose Tremain's *The Road Home*." *Hard Times* 84 (Autumn
    2008): 45–47.
Ricoeur, Paul. *The Course of Recognition*. Trans. David Pellauer. Cambridge, MA, and London:
    Harvard University Press, 2005 [2004].
Salaverría, Heidi. "Anerkennbarkeit: Butler, Levinas, Rancière." *Alterität und Anerkennung*.
    Eds. Andreas Hetzel, Dirk Quadflieg, and Heidi Salaverría. Baden Baden: Nomos, 2011.
    35–53.
Saner, Emine. "'I couldn't get her voice out of my head.'" Interview with Kate Clanchy. *The
    Guardian* 11 June 2008. http://www.theguardian.com/books/2008/jun/11/women.kosovo
    (6 October 2013).
Sceats, Sarah. "Appetite, Desire and Belonging in the Novels of Rose Tremain." *The
    Contemporary British Novel*. Eds. James Acheson and Sarah C. E. Ross. Edinburgh:
    Edinburgh University Press, 2005. 165–176.
Singh, Anita. "Author Rose Tremain wins the Orange Prize for Fiction." *The Telegraph* 4 June
    2008. http://www.telegraph.co.uk/news/uknews/2075042/Author-Rose-Tremain-wins-
    the-Orange-Prize-for-Fiction.html (12 September 2013).

Swanson, Jacinda. "Recognition and Redistribution: Rethinking Culture and the Economic."
    Theory Culture & Society 22.4 (2005): 87–118.
Tremain, Rose. *The Road Home.* London: Vintage, 2008 [2007].

Romain Nguyen Van

"The Last Voice of Democracy": Precarity, Community and Fiction in Alan Warner's *Morvern Callar* (1995)

I

"There are girls trapped in deathly jobs all over the world. Morvern exists okay, she was a girlfriend". Such was Alan Warner's response when he was asked if there was anything "real" in his portrayal of Morvern Callar, the eponymous heroine of his 1995 début novel (Thomson 1997). Published during John Major's term, *Morvern Callar* describes the neoliberalization of working conditions from within, i.e. through the life of a young female "prole outsider" (Thomson 1997). After discovering her boyfriend lifeless by the Christmas tree on the floor of their apartment, Morvern – a supermarket employee in a poverty-stricken village of the Scottish Highlands – engages in a rebellion against her supervisor, "Creeping Jesus", by taking good care of her "discipline record" (9)[1] and eventually failing to show up. She then flees to Spain, treating herself to a little vacation, "dancing and lying on the beach till [her] money ran up" (169). With her sidekick and colleague Lanna, she experiences the debauchery of the "holiday brochures" she coveted, smokes silk cuts, succumbs to consumer fetishism and enjoys the fictional lifestyle of the author whose identity she has usurped, squandering the advance money she has received for the book left by her boyfriend – a novel she pretends to have written – before eventually going back to Scotland in search of a new job.

The present chapter studies Warner's novelistic representation of precarity in late twentieth-century Britain. I prefer to use the term "precarity" rather than that of "precariousness", in accordance with Judith Butler's distinction between the two notions. Butler famously defines "precariousness" as the fact that one's life is always in some sense in the hands of the other (2009, 14). "Precarity", she characterizes as a particular case of "precariousness": as "that politically induced condition in which certain populations suffer from failing social and economic networks of support and become differentially exposed to injury, violence, and death" (2009, 25). Those who suffer from precarity "are at heightened risk of disease, poverty, starvation, displacement, and of exposure to violence

---

1 All page references for Warner's novel refer to the Vintage edition (1996).

without protection" (2009, 25–26). Poverty is therefore one of the potential modes of precarity (alongside disease, injury and death). Precariousness engages more global, "socio-ontological" issues (Lorey 2011, 1): it suggests "a dependency on people we know, or barely know, or know not at all", implying by the same token "obligations toward others" (Butler 2009, 14).

Morvern Callar may be read as one of the few works of fiction – among which should be included some novels by Martin Amis, Iain Sinclair, and to some extent, those of Toby Litt and Jonathan Coe – that, roughly since the beginning of the 1990s, have sought to describe precarity as one of the major consequences of the neoliberal order set up in the Thatcher years. In Warner's novel, it is "Morvern from the superstore" (32) herself who tells about her own living and working conditions. Her narrative of poverty thus abounds in colloquialisms, phonetic transcriptions and the odd spelling mistake, which are all meant to 'translate' Morvern's oral world into writing. Fiction here seems to illustrate Le Blanc's "philosophy of translation": narrating the lives of the poor through fiction is "the only way to renew social criticism, by bestowing on it the task of restoring the voice of those who suffer from precarity" (Le Blanc 2007, 18). Translation may be literal, literary, or carried out by sociologists, Le Blanc argues, but always it conveys, transcribes, makes audible the voice of the speechless poor.

For Morvern's voice is not the expression of a singularity. With its idiosyncratic language, its spoken style and its frequent errors, *Morvern Callar* endeavours rather to report the voices of all those who live precariously in Britain. Evidence of this may be found in the novel's polyphonic mode: within the framing story several other poverty narratives are embedded, reverberating with the main, primary narrative. Morvern's role also consists therefore in lending a voice to a gallery of secondary characters who, like herself, are either unemployed or about to be "given the boot" (103) from the local supermarket. This embeddedness of narratives of poverty suggests that precarity is always a relational phenomenon, an experience to be told, related to others, made into a story. The two publishers Morvern meets to discuss her boyfriend's book, do not tell stories – "[t]hey didn't tell stories, they just discussed" (164): they merely jabber on, a view that Warner as a writer seems to share, calling publishers "philistine bloodsuckers" (Thomson 1997). It is "the others", the working poor of the novel, who "tell stories", i.e. turn their experience of poverty into narratives which end up being collected in Morvern's first-person immoral tale of mourning.

This chapter suggests that the narrative economy of *Morvern Callar* – a novel regarded as representative of those "'state of the nation' texts that offer themselves as [a report] on Thatcherite (and post-Thatcherite) Britain" (Hutchinson 2007, 228) – paradoxically establishes discontinuity as a major structural, thematic and aesthetic device for dramatizing neoliberalism at work. This chapter also endeavours to formulate the covert political statement of Warner's novel about 'class' and 'community', two collective structures that are shown by Warner to be on the brink of collapse. Although contemporary British fiction has been accused of eluding class issues (Driscoll 2009), I argue on the contrary that *Morvern Callar* manages to translate the voice of the working poor, and thus to sketch through fiction some sense of a new, complex political community. In that respect, Morvern's voice may be said to represent "the last voice of democracy" (Le Blanc 2007, 25).

II

One of the possible – though disputed – etymologies of 'risk' seems to be part and parcel of the history of commerce and capitalism. According to the *OED* (2013a), 'risks' may first and foremost have meant losing or damaging a merchandise at sea. Indeed, economic risks may be said to shape all poverty narratives, and Warner's novel is no exception to the rule. What remains to be seen, however, is the very nature of the 'shaping': how each poverty narrative rearranges the risks into a structure, or into what I shall call a 'narrative economy'. Still according to the *OED* (2013b), the term 'economy' finds its origin in the "classical Latin *oeconomia*" and may designate an "arrangement of material by an author". In this sense, the 'narrative economy' of a novel may be regarded as an organic body – 'a corpus' – whose limbs or parts an author arranges for rhetorical or aesthetic effects. It seems, however, that one should also take into account the economic risks run by the various characters, the balance of economic gains and losses faced by them, their management of financial resources in a certain economic context. A study of the novel's 'narrative economy' would therefore imply focusing on the narrative structure which such an economic context contributes to creating: losing one's job, looking for a new one, visiting the Job Centre on a daily basis, saving money and spending it, inheriting money, gambling it, winning the lottery, losing one's bet – such are the possible economic 'events' that, combined in a limitless number of possible scenarios, may form the 'narrative economy' of a plot.

By 'economic context', I shall mean here the dominant neoliberal ideology that is represented in the text, as well as the particular economic system constraining the lives of the novel's characters, a concrete economic system which I broadly refer to as the 'neoliberal order'. My main source of inspiration for such phrases is a short essay by Pierre Bourdieu, called "The Essence of Neoliberalism", which focuses on what Bourdieu calls the "precarious arrangements" that now characterize working conditions (1998, 3). According to him, "the new economic order" can only thrive by "produc[ing] insecurity", which also implies "the methodical destruction of the collectives" (1998, 3), without which, however, our present economic order cannot survive. To some extent, Alan Warner's groups of characters embody those collective structures Bourdieu refers to – the family, organized labour and trade unions, but also the informal solidarities or modes of organization and resistance at work within the new economic order. But such structures are shown to be at risk, threatened by the very nature of the new economy and its attendant ideology. Indeed, neoliberal rulers have tried to persuade us that we now live in a classless society, that individuals are all that matters, although some commentators like David Harvey have suggested on the contrary that neoliberalism ended up restoring the class divides whose importance had somewhat been softened by the post-war consensus in Europe (2005, 16).

It has been noted that just as there had been "political pressure to erase class in the period from Margaret Thatcher to Tony Blair" – who famously declared class warfare "over" at the 1999 Labour conference (Driscoll 2009, 1) – so had contemporary British fiction, with its "canonized middle-class authors", evaded the class question (Driscoll 2009, 1). In Driscoll's words, the British contemporary novel "both articulates and silences questions of class" (2009, 1). Alan Warner's position in such a vision of British literature is made particularly conspicuous. Even though an author's supposed or known social background cannot be sufficient for defining a text's social or political implications, it is impossible to ignore that this Highland autodidact is neither a Cambridge graduate nor a 'middle-class author'. Still, if *Morvern Callar* is definitely not a 'middle-class text', it nevertheless relies on a double-edged discourse about class consciousness. But, I wish to argue, this is precisely what a fictional narrative permits: the elision of class discourse is carried out in a dialectical manner through the narrativization of poor lives.

Money, or rather the lack thereof, has quite naturally determined all poverty narratives, starting with Dickens's *Oliver Twist*. It is indeed a defining feature of the genre that deficit should be essential to both plotline and characterization. Again, *Morvern Callar* is certainly no exception: when the novel opens, Morvern does not have "enough till payday" (5). What is specific to Warner's poverty narrative, however, is that its plot is determined by the main character's desire to make good a *chronic* deficit. For, as a matter of fact, money comes fairly easily to her, and the manna she receives on three occasions even enables her to escape the gritty realism of her employed life: she first lives off her late boyfriend's account balance – £6,839 (55) –, later enjoys the advance money of the book he wrote (111), before she finally receives a £44,771.79 inheritance from her boyfriend's father (186). This is not to say that the narrative economy of the book is not about losses too: for the novel depicts Morvern squandering her capital without rhyme or reason, before finding herself bankrupt again on several occasions. The novel's main focus is not therefore about whether the main protagonist can, in imitation of the paradigmatic model of bourgeois social climbing narratives, amass a fortune: in *Morvern Callar*, the successive improvements and degradations of living conditions, the rapid alternations of various states of impoverishment and destitution, form the driving force behind the novel's narrative economy.

The first movement of the novel depicts in a dispassionate manner the working conditions and the precarious lives and loves of several characters. The reader is introduced to a number of equally yet differently precarious lives, a collective portrait including the unemployed youth of a remote, unidentified Highland port whose sole option is to "sign on", a middle-aged train driver (Morvern's foster-father) who is sacked just before retirement, and elderly people who are too poor to afford even heating (34). After Morvern has left "the port" with her undeserved treasure, she starts to enjoy a consumer-driven lifestyle outside the wage-system, which constitutes the second movement of the narrative. In the last third of the novel, precarity enters a new and climactic phase, epitomized by the numerous passages in which Morvern is depicted asking for money and falling on her knees to pray to some unknown divinity (165). In that respect, the novel is literally true to the etymological roots of the terms "precarity" and "precariousness", which, the *OED* (2013c) explains, derive from the classical Latin *precarius*, which means "depending on the favour of another".

Morvern seeks shelter in the fiction of a fragile autonomy while she pretends to be a writer, but the end of the novel apparently upolds the assertion made by her foster-father, Red Hanna, who bitterly rants that "[t]heres no freedom, no liberty; theres just money" (44). Morvern's final return to wage labour suggests that freedom under neoliberalism is indeed a mere fallacy, and the narrative economy of the novel exposes the "false transparency of consent" (Lordon 10, 79). Morvern eventually surrenders to the 'economic order' she has tried to escape, finally giving in to the "injunction to work" (Cingolani 2005, 120) she initially received, by agreeing to make her life finally 'productive':

> Looking for job to be honest.
> Work? went the girl.
> Aye. Know anything going?
>
> Phew bad time of year; you qualified in anything, you a student or that? Says the baldy.
> Nut. I'll do anything though. I mean anything not in the port. (Warner 1995, 221)

Morvern's newly regained desire for productivity is not only evidence of a willing alignment with neoliberal orthodoxy, but also of her incapacity to 'produce' a new life of her own. This perfect alignment is in Lordon's view inherent in the "fabrication of consent" that is so characteristic of the "neoliberal order" (Lordon 2010, 80). As an ultimate twist in the plot, the very last sentence of the novel suggests that the protagonist's return to employed work may in fact be linked with her pregnancy, but this explanation is never explicitly given. This finale rather exemplifies the sham of Morvern's "wilful servitude" (Lordon 2010, 79). Unexpected though it might be in terms of narrative economy – why should she return to work when she has just inherited a comfortable sum? – Morvern's final choice precludes any simplistic interpretation of Warner's fiction, as it disturbingly seems to espouse the dynamics of consent prevalent on the neoliberal job market, torn between what Lordon calls "problematic consent" and "it's-my-own-choice" rhetoric (2010, 80).

The novel presents a gallery of secondary characters who all experience the instability and insecurity of a post-Fordist economy of service in which people are rendered docile – and therefore productive – by the job market. As a matter of fact, their lives exemplify what Cingolani calls the "biographical discontinuity which characterizes conditions of social and economic precarity" (2005, 82). To be more accurate, precarity should be defined as a combination of different kinds and degrees of discontinuity: low and discontinuous incomes; poor and discontinuous social protection and security; intermittent work "shifts" (Cingolani 2005, 21). The condensed form of such discontinuities in Warner's novel is the supermarket, a paradigmatic site of both consumer-driven capitalism and service economy. The economic forecast Red Hanna makes up to Morvern is indeed very gloomy: "heres you twenty-one; a forty-hour week on slave wage for the rest of your life" (44). Precarity is presented as a stable, almost unchallengeable principle, as though life itself could be nothing but a precarious, life-long balance between security and poverty. With its oxymoronic quality, the "slave wage" metaphor is reminiscent of Marxist thought by assimilating employed work to downright exploitation.

In addition to the smallness of incomes, references to job insecurity abound in Warner's novel. Lanna narrates how one of their colleagues "got given the boot from work" (103), thus falling prey to seasonal work – another form of discontinuous employment – in the neighbouring "superquarry" (103). The Hiphearan, another secondary character, represents a yet more spectacular form of precarity:

> The Hiphearan came in carrying a plastic bag with the superstore name written off it. The Hiphearan's only way of getting money, apart from signing on, was to leap off the railway

pier in High Season wearing his tackity boots, if the young holiday makers would pay him a fiver. (58)

This vignette further illustrates the variety of situations of precarity the narrative manages to record. Unemployment benefits and unemployed work are combined to escape poverty, and some odd jobs are particularly precarious, both temporal-ly – they depend on the High Season – and physically – making a living consists in literally 'taking the leap'. This spectacular episode is one where precarity sud-denly becomes visible to the rest of society, as if on show. But the preferred rep-resentational mode for depicting those whom Bourdieu (1998, 3) calls "the re-serve army" of neoliberal capitalism remains narration: the structure of Warner's novel relies on a system of embedded stories introduced through dia-logue. For example, one of the secondary characters, a home help, mentions the difficulties of "some old folk [who] can't afford heating as if poor people were in a war no one else was" (34). Story-telling makes up for the inaudibility of the poor, and the war metaphor employed here once again carries clear Marx-ist undertones, suggesting the permanence of a "master narrative" of historical development (Jameson 1981, 33).

Red Hanna's resentful comment after his layoff may indeed be read as a def-inition of neoliberalism's ideological premise: "You get told if you work hard you get money but most work hard and end up with nothing. I wouldn't mind if it was shown as the lottery it is but oh no" (44). The passage once again illustrates the powerful "injunction to work" which constitutes the backbone of neoliberal ideology, exposed here as a fiction: the lottery metaphor is used to express the arbitrary nature of economic forces and of their impact on the lives of individu-als. What Red Hanna does not understand, however, but is nevertheless suggest-ed through the sheer accumulation of similar stories, is that precarity is a vital necessity for the new market economy. Far from being a lottery-like process, pre-carization is thus made to appear as an 'arrangement' that is inherent in the neo-liberal economic order, seeming thus to illustrate Bourdieu's theory:

> Without a doubt, the practical establishment of this world of struggle would not succeed so completely without the complicity of all of the precarious arrangements that produce inse-curity and of the existence of a reserve army of employees rendered docile by these social processes that make their situations precarious, as well as by the permanent threat of un-employment. [...] the ultimate foundation of this entire economic order placed under the sign of freedom is in effect the structural violence of unemployment, of the insecurity of job tenure and the menace of layoff that it implies. (Bourdieu 1998, 3)

Cingolani goes as far as to argue that part-time work and precarity have become the fundamental mechanism through which neoliberalism manages to sustain itself (2005, 37). Warner's novel may therefore be said to be 'dialogic': while lending a voice to the exploited, it simultaneously partly invalidates the character's analysis through narrativization, implicitly drawing on contemporary sociology to consolidate its implicit political discourse. Between the lines, *Morvern Callar* thus becomes a genuinely *political text*.

Still, the political nature of the novel is to be grasped most of the time at an explicit level, notably in the reflexive moments that pepper Morvern's narrative, which both constitute autobiographical turning points when Morvern's subjectivity gradually reconstructs itself, and sketch the contours of a thought-through critique of the neoliberal order. In her narrative of how she got illegally hired by the supermarket when aged thirteen, a specific place is indeed dedicated to 'part-time work'. *Morvern Callar* is one of the very few contemporary British novels to turn its gaze on teen work, and to present it, in the narrator's own words as a major cause of school drop-out:

> Cause of the tallness I had started part-time with the superstore when thirteen, the year it got built. The superstore turn a blind eye; get as much out you as they can. You ruin your chances at school doing every evening and weekend. The manager has you working all hours cash in hand, no insurance, so when fifteen or sixteen you go full-time at the start of that summer and never go back to school. (10)

Opening the narrative of her career path with an autobiographical 'I', Morvern rapidly shifts to an impersonal 'you', which, although common enough in everyday spoken English, both creates some sort of antagonism between 'you' and 'them', and facilitates some identification between the reader and 'you', while at the same time her vocabulary and syntax are endowed with the vernacular quality of a popular idiom that is customarily not given voice to, most notably when discussing socio-economic relations. As those left behind recover the voices they have lost, such autobiographical fragments initiate what Jacques Rancière would certainly call a "democratic process", inasmuch as they call for a new "sharing of the perceptible" (2011, 7). Because Morvern has her say not only as a superstore employee but also first and foremost as a centre of perception and interpretation, her voice, although it does not carry immediate political or militant overtones, commits the text to a cause. Warner's renowned talent for rendering orality thus pays homage to the fundamental "democracy of writing" (Rancière 2011, 13), using his paper character as a mouthpiece for all the precarious workers of neoliberalism.

In Bourdieu's theory, precarity is an economic and psychological weapon relying on the fear of being dismissed to ensure the domination of some economic actors over others, sometimes in violation of the law. This violence is admirably rendered in the description of the strategies of power adopted by Creeping Jesus, from the one-way glass behind which he spies on his employees (11), to his exploitation of them beyond the legal obligations of their contracts: "After service me an Smiler let the section run down but Creeping Jesus made us stock up just before the supermarket shut so there would be tons to take off after the shoppers left though we werent paid a penny after closedown" (11). The opposition between two conflicting systems of quantification – the "tons to take off" on the one hand, the nullity of the reward on the other – emphasizes the process whereby the supermarket illegally generates profit. Still, the managerial domination that employees are submitted to is both denounced and muted by those who are its victims. The political nature of Lanna's criticism sounds like some unconvincing understatement, which is also the case when she complains about how "bakery [kept] her over five hours without break [although] there was a law against it" (7). The employees' voices seem to have lost their political and polemical force: because they display complete ignorance of the specific legal dispositions that protect workers, and their complaints elicit neither response nor support from their colleagues, the working poor are also represented as consenting to neomanagerial techniques.

The absence of any collective organization in the novel further emphasizes the divisions that precarity creates: the "striating" effects of precarity (Lorey 2011, 1) divide workers instead of uniting them. With precarity and discontinuity ensuring the success of neomanagerial techniques in the workplace, *Morvern Callar* offers thus a realistic picture of working conditions under neoliberalism, in terms which are strongly reminiscent of those used by renowned contemporary sociologists, seeming thus to call into question the distinction that is usually made between sociological and fictional discourses. What fiction adds to the documentary dimension of any sociological enquiry, however, is to be attributed to the degree of empathy the narrativization of working conditions suscitates, thanks notably to the use of the first-person narrative.

The weakening of collective organization in the younger generation of employees, the lack of relational ties combined with the absence of any collective rhetoric to respond to managers, is not only a dominant motif in the novel; it is also an inquiry into one of the principal methods of neoliberalism, what Bourdieu calls its "programme of the methodical destruction of the collectives" (Bourdieu 1998, 3). If *Morvern Callar* can indeed be called a "'state of the nation' text" (Hutchinson 2007, 227), it is because the weakened response to working conditions depicted in the novel also illustrates the confrontation of neoliberalism with any type of organized labour. Red Hanna is portrayed as a disillusioned, defeated man, pointing to the weakening of unionism as a collective structure in post-Thatcherite Britain. This theme is also exploited in Jonathan

Coe's *The Closed Circle* (2004) and in David Peace's *GB 1984* (2004), with perhaps an even more overtly political dimension than in Warner's novel.

The novel form is then used to dramatize the collapse of solidarities as one of the major consequences of a managerial discourse which creates pressure notably through "the techniques of participative management" (Bourdieu 1998, 3). Morvern remarks that "self control" and "involvement" are not enough to ensure promotion when not combined with total submission to disciplinary discourse: "Smiler told about Smugslug and how I shouldve been Section Supervisor. I just looked at him and goes, Mmm, cause with the discipline record and the way Creeping Jesus was browned-off at me I was stuck in that job for ever" (9). However unruly Morvern may be, her manager seeks to induce in her a defense of the work team:

> It's not just me suffers you know Morvern, the whole section suffers, working a man short. I'm not a man. (172)

This is also what fiction achieves: by dramatizing the force of neoliberalism's discursive strategies, it exposes the contradictions within which poor workers are caught. In his rhetoric, Creeping Jesus moves from the singular to the collective and gives "a man" an anonymous and universal value, which Morvern feigns not to understand by hiding behind a rather lame gender argument. Meanwhile, the novel gives access to the thoughts of a *female* exploited worker, which is enough to establish a distance between an unarticulated contestation of the dominant discourse and a managerial discourse which summons irrelevant ideals of collective cooperation towards the creation of surplus value.

While class relation issues ran throughout twentieth-century British fiction and were often translated in terms of 'us' and 'them' dichotomies – an antagonism present in the works of the Angry Young Men, for instance – the advent of the 'postmodern' seemed to shift such problems to the background, not so much because they had become less pressing issues, but because they were said to have become so. Even in academia, issues of poverty seemed to lose ground in the 1980s, when identity issues – 'race', or 'gender' issues for instance – got the upper hand. Philip Tew claims that "class blindness [...] haunts contemporary British fiction and academic exegesis" (Keulks 2006, 73), and Driscoll asserts that "the contemporary British novel, assisted by 'class blind' post-ideological literary theories, [...] [has helped enable and sustain] the ideological notion of a 'classless' contemporary British literature and culture" (2009, 1). It may be argued, however, that Alan Warner's novel is perhaps not as "class blind" as the vast majority of the 'middle-class' texts Driscoll draws his analysis from – the novels of Martin Amis, Zadie Smith, Ian McEwan or Alan Hollinghurst. Warner himself claims that *Morvern Callar* is "a novel about Morvern's rejection by that artistic, middle-class world" (Warner 1998). What *Morvern Callar* does, in fact, is to dramatize the changed contours of a class-based society, questioning the very notion of a viable 'community'.

That is profoundly why Warner's text and characters seem to cultivate a somewhat schizophrenic relationship to issues of class. Indeed, Morvern seeks to escape her own class rather than engage in class warfare. As we have seen, the novel summons class-inspired reflections while suggesting at the same time that such categories may have become irrelevant or insufficient as a response to the aggressions of neoliberalism. Class issues do feature large in the novel, but they are not explicitly commented upon and do not constitute the novel's main argument. As Driscoll would put it, *Morvern Callar* thus simultaneously "silences and articulates class issues" (2009, 1). Lynne Ramsay's screen adaptation of the novel (2002) undoubtedly added grist to Driscoll's mill. But some fragile remnants of class discourse do survive in the novel, despite the fact that class consciousness and class politics seem to recede in the background of a nation of shoppers. As individual lives get narrated in the novel's embedded narratives, they merely form a collection of unrelated stories which, at first sight at least, fail to coalesce into a coherent political community.

The classic 'us' and 'them' dichotomy is in fact all that seems to have survived from a consistent Marxist interpretive paradigm. An awareness of the class divide makes itself heard when Morvern describes the "well-to-do South voice" of a customer (10), a vocal synecdoche that is constantly confronted, in Morvern's narrative, with another common synecdoche, the hands of the poor, notably Morvern's own "hands all soil" (8) – the North/South divide being of course a powerful theme in British representations of poverty and class since at least the second half of the nineteenth century, an antagonism best illustrated by Elizabeth Gaskell's title, *North and South* (1855). A wealth of other such details suggest that Morvern is sensitive to issues of inequality related to different living standards: the houses where "only well-to-do live" (22) are opposed to the council flat she grew up in (41); some can afford a higher education and some others cannot (27); the wealthy people use credit cards which makes it easier to avoid tipping those who work for them (11).

In the specific context of neoliberal Britain, Morvern's precarity is the reverse side of the lives of the wealthy as she fantasizes them, symbolized by the "holiday brochures" (28) which constitute a recurrent fictional counterpoint to her own working conditions. The glossy travel brochures suggest the out-of-reach world of the rich, which Morvern will eventually grow familiar with during her Spanish vacation. Such ambivalence explains why Morvern's contempt of Southern accents is never explicitly 'translated' into any sense of being part of a social or political class. Red Hanna, whose name is credit enough to his former years of communism, represents an extinct world, where class identities and unionism used to walk hand in hand, and where the Marxist interpretive "master code" (Jameson 1981, 10) would make it easy to think of oneself as part of a community welded by solidarity. Indeed, the specificity of this novel's representation of precarity lies not in a coherent Marxist sense of class warfare, but rather in its capacity to produce a sense of community grounded both in and *out of* class-based interpretations.

It is precisely because precarity endangers the collective dynamics of solidarity that the recognition of the shared precariousness of all life in the novel is not presented as a cohesive and constant mode of being for the main protagonist, but rather as sudden flickering moments and fragile narrative constructs constantly impeded by various forms of discontinuity. Precarity opposes individuals, whereas precariousness brings them together, under a shared acknowledgement of the value of human life (Butler 2009, 19). In *Morvern Callar*, things happen as if the poor themselves validated the neoliberal notion that "there is no such thing as society" (Thatcher 1987), as if the political relevance of any collective organization were now a thing of the past. But it is precisely such a sense of a lost relationality that is diagnosed by Butler when she claims that "we are compelled to take stock of our interdependence" (Butler 2004, 27). In similar fashion, *Morvern Callar* seeks to represent the segmented state of society under neoliberalism, but paradoxically, however, it is also during Morvern's individualistic and consumerist trip that her capacity to 'be with' and 'feel for' is eventually restored.

The first part of the narrative depicts a rather callous Morvern:

> Watching telly while eating you only saw men machine-gunning in a ruined town. It was Yugoslavia then there was a picture of a girl human with the head missing. I put off the channel and watched the video of Bad lieutenant while trying the bits of the pedicure set. (50)

Morvern's impassivity in front of the image of the beheaded girl should indeed be read as a metaphor of her initial incapacity to acknowledge the reality of another's precarious life. The cold, placid description of the headless girl is aptly rendered by the matter-of-factness, the 'poverty' of the description itself. Morvern uses an impersonal "you" which testifies to her lack of sympathy for the pain of that Other. One should note, however, that the uncommon inversion of noun and adjective ("a girl human") disturbingly shifts the emphasis on the potential *humanity* of the headless girl. Still, the war narrative experienced in the televised frame is just a possible narrative among others for Morvern, who therefore prefers to substitute aesthetically pleasant for real, potentially disturbing violence. Morvern's individualism, and the illusory autonomy she finds shelter in, forbids her to recognize the shared precariousness of all human beings and to apprehend lives in terms of one's ethical "obligations toward others". The novel thus initially narrates the failure of "regard" (Butler 2009, 25). This episode also symbolizes Morvern's desire to sever the ties that connect her with Others, and the mangled body of the girl may well constitute a preview of her boyfriend's gruesome dismemberment (81).

Yet, Morvern seems to gradually depart both from her previous spatial fixity and from her initial callousness, and to retrieve that lost capacity to acknowledge the precariousness of all lives. One scene in particular may be read as a pivotal moment:

> The guy came straight up and opened [the door] my age but shorter, his face was red with the greeting. He looked right at me.
> Are you all right? I says. (132)

The boy's physical description is marked by the comparison Morvern makes between their respective ages, as if Morvern were now capable of seeing herself in others. The emphasis she puts on the young man's face is evidence of the Other's perceived humanity, which is the condition for "ethical obligations" towards the Other to emerge (Butler 2009, 22). The boy's weeping face thus serves as a counterpoint to that of the disfigured, and therefore dehumanized girl. The young man has just lost his mother, and Morvern tells him about her own foster-mother's funeral (134), underscoring once again some implied analogy between self and other. Their shared grief, their common loss has a universal feel to it, that of a motherless child's vulnerability and sorrow. The few words they exchange thus create a space where a flickering sense of relationality is experienced, as if voice were also the necessary condition for a face to come out (Le Blanc 2007, 19).

The novel's indictment of the loss of collective modes of being and relational ties, on the one hand, and the successive modes of Morvern's personal mourning, on the other, raise an important political issue: that of grief as an essential ingredient of ethical responsibility (Butler 2004, 22). Grief is not privatizing, *Morvern Callar* seems to suggest, but is constitutive on the contrary of a renewed sense of dependency, and, as a consequence, of a new political community. It has been convincingly argued that "the mourning of the communitarian ethos evident in [*Morvern Callar*] is, it seems, symptomatic of a general reassessment of 'community' throughout the post-Thatcherite left in Britain" (Hutchinson 2007, 228). *Morvern Callar* is not only about the mourning of a communitarian ethos; it is also about its potential rebirth as it sketches the contours of a political community which spreads both within and *beyond* the terms of class relations.

The novel's general mood is definitely not compatible with the traditionally anticlerical strategies of Marxist thought. The text of course claims no religious doctrine, but it accommodates a variety of Christian, mainly Catholic, subtexts: the story opens with the suicide of Morvern's lover at Christmas time; the tune "Oh Little Star of Bethlehem" is played several times (13, 25); the Virgin Mary is summoned (153) as if to prepare Morvern for the "immaculate conception" of the final pages (229); Morvern prays on several occasions (174, 228); and although her behaviour is less than devout (165) she finds shelter in a church (174). Such religious references do create an implicit pattern whereby the sense of a spiritual community is ultimately derived both from the novel's indictment of poverty and exclusion, and from its sketching of a spiritual horizon. This implicit spiritual community partly replaces a purely political community, but because it denounces neoliberalism at work, it also seems fairly close to some form of 'Christian leftism'. If *Morvern Callar* may be described as a working-class novel, it nevertheless offers a more comprehensive ideological positioning, where class-inspired reflections and Roman Catholic reminiscences are not mutually exclusive. When asked to comment on the 1997 landslide Labour victory, Warner claimed that, as a "trade unionist, out to better the work conditions of people, [he found] it hard to support a party that [had] abandoned core beliefs that the majority of its supporters in Northern England and Scotland still believe in", before suggesting that "New Labour may be a party of nihilism" (Warner 1998).

III

The complexity of *Morvern Callar* as a poverty narrative should not therefore be underestimated: working-class characters are featured in a fiction which, on the whole, remains evasive about the political implications of poverty and precarity. But when they seek to articulate their economic predicament, the singular voice of Morvern's narrative and the embedded narratives of the secondary characters manage to construct some kind of fragile political community, while simultaneously acknowledging its inevitable demise. As a matter of fact, the admission of a de-politicization of social life as a result of precarity seems to be part of the novel's political statement about neoliberalism, although the discordant concert of voices is also used to restore some power, albeit a symbolic one, to those who have been absent from mainstream contemporary literature for too long, thereby asserting the essentially polyphonic nature of the novel. Morvern remarks that her name, *callar*, means "silence" or "to say nothing" in Spanish (125), which is indeed the condition of the precarious poor whose voices have been silenced in neoliberal societies. Fiction grants a voice to such silences; it makes precarious lives audible again, while also mapping out through narrativization the changed contours of precarity under neoliberalism. The mere fact that Morvern should include stories other than hers in her narrative, and use them to augment the stuff of her own self-narrative, testifies to the capacity of the novel to recreate the collective voice that neoliberalism has sought to destroy. Le Blanc argues that while "ordinary lives" are concerned mainly with their own "creative power", precarious lives are on the contrary mostly defined through the "deprivation of that creative power" (2007, 18). This is precisely what the novel underscores: by turning a story of precarity into a self-narrative, it allows Morvern to become the author of her own life, which inevitably includes a certain degree of creative self-fictionalization.

Works Cited

Bourdieu, Pierre. "The Essence of Neoliberalism." Trans. J.J. Shapiro. *Le Monde Diplomatique* English edition (March 1998): 3.
Butler, Judith. *Frames of War: When Is Life Grievable?* London: Verso, 2009.
——. *Precarious Life: The Power of Mourning and Violence*. London: Verso, 2004.
Cingolani, Patrick. *La Précarité*. Paris: Presses Universitaires de France, 2005.
Driscoll, Lawrence Victor. *Evading Class in Contemporary British Literature*. New York: Palgrave Macmillan, 2009.
Harvey, David. *A Brief History of Neoliberalism*. Oxford: Oxford University Press, 2005.
Hutchinson, Colin. "The Abandoned Church and the Contemporary British Novel." *The Yearbook of English Studies* 37.1 (2007): 227–244.
Jameson, Fredric. *The Political Unconscious: Narrative as a Socially Symbolic Act*. London: Routledge, 1981.
Keulks, Gavin, ed. *Martin Amis: Postmodernism and Beyond*. Basingstoke: Palgrave Macmillan, 2006.
Le Blanc, Guillaume. *Vies ordinaires, vies précaires*. Paris: Seuil, 2007.
Lordon, Frédéric. *Capitalisme, désir et servitude: Marx et Spinoza*. Paris: La Fabrique, 2010.
Lorey, Isabell. "Governmental Precarization." Trans. Aileen Derieg. *eipcp* January 2011. http://eipcp.net/transversal/0811/lorey/en (15 June 2013).
OED. "risk, n." Etymology. *The Oxford English Dictionary*. Online Edition 2013a. http://www.oed.com/view/Entry/166306?rskey=dLVNIw&result=1&isAdvanced=false#eid (12 November 2013).
——. "economy, n." Etymology. *The Oxford English Dictionary*. Online Edition 2013b. http://www.oed.com/view/Entry/59393?redirectedFrom=economy#eid (12 November 2013).
——. "precarious, adj." Etymology. *The Oxford English Dictionary*. Online Edition 2013c. http://www.oed.com/view/Entry/149548#eid28800616 (12 November 2013)

Rancière, Jacques. *Politics of Literature.* Cambridge: Polity Press, 2011.

Thatcher, Margaret. "No Such Thing as Society." Interview with Douglas Keay. *Woman's Own* 23 September 1987: 1.

Thomson, Graham. "Interview with Alan Warner." *Barcelona Review* 1997. http://www.barcelonareview.com/arc/r2/eng/warnerint.htm (15 June 2013).

Warner, Alan. "Alan Warner, the Wild Man of Letters." Interview with Tobias Jones. *The Independent* 24 May 1998. http://www.independent.co.uk/life-style/interview-alan-warner-the-wild-man-of-letters-1157673.html (15 June 2013).

—. *Morvern Callar.* London: Vintage, 1995.

Georg Zipp
Life on the Streets: Parallactic Ways of Seeing Homelessness in John Berger's *King: A Street Story* (1999)

1 Homelessness as Precarious Life

The task of the humanities is, according to Judith Butler, "to return us to the human where we do not expect to find it, in its frailty and at the limits of its capacity to make sense" (2004, 151). Butler urges her readers "to interrogate the emergence and vanishing of the human at the limits of what we can know, what we can hear, what we can see, what we can sense" (2004, 151). Art critic Hal Foster, surveying art works of the first decade of the twenty-first century, argues that there is "no concept [which] comprehends the past decade, but there is a condition this art has shared, and it is a precarious one" (2009, 207). Foster reminds his readers that precariousness – which he understands in the sense of the French *précarité* and hence as predominantly socioeconomic insecurity (2011, 106) – is not a new phenomenon, but that, accelerated through the excesses of neoliberalism, the precarious condition has become

> all but pervasive, and it is this heightened insecurity that much art has attempted to manifest, even to exacerbate. This social instability is redoubled by an artistic instability, as the work [Foster surveys] foregrounds its own schismatic condition, its own lack of shared meaning, methods, or motivations. Paradoxically, then, precariousness seems almost constitutive of much art, yet sometimes in a manner that transforms this debilitating affliction into a compelling appeal. (2009, 207)

The novel *King* (1999), by the art critic, writer and Marxist John Berger, came out on the cusp of this precarious decade, and it pre-empts the theme that was going to occupy not only the art world in the following years: both in form and content, the novel is precarious. It depicts life on the street, and it does so in a manner that explores possibilities for disrupting established ways of seeing the homeless and dispossessed.

In her discussion of "Precarious Life", Judith Butler invokes the Levinasian concept of 'face' as "a figure that communicates both the precariousness of life and the interdiction of violence" (2004, xviii):

> [It] is not precisely or exclusively a human face, although it communicates what is human, what is precarious, what is injurable. The media representations of the faces of the 'enemy'

efface what is most human about the 'face' for Levinas. Through a cultural transposition of his philosophy, it is possible to see how dominant forms of representation can and must be disrupted for something about the precariousness of life to be apprehended. This has implications, once again, for the boundaries that constitute what will and will not appear within public life, the limits of a publicly acknowledged field of appearance. Those who remain faceless or whose faces are presented to us as so many symbols of evil, authorize us to become senseless before those lives we have eradicated, and whose grievability is indefinitely postponed. Certain faces must be admitted into public view, must be seen and heard for some keener sense of the value of life, all life, to take hold. (2004, xviii)

As will be discussed below, those deemed 'evil' in Berger's novel are the precarious homeless, and they are obliterated as soon as they become visible in the spotlight of the bulldozer which makes them homeless, again. As Butler further emphasizes,

[t]he structure of address is important for understanding how moral authority is introduced and sustained if we accept not just that we address others when we speak, but that in some way we come to exist, as it were, in the moment of being addressed, and something about our existence proves precarious when that address fails. More emphatically, however, what binds us morally has to do with how we are addressed by others in ways that we cannot avert or avoid; this impingement by the other's address constitutes us first and foremost against our will [...]. (2004, 130)

The face implies not only an address, however, but also a look, and a gaze, and effects a double moral obligation: only when we choose to look at the other does this other come into existence, but with this act of violently willing the other into existence comes a moral obligation to avoid a voyeuristic gaze. 'Literary' fiction, which is possibly more ambitious in scope than its more 'popular' counterparts, offers a vast space to experiment with aesthetic and ethical conventions in attempts to approximate those spaces of precarious existence where the ability to make sense is elusive. *King* attempts to change the way readers *see* poverty by way of what could be termed, upon readers' recognition of their own and other people's vulnerability and insecurity, a visual "dislocation from first world privilege" (Butler 2004, xii).

2 The Parallax Effect

This strategy of visual dislocation is an indication of a parallax, which a dictionary quoted by Frederic Jameson (2006) defines as "the apparent displacement of an observed object due to a change in the position of the observer". Immanuel

Kant's concept of the parallax was recently revived in philosophical debate by Kojin Karatani and subsequently popularized by Slavoj Žižek. For Žižek,

> putting two incompatible phenomena on the same level [...] is strictly analogous to what Kant called 'transcendental illusion', the illusion of being able to use the same language for phenomena which are mutually untranslatable and can be grasped only in a kind of parallax view, constantly shifting perspective between two points between which no synthesis or mediation is possible. Thus there is no rapport between the two levels, no shared space – although they are closely connected, even identical in a way, they are, as it were, on the opposed sides of a Moebius strip. [...] In short, [this is] the occurrence of an insurmountable *parallax gap*, the confrontation of two closely linked perspectives between which no neutral common ground is possible. (2006, 4)

One well-known example of the parallax effect is an observer's thumb on the outstretched hand, which starts jumping to and fro when the eyes are closed in rapid succession. Another well-known example is the Rubin (or figure-ground) vase. For the latter, Žižek emphasizes that "one either sees the two faces or a vase, never both of them – one has to make a choice" (2004, 128). Similarly, when faced with stark global inequality, for example,

> [t]here is no neutral language enabling us to translate from one to the other, still less any attempt to posit the 'truth' of one from the perspective of the other. All one can do in today's conditions is to remain faithful to the split as such, to record it. An exclusive focus on First World issues of late-capitalist alienation and commodification, of ecological crisis, of racism, intolerance and so on, cannot avoid seeming cynical in the face of Third World poverty, hunger and violence. On the other hand, attempts to dismiss First World problems as trivial in comparison with the 'real' problems of the Third World are no less fake; a form of escapism, a means to avoid confronting the antagonisms in one's own society. (Žižek 2003, 24)[1]

What is important about the concept of the parallactic view is the "multiplicity of observational sites", or the duplicity of perspectives: like the optical illusion of the figure-ground vase, the descriptions of both the face and the vase are in productive tension and cannot easily be resolved into a compromise. Jameson (2006) stresses therefore that cultural critics should "perpetuate the tension and the incommensurability rather than palliating or concealing it". In other words: mutually exclusive interpretations are not necessarily a problem but prove productive in changing readers' perspectives and understanding. The

---

1 Or, as Žižek writes more succinctly elsewhere, "in today's globalized universe, marked by irreconcilable gaps between different levels of our life, such a fidelity to parallax views, to unresolved antagonisms, is the only way to approach the totality of our experience" (2004, 134).

inner gap at the centre of the parallax, however, is un-representable, and can only be approximated by triangulation.[2]

3 Ways of Seeing in *King*

Parallaxes run deep through the structure of Berger's novel: they manifest themselves at various structural and interpretative levels and constitute attempts to make readers question their positions *vis à vis* poverty and to thus change the way they see poverty. Three parallaxes and their dichotomies prove crucial to Berger's project of not merely conveying a sense of the conditions of precarious living but also of changing the ways this precariousness is seen. Subsequently, they will be discussed in the following order: (i) First World vs. Third World poverty, (ii) author vs. narrator, and (iii) dog vs. human. First, however, the novel's central triangulation will be considered.

Parallaxes can be determined by triangulation. In Berger's story, this is represented through a mediation between what can be seen and what can be told, and the perception of one influencing the other.[3] While the reader is invited, on the back cover of the first edition, to "*listen* to King as he tells the story" (emphasis mine), he or she actually *reads* what King, the narrator, can see and therefore *describes* in words, namely "the coat", a forgotten and overlooked space in the vicinity of the motorway M1000:

> Twelve kilometres from the city centre and four from the sea there is a zone where people never stop unless obliged. Not because it's dangerous but because it has been forgotten. Even those who do stop for a moment forget it immediately afterwards. It's empty, yet it is large. (2)[4]

---

2 In physics, triangulation and the parallax effect are used to calculate distances between faraway stars. The parallax at the heart of physics itself is that light displays properties of waves (Christiaan Huygens) and of particles (Isaac Newton), phenomena which, despite capturing correct interpretations of reality, have so far been incompatible when it comes to reconciling them in a single 'world formula'. The effect is similar for the description of social phenomena, where two theories can be correct but still incompatible.
3 As Berger stresses in *Ways of Seeing*, "[i]t is seeing which establishes our place in the surrounding world; we explain that world with words, but words can never undo the fact that we are surrounded by it. The relation between what we see and what we know is never settled" (1972, 7). What can be seen and how that which is seen is described influence each other mutually: "[t]he way we see things is affected by what we know or what we believe" (1972, 8).
4 All pages numbers for Berger's novel refer to the 1999 edition.

These words form the opening of the novel and the author makes it clear that he wants to remind his readers of the existence of this forgotten industrial-urban space and to make it visible to them again: the assumption of 'forgetting' is that this is a space which used to be known but has been obliterated. The story, for all its descriptions, visual clues, flashbacks and memories, invites readers to vividly picture the wasteland, but still fails to capture its totality. The text is aware of this impossibility of describing in its entirety what can be seen. Therefore, King acknowledges, from the very beginning of the novel, the impossibility of his task: "*I am mad to try*", "mad to try to lead you to where we live" (2). Just like images, words fail to capture all of the landscape that Berger's homeless characters live in. Both words and images are only approximations and pointers to a reality behind the representation.

The setting of "the coat" cannot be located on a real-world map but alludes to features that most European wastelands have in common: it includes references to real-world places like Berlin's Treptower Park, the metro in Paris, and other scenarios of European cities. It is not quite clear whether these pointers are all merged in St Valéry or whether they are remembered by King, who, throughout his life, has crossed from one forgotten space to another. The setting by itself therefore forms a snapshot of the totality of a precarious experience at the historical juncture in the wake of the fall of the Berlin wall, which is referred to indirectly as "the second barbarism [which] kills a man and takes everything whilst it promises and talks of freedom" (213).

The plot is rather spare, seemingly arbitrary and interspersed with the characters telling jokes,[5] stories or anecdotes, and King reminiscing about the past. The narrator tells the story of Vico and Vica, who, having survived the winter in their tenement ("the Hut"), engage in a day of activity: Vica and King fetch water (relying on their ability to outwit a petrol station owner), then Vico attempts to sell his camera (and, by proxy, his memories), King fights off intruders. A sense of foreboding comes when the slumlord who manages the settlement returns crestfallen from a meeting with developers; rumours have it that the settlement is to become the building site for an Olympic stadium. King plays games with a boy, Vico and Vica try to sell radishes, drink beer, fall asleep with exhaustion, and then make their way back to the settlement where they arrive just as a crawler is destroying it. The inhabitants of "the coat" are to be carted off for resettlement. After the inhabitants' futile attempts to resist – using knives, Molotov cocktails and guns – they are defeated by the combined forces of bulldozers

---

5 "My friend, have you ever seen a man-eating lion? No, but I have seen a man eating herring!" (191).

and tear gas. King finally imagines that his fellow inhabitants are being transformed into dogs but eventually realizes that he has fled from the destroyed settlement alone.

This 'plot' summary already suggests that, in the world of the story, the tenuous link between signifiers and signified has broken down. In Berger's version of capitalism, even words appear to have lost their property and properties: "There are no words for what makes up the wasteland because everything on it is smashed and has been thrown away, and for most fragments there are no proper names" (3–4). Vico and Vica too have lost their original names: Vico used to be called Gianni (121), and his new name carries the spectre of Vico Giambattista, of whom he claims to be a descendant; it is also the Italian word for a (downtrodden) street (102).[6] Vica's name suggests that she is, figuratively, the only 'property' Vico has left.

A first step for Berger is therefore to re-inscribe the forgotten and overlooked back into the picture. The descriptions of what can be seen in "the coat" are an invitation to readers to re-focus their attention, since looking "is an act of choice. As a result of this act, what we see is brought within our reach" (1972, 7–8). By 'painting' his homeless couple back into the picture, Berger seeks to re-assert their existence. This mirrors Butler's invocation of the 'face' and her assertion above that the genesis of the existence, which begins at the moment of being addressed, "proves precarious when that address fails" (2004, 130). The reader's 'seeing' of Vico and Vica therefore puts forward an ethical demand.

The narrator is aware, however, that mere representation and increased visibility are not enough. Sometimes the characters' invisibility is vital. If they were merely noticed by more people, that "would be intolerable" (106). Representation without consequences would fall prey to voyeurism. To counter this, Berger's narrator tries to re- and deflect conventional expectations of what the reader is going to see when laying eyes on a homeless man, and to destabilize tacit assumptions about the illiterate poor: Vico and Vica originate from the middle class; they used to own a factory and were impoverished not through their own fault but due to insufficient fire insurance. Vico may look like an illiterate man "who when it is snowing shambles into the public library to keep warm", but he is "not this man. He had read thousands of books in his life, but he had come to look like this man" (53). In another scene, the narrator, aware of the reader's gaze, gently deflects indecent attention from Vica when she is "relieving herself as she does every morning behind the tyres" and explains:

6 The double meaning of "street story" is consequently not just that it is a story from the streets but also of (a) Vico.

"When a woman has so little privacy, it's good at certain moments if a small curtain can be made for her with words. So I'll tell the story about the swallow" (29). Seeing the homeless is complicated when the narrator describes what a third person sees when looking at Vico and Vica and counts on the reader's allegiance with King and the homeless couple:

> The sight we offer, the three of us – an old man, an old woman and their dog in a delivery doorway screeching at each other and standing on pieces of cardboard, hands grubby and swollen, eyes misty, making no effort to improve their lot, indifferent to hope and reasoning – this sight is disgusting and infectious. It saps confidence and a lack of confidence diminishes immunity.
> Flush them out, mutters a man with a telephone in his hand, they should be hosed off the street. (138)

These examples represent the didacticism with which some reviewers charged Berger; they also show, however, how Berger aims for a new kind of solidarity, and to change the way readers see and interact with those dehumanized by the system.[7]

The narrator also constantly undermines the credibility of what is related, and what the reader sees: "I'm not sure. When people here talk about the past, they tend to exaggerate, because sometimes the exaggerations too help to keep them a little warmer" (7). This introduces a precariousness on a textual level and unsettles the relationship between words, images and reality further. It is a mimesis through which the literary work foregrounds "its own schismatic condition", as Hal Foster diagnoses in the case of precarious art installations. And indeed, the novel and the world it depicts resemble installation art. After introducing the reader to "the coat", King goes on to describe details of the setting:

> The terrain is used as a dump. Smashed lorries. Old boilers. Broken washing machines. Rotary lawn mowers. Refrigerators which don't make cold any more. Wash-basins which are cracked. There are also bushes and small trees and tough flowers like pheasant's eye and viper's grass. (4)

---

7 And be it only because they might be next in line: in the novel, a fear of contagion is associated with the dispossessed and likened to a plague because no one seems to know how the economic system works, and whose livelihood might become precarious, and why: "The passersby see three more plague victims. Deep down everybody knows that nobody is telling the truth about this plague. Nobody knows whom it selects and how. And so everywhere there is a fear of infection" (138).

Everything and everyone is consumed, used up and ultimately ends up among the detritus that is amassed in the narrative. Words, things and people are discarded. Once removed from the circuit of desire that sustains capitalism, they come under strain not only from their fossilization and reification, but also from their being overcharged with religious, allegorical or banal connotations. Functional textiles, for instance, have lost their 'function' and are re-contextualized as trash, also because their 'meaning', always already on the verge of breaking down, has been lost: "The Gore-Tex membrane is made of two different polymers – polytetrafluoroethylene (e.PTFE), which is hydrophobic, and another polymer which is oleophobic. The e.PTFE membrane contains nine billion pores per square inch" (97).[8] While in *Ways of Seeing* (1972) Berger discusses publicity as a promise directed towards the future, in *King* he seems intent on exploring the backside of our material culture: the ramifications of what happens when those products have become the past. Detritus can be re-appropriated and re-contextualized into ready-made art, however. The cited quotes of seemingly random and excessive words highlight the novel's kinship with contemporary visual culture. Installation art can "evok[e] our everyday world as a precarious Plato's Cave of flitting shadows without enlightenment" (Foster 2009, 209). Its fleeting impressions are mirrored in Berger's novel by short, disjointed paragraphs which flit, sometimes arbitrarily, from object to object. However, it is almost impossible to read a story without trying to impose a sense of order and an interpretation. While such sense-making mechanisms are precariously unsettled by Berger, the overall effect is not one of arbitrariness. Rather, the fresh imagery and contradictions, which cannot be unambiguously dissolved, invite the reader to actually look at homelessness, to see it anew, with Berger's ideas in mind. The novel's productive tension is therefore one between the disruptive methods of installation art and the linear order of text. Hal Foster notes that precarious installation art today has abandoned the project to "attempt to capture the lack of consistent and repeatable meanings in the culture – to capture the lack and make it over into form"; instead, it has given over to "letting this formlessness be, as it were, so that it might evoke, as directly as possible, both the 'confusion' of ruling elites and the 'violence' of global capital" (2009, 208). Berger's novel, by contrast, opens complex interpretative routes through the use of parallaxes and ultimately leads to the conclusion that the sense of order and of meaning which were lost can be re-imposed onto fragmented realities through the use of voice.

---

8 See also the following reference to a lemonade and how its 'meaning' has been charged through advertising: "A motorcycle messenger has stopped to buy an Orangina at the Pizza Hut. Helmet off, sitting astride the bike, he pours the juice down his throat and it washes away the dirt, and its coldness puts a sweet hand on his fatigue. Orangina" (114).

First World and Third World

The "coat's" inhabitants live in makeshift tenements, and only that of Jack, the slumlord, disposes of "floorboards and a proper gutter system" (7). One character lives in a former transformer shed (8), and another underneath "a giant lorry tarpaulin" (10). The residents have to pay rent for their patch of land. This scenario reflects Berger's vision that capitalism is all-encompassing: even though they have already been pushed towards the margins, the inhabitants of "the coat" cannot escape the system. Society is structured like a Matryoshka doll, or a box in a box in a box, where you wake from the nightmare of having been failed in the capitalist system, only to wake up having to play the game all over again, on a smaller scale. Not being able to afford their former home, Vico and Vica now have to pay the slumlord. They live in a post-apocalyptic wasteland of absurdity, on a level with that of Winnie and Willie in Beckett's *Happy Days*,[9] i.e. in a state in which all time seems to have stopped, and where the past is perpetually slipping away without giving way to a future (at least not one that is of this world); that is why King claims that "sleep is best" (33).[10]

Significantly, the "coat" also resembles shantytowns in the Global South, and Berger's first parallax therefore offers a vision of Third World poverty which is taking place in the heart of Europe. This is unusual because we have become accustomed to seeing poverty and slum settlements from a safe distance. If one follows Žižek's implication about the parallactic "split" (see above), then a focus on late-capitalist inequality in the First World, and one on Third World hunger and violence cannot be reconciled under the same label 'poverty'. Berger complicates this further: his novel reminds readers that both seemingly irreconcilable varieties of poverty (the 'absolute' one that is supposedly anachronistic in Europe, and the 'relative' one) do co-exist in the same place and right at the centre of Europe. Arguably, Vico and Vica have something in common with both Mexican slum dwellers and with European city dwellers.

---

9 A reviewer noted that they are "like the tramps in *Waiting for Godot*, philosopher-beggars inhabiting a world of abstractions" ("With a Bark not a Whimper" 1999).
10 Sleep, as death's little brother, is the closest they can come resembling a state of rest, even though their life has effectively come to a standstill: restless immobility is another paradox of the homeless condition.

Author and Narrator

A second parallax operates at the level of author vs. narrator. The cover of the first edition omitted Berger's name;[11] therefore the novel's title *King* could be taken for the name of the author and narrator, and *A Street Story* as the novel's title. If author and narrator thus coincide in the figure of King, Berger appears to renounce his author function in order to join the ranks of those dehumanized and forgotten. It then becomes unimportant as to who tells the story: in the words of Roland Barthes, it is "language which speaks, not the author" (1988, 143). By consequence, Berger's novel constitutes not a subjective tale by an individual but one of a truth that reaches beyond the horizon of a single person. If authorship and narratorship coincide, the novel is also something of a frontline report, a quasi-authentic documentary and testimonial of someone living "A Street Life". The tale's universal applicability is therefore achieved through radical subjectivation of the telling and writing 'through' or by King.

If, on the other hand, there is no identity between narrator (King) and author (Berger), as the marketing of the paperback version suggested – it featured the author's name on the cover – then the author can exercize his entire cultural capital in order to speak on behalf of the disenfranchised. This opens up other interpretative routes by making it possible to link themes of the novel with some of the concerns Berger raises in earlier works, especially in *Ways of Seeing* and his essay "Why Look at Animals?", which was originally published in 1977.

Animal and Human

The third and most important parallax in the novel is that of animal vs human: the question as to whether the protagonist-narrator King is a dog who can talk or a human reduced to thinking that he is a dog. The hardcover's back matter flags

---

11 Berger explains this in an interview: "First of all, the story claims to be told by a dog so it's not me. More importantly when the author's name is on the cover and especially if it's an author like me or who has written quite a lot of books, the book is first seen as a kind of literary event – there's a new book by Berger. I wanted it to be a story that comes from the street, this is a story where very few printed stories come from. It was to minimise its literary signification if you wish, and I wanted it to be announced as a street story rather than as a new novel by John Berger" (Koval 2000).

this question,[12] and the narrator self-consciously questions his status as he finds himself in a world in which madness seems a prerequisite for survival: "Everyone at Saint Valéry needs a madness to find their balance after the wreck. It's like a walking stick. Madness is the third leg. Me, for instance, I believe I'm a dog. Here nobody knows the truth" (129). In an interview, Berger confirms that he left the question of the narrator's animal or human state intentionally open:

> [R]eaders can take their choice. Or maybe at different moments exchange their view of the dog for another view of the dog. There are two possibilities, both of them are somewhat unexpected. [...] maybe it is a dog but then it's a dog who can talk and a dog who knows a great, great deal. Maybe it's a person who calls himself a dog, because almost everybody in that group of homeless people change their names. It's not so much that they invent characters for themselves, but they are no longer the same people that they once were, they have been transformed by this terrible trauma and these hardships. And so maybe, maybe this is a man who tells himself or tells others that now he's a dog. (Koval 2000)

Throughout the text, there are clues to indicate one or the other: King's style of narration suggests that he has a very short attention span. He licks people's faces, fingers, eyelids and legs, he barks, sleeps with Vico and Vica to guard them and pulls their "chariot" (a shopping trolley) to fetch water. He is even recognized by a passing woman as a dog (49). Most of this suggests that he actually is a dog. However, the trolley is not unambiguous: King might be human and still wear a harness to pull the chariot; this would underline his state of dehumanization in a show of quasi-masochism like Lucky's in *Waiting for Godot*. Other qualities seem to indicate more clearly that he is a human being: he is able to understand speech and speak himself – it is not clear whether he only speaks to the reader and 'communicates' with the novel's characters mutely, in his thoughts. He confesses that he used to be an alcoholic who hung around bars, where he is still not seen as a stranger (204), and, in a more disconcerting scene, King relates his sexual encounter with a woman named Marina (177–178). Moreover, if King really was a dog, he should have a better sense of smell and worse eyesight. There is a curious lack of smell in the novel, and when a smell is invoked, it is usually coded in a visual simile: "Geraniums smell like wet silver" (108), or petrol smells of "high octane", "like diamonds" (6), which suggests that King perceives the world more like a man than a dog. Instead of deciding which is more likely – in parallactic thinking a futile endeav-

---

12 "In this book you will be led to a place you haven't been, from where few stories come. You will be led by King, a dog – or is he dog? – to a wasteland beside the motorway [...]" (back cover).

our anyway – it is instrumental to consider the implications of either option and discuss the productive tension that results for the reader. If King is a dog, then this solves a dilemma of plausibility: King is a guide and a teichoscope. If he is a human being, then the text becomes a disturbing indictment (and one in which the ability to swap perspectives might ease the reader's conscience).

If King is a dog, then this has consequences on two levels. On a symbolic level, it taps into a vast reservoir in the cultural imaginary,[13] with anthropomorphic animals usually being relegated to children's fiction, satire or fables. As Berger writes in "Why Look at Animals": "Animals are born, are sentient and are mortal. In these things they resemble man. In their superficial anatomy – less in their deep anatomy – in their habits, in their time, in their physical capacities, they differ from man. They are both like and unlike" (2009, 13). However, in Berger's view, animals have become marginalized in the modern world, and this was "followed by the marginalization and disposal of the only class who, throughout history, has remained familiar with animals and maintained the wisdom which accompanies that familiarity: the middle and small peasant" (2009, 36). Arguably, *King* demonstrates that this marginalization and disposal is now repeated with the poor and homeless, who, in the cultural imaginary, are also thought to have a close bond with their animal companions.[14] The mythological appeal of animals, according to Berger, lies in the fact that they "came from over the horizon. They belonged *there* and *here*" (2009, 15–16). Their mere presence can therefore be seen to communicate truths, or to be an intermediary between the real and the metaphysical, offering consolation for an existential solitude.[15] An animal cannot verbally translate between there and here, however, so that "its lack of common language, its silence, guarantees its distance, [...] its exclusion from and of man" (Berger 2009, 14). It is appealing for man to imagine what an animal might say, since it has "secrets which, unlike the secrets of caves, mountains, seas are specifically addressed to man" (Berger 2009, 14). If,

---

13 "The parallelism of their similar/dissimilar lives allowed animals to provoke some of the first questions and offer answers. The first subject matter for painting was animal. Probably the first paint was animal blood. Prior to that, it is not unreasonable to suppose that the first metaphor was animal" (Berger 2009, 16).

14 In online reviews, readers commented on how the reading of *King* altered their associations of dogs with the homeless (for example, a comment by user "Phillip Edwards" on Goodreads. com [27 February 2007]). Barbara Korte's chapter in this volume mentions the best-selling success of James Bowen's memoir *A Street Cat Named Bob* (2012), which was unusual in that the homeless man's companion was a cat instead of a dog.

15 "With their parallel lives, animals offer man a companionship which is different from any offered by human exchange. Different because it is a companionship offered to the loneliness of man as a species" (Berger 2009, 15).

in a suspension of disbelief, King can therefore be accepted as an actually speaking animal, he becomes the arbiter of metaphysical truth. (And the dog, read backwards, thus becomes an omniscient god.[16])

The second consequence of reading King as a (speaking) dog is a more pragmatic one: King becomes the reader's guide (as announced on the cover) to the wasteland, which would otherwise be a speechless and inarticulated space, not just invisible but also unheard. Writing on behalf of the dispossessed can be a critical endeavour: in almost any literary text about poverty there is a (subjective, spatial or temporal) gap between that which is represented and the person narrating it; thus there might even be an issue of legitimacy if a (middle-class) author writes on behalf of the disenfranchised.[17] At the same time, supposedly authentic narratives by 'really' poor authors raise questions of access, both institutionally as well as in terms of aesthetics.[18] On a textual level, this dilemma is reproduced in the question of narrators and characters of poverty: how can the way in which a narrator tells his or her tale be made plausible, and in words that are neither implausibly educated nor patronisingly simple? How to account for the way in which the events are relayed? The angle, for example, of a character who rises out of poverty and narrates from memory, is viable, but remains a specific angle.

This is where King as a dog-narrator is a useful teichoscopic device: he is able to 'look over the wall' and to describe to the reader what is going on 'on the other side', effectively being able to guide, translate and comment. The dog is insider and outsider at the same time. He roams around on his own but chooses to become a member of the community at his will. Since he acts as an intermediary, the direct, voyeuristic gaze of the reader on the homeless characters is deflected, and once it is accepted that a dog can speak, this is less strange than an intrusive human interpreter would be. Indeed, King's 'dogness' helps to underline the common humanity as well as the class differences between the novel's readers and the homeless whose existence is described. King as a dog is *not* mad but free to tell things as he sees them, and thus as they (supposedly) are. By giving a voice to the wasteland, Berger therefore extends the boundaries of "what will and will not count as a viable speaking subject and a reasonable opinion within the public domain" (Butler 2004, xix). King, as an outsider to this debate, does not have to be afraid of losing, in Butler's

---

16 As outlined in the novel, according to Giambattista's theory of the cycle of the ages, the "Age of Gods" will be followed by the "Age of Heroes", the "Age of Men" and the "Age of Dogs" before restarting with a new "Age of Gods" (180).

17 For a further discussion on this, see Korte (2010, 295).

18 See Krishan Kumar on examples of "vapid naturalism" (1995, 24).

words, his "status as a viable speaking being" (2004, xix–xx) and can openly say what crosses his mind. The partial answer to the problem of representing precariousness is therefore that poverty writing of sufficient complexity can emanate from any writer gifted with imagination. Just as animals and human beings are "both like and unlike", so are the precarious and the non-precarious in literary representations. Certain material realities cannot simply be declared null and void, as there is a fundamental difference in that the readers venturing to 'that place they've never been' have the money and power which the precarious do not. At the same time, empathy should enable readers to imagine – to certain limits – what it must be like to be poor, and possibly without sentimental or self-gratifying reactions of the type Carolyn Betensky describes (2004 and her chapter in this volume). Berger's novel cautions that "only those also resisting know how my friends resist" (202), and its narration also eschews another pitfall of poverty narratives, namely a false sense of radical difference, furthered by voyeuristic and sensationalist depictions through which the dispossessed are posited as people entirely *other* from the readers.

If King is read as a human being who believes that he is a dog, the text becomes a disturbing indictment of the conditions of living that can drive people crazy, and make them forget the essence of their identity. As King says in the novel: "I have a strange way of talking, for I'm not sure who I am. Many things conspire to take a name away. The name dies and even the pain suffered doesn't belong to it any more" (70). The pretence of being a dog thus becomes the metaphor through which the person who suffers can bear the debasement. Not only does King have to eke out a living by scrambling for scraps among the scrap heaps, but he has also forgotten what makes him human, apart from speech. And this speech alone, constantly threatening to collapse its meaning, and having severed most connections between signifiers and signifieds, does not offer much shelter from this precarious condition. Bar his speech, much of King's comportment has become that of a dog; as mentioned before, he licks other people's faces, barks, and pulls the trolley. If language fails him, too, then King is close to becoming an animal. As Berger writes in "Why Look at Animals": "What distinguished man from animals was the human capacity for symbolic thought, the capacity which was inseparable from the development of language in which words were not mere signals, but signifiers of something other than themselves" (2009, 18). If King is only metaphorically an animal but really a human being, then his condition is equivalent to that of an animal in the zoo, which is *"rendered absolutely marginal"* (Berger 2009, 34). This implies that he is irredeemably and utterly reduced, and more insidiously so, since "[t]he animals of the mind cannot be so easily dispersed" (Berger 2009, 25), that is, internal dehumanization cannot be disrupted off-handedly. It is in this context that the novel's indictment of neoliberalism as "the second barbarism [which] kills a man and takes everything whilst it promises and talks of freedom" is to be understood – the precarious subject's subjection under the regime of power has become naturalized and internalized while retaining the surface illusion of liberty and free will, just like Berger's zoo animals,

> isolated from each other and without interaction between species, have become utterly dependent upon their keepers. [...] What was central to their interest has been replaced by a passive waiting for a series of arbitrary outside interventions. [...] At the same time this very isolation (usually) guarantees their longevity as specimens and facilitates their taxonomic arrangement. (2009, 34)

Berger himself notes the clumsy parallel between zoos and other "sites of enforced marginalization – ghettos, shanty towns, prisons, madhouses, concentration camps" (2009, 36), but in his novel King has memories of refugee or detention camps (177), and there are further parallels. The gaze of animals in a zoo "flickers and passes on. They look sideways. They look blindly beyond. They scan mechanically. They have been immunized to encounter" (Berger 2009, 37). In the novel, King's fellows have been reduced to this state, while King, as human being, appears to have conserved a notion of what it used to mean to be a man. For Berger, the difference between human being and animal is that "[o]ther animals are held by the look. Man becomes aware of himself returning the look" (2009, 13). King is still aware of the effect the gaze has since he directs it by telling the story. His awareness of being looked at, and of returning this look, reflecting it back onto the reader, therefore reconnects to Butler and redoubles the ethical plight of the face and the precarious subject. It is in this sense that the entreaty of the precarious, as outlined at the beginning of this chapter, always "carries the force of accusation".

The readers, those in power, cannot evade the look, and cannot reply to Vico's powerless cry that he and his community "are being wiped off the earth, not the face of the earth, the face we lost long ago, the arse of the earth, il culo. We are their mistake, King, listen to me!" (210) And, as Vico elaborates further: "A mistake, King, is hated more than an enemy. Mistakes don't surrender as enemies do. There's no such thing as a defeated mistake. Mistakes either exist or they don't, and if they do, they have to be covered over" (211). The angry reactions provoked by confrontation with this kind of poverty, be it in reality or through mediated discourses, seems to suggest that there is a short-circuit of ego-based fantasies where the perpetrators substitute the fear of becoming 'like' the poor with pre-emptive aggression, so as to assert their maximal difference, or, as in the case of the construction workers who destroy "the coat", to wilfully look away, asserting that they are only doing a job required by the system. Ultimately it is the reader, who by choosing to look away at this point, will have collaborated in the creation of this mistake and therefore in the continued subjection of the precarious subject. Berger's novel posits that hatred results when the precarious cannot be willed away by being overlooked, that is, when the indictment inherent in the entreaty actually reaches the addressee:

> The hatred which the strong feel for the weak as soon as the weak get too close is particularly human; it doesn't happen with animals. With humans there is a distance which must be respected, and when it isn't, it is the strong, not the weak, who feel affronted, and from the affront comes hatred. (24)

The parallactic shift between King-the-animal and King-the-human precludes such a hatred; by stating the possibility of hatred explicitly, forcing the reader's acknowledgement of this potentially emotional response, the novel ultimately strives to transform it into recognition and understanding. This is why, in the best sense of Butler's theory, the novel's ethics "rests upon an apprehension of the precariousness of life, one that begins with the precarious life of the Other" (2004, xvii-xviii). It allows one to respect the other's agency, and to listen without looking down. Its success lies in the fact that it manages to eschew the voyeuristic potential that is often inherent in representations of homelessness. The ethical maxim of the novel is for these precarious faces "to be admitted into public view" before their destruction happens; the reward will be that "some keener sense of the value of life, all life [can] take hold" (Butler 2004, xviii). According to Berger's novel, capitalism's ethics work differently: the inexorable move of capital only remembers a forgotten space when a price tag can be put on it. Thus made visible, the inhabitants are blamed for their very existence, rather than the system which failed them in the first place: the vindictive system, teasing the inhabitants with the words "[s]o you are asking for it – are you?" (223),[19] punishes the precarious for who they are under the pretence of punishing their acts of resistance.

4 New Ways of Seeing – New Voices?

The parallaxes outlined above cannot be defused easily. By way of conclusion, it is therefore helpful to consider the novel's ending, which implies the need for the

---

19 "This is the most common phrase which precedes torture, rape or killing. That much I know. On this occasion it announced the last clumsy phase of an ill-organised operation for the flushing out of illegal squatters from land which had been bought for investment" (223).

homeless to find a voice. As the bulldozer – ironically a "Liebherr" (188) – is levelling the site of "the coat", King imagines that its inhabitants are transformed into dogs; different breeds, but dogs all the same. Their coughs emanating from the tear gas attack on "the coat" are transformed into barks, by which they assert their presence:[20]

> A bark is a voice which breaks out of a bottle saying: I'm here. The bottle is silence. The silence broken, the bark announces, I'm here.
> Joachim's cough barked again. Alfonso barked. The bark of another one prods your ears, presses on your tongue, and forces the jaw to open in reply: I'm here! Saul barked, throwing out the diabolic gas he'd swallowed. Malak barked, twisting the ring on her finger. They did not know where to go. They were like me. Liberto barked. They were like me.
> After a while you forget you're barking, and when this happens you hear the others, you hear the chorus of barks and, although not one of them has changed and each is distinct, so distinct that it can break a heart, the barking is saying something different now, it's saying, We're here! and this *We're here* blows on an almost dead memory [...]. (227)

With the knowledge that each of them is distinct – the precariat is not a unified class – the bark asserts their presence and makes them heard. It becomes a first step in transforming an accusation into active resistance, and regaining agency. As Nick Couldry writes: "Articulating voice – as an inescapable aspect of human experience – challenges the neoliberal logic that runs together economic, social, political and cultural domains, and describes them exclusively as manifestations of market processes" (2010, 13). In *Ways of Seeing*, Berger claimed that "[a] people or a class which is cut off from its own past is far less free to choose and to act as a people or class than one that has been able to situate itself in history" (1972, 33). If one continues this line of thought, then in his novel, the impossibility of recovering the past prevents this kind of class consciousness. In the end, King realizes that everyone's transformation into a dog was just an illusion and that he has fled from the devastated settlement alone. The dog-narrator, in the end, is alone like everyone else, who are all dying isolated, individual deaths. All voice is fiction, Berger seems to imply, but even the strategic essentialism of everyone pretending that they are dogs might help to enact collective action: King is a solitary figure, but one which potentially projects hope, in that he was the first to find his voice – and the others might yet follow suit. The "revocable tolerance" (Foster 2009, 209) of the precarious condition therefore operates both

---

20 The importance of the barking scene is prefigured by the quote from the poem "La casada infiel" by Federico García Lorca which introduces the novel: "y un horizonte de perros ladra muy lejos del río", or: "and a horizon of dogs barked very far from the river". For the English translation, see García Lorca (2005, 295).

ways: it is not merely that those forcing the other into a precarious condition can revoke it, but also the other way round. When they find a voice, Berger suggests, the precarious can revoke their willingness to endure the situation. This might still be an illusion, since King has been barking alone, but it is a potential beginning for change.

King's utopian hope lies in a reconstitution of sense and of voice. It is hoped that readers, when faced with the precarious condition, will decipher the underlying reality and, for all their differences, act in unity. There is, without a renewed collective voice, as Berger asserts, no way to recover the political consciousness or class solidarity that distinguished the former proletariat from today's precarious existences. Without explicitly saying so in the novel, Berger calls for a (Marxist) awareness in order to make sense of the present situation, and postulates that a first step towards establishing this new kind of solidarity is to change the way readers see and interact with those dehumanized by the system.

Works Cited

Barthes, Roland. "The Death of the Author." *Image – Music – Text: Essays*. Ed. & trans. Stephen Heath. New York: Noonday Press, 1988. 142–148.

Berger, John. "Why Look at Animals?" *Why Look at Animals?* London: Penguin, 2009 [1977]. 12–38.

——. *King: A Street Story*. London: Bloomsbury, 1999.

——. *Ways of Seeing: Based on the BBC Television Series with John Berger*. 28th reprint ed. London: Penguin, 1972.

Betensky, Carolyn. "Princes as Paupers: Pleasure and the Imagination of Powerlessness." *Cultural Critique* 56 (2004): 129–157.

Butler, Judith. *Precarious Life: The Powers of Mourning and Violence*. London: Verso, 2004.

Couldry, Nick. *Why Voice Matters: Culture and Politics after Neoliberalism*. London: Sage, 2010.

Foster, Hal. "Towards a Grammar of Emergency." *New Left Review* 68 (2011): 105–118.

——. "Precarious: Hal Foster on the Art of the Decade." *Artforum* 48.4 (December 2009): 206–209, 260.

García Lorca, Federico. "The Faithless Wife." *The Selected Poems of Federico García Lorca*. New York: New Directions, 2005. 75–78.

Jameson, Fredric. "First Impressions." *London Review of Books* 28.17 (2006). http://www.lrb.co.uk/v28/n17/fredric-jameson/first-impressions (15 October 2013).

Korte, Barbara. "Can the Indigent Speak? Poverty Studies, the Postcolonial and Global Appeal of *Q&A* and *The White Tiger*." *Connotations* 20.2/3 (2010): 293–317.

Koval, Ramona. "A Dog's Life: Interview with John Berger." *Headspace: Animals. Call of the Wild* 18 (2000): n. pag. http://www.abc.net.au/arts/headspace/rn/booksw/dogs/default.htm (15 October 2013).

Kumar, Krishan. "Versions of the Pastoral: Poverty and the Poor in English Fiction from the 1840s to the 1950s." *Journal of Historical Sociology* 8.1 (1995): 1–35.
"With a Bark Not a Whimper." *Telegraph.co.uk* 27 February 1999. http://www.telegraph.co.uk/culture/4716922/With-a-bark-not-a-whimper.html (15 October 2013).
Žižek, Slavoj. *The Parallax View.* Cambridge, MA: MIT Press, 2006.
——. "The Parallax View." *New Left Review* 25 (2004): 121–134.
——. "Parallax." *London Review of Books* 25.22 (2003): 24. http://www.lrb.co.uk/v25/n22/slavoj-zizek/parallax (15 October 2013).

Barbara Korte
Poverty on the Market: Precarious Lives in Popular Fiction

1 Poverty and the Popular

The *Oxford English Dictionary* gives the following definitions for 'poverty', 'popular' and 'popular culture':

poverty:
Destitution[:] The condition of having little or no wealth or few material possessions; indigence, destitution. (*OED* 2013a, Def. I.1.a)

popular:
Of a belief, attitude, etc.: prevalent or current among the general public; generally accepted, commonly known. (*OED* 2013b, Def. A.1.)
Of, relating to, deriving from, or consisting of ordinary people or the people as a whole; generated by the general public; democratic. (*OED* 2013b, Def. 3.a.)
Of cultural activities or products[:] Intended for or suited to the understanding or taste of ordinary people, esp. as opposed to specialists in a field; *spec.* (of literature, etc.) intended for and directed at a general readership. (*OED* 2013b, Def. 4.a.)
Liked or admired by many people, or by a particular person or group. (*OED* 2013b, Def. 7.a.)
Designating forms of art, music, or culture with general appeal; intended primarily to entertain, please, or amuse. (*OED* 2013b, Def. 7.b.)

popular culture: The cultural traditions of the ordinary people of a particular community; (now) esp. pop culture[:] culture based on popular taste rather than that of an educated elite, usually commercialized and made widely available by the mass media. (*OED* 2013c)

These definitions at first sight suggest that poverty and the popular make strange bedfellows. Of course, political organizations and charities have an interest in making poverty widely known to the general public. But while the popular is that which is liked by many people, being poor is rarely desirable. The popular suggests community, but poverty is widely associated with social exclusion. An articulation of poverty with the popular seems even more awkward and vexed when culture comes into play. Although the term 'popular culture' retains a meaning that defines it as a culture produced by the people, and although there is a tradition in which 'ordinary people' have spoken about poverty, popular culture today is most frequently understood as produced by a cultural industry that aims to entertain its consumers and to succeed on the market. As Ken Gelder notes for popular literature:

188 —— Barbara Korte

> Two key words for understanding popular fiction are *industry* and *entertainment* [...]. Literary fiction is ambivalent at best about its industrial connections and likes to see itself as something more than 'just entertainment', but popular fiction generally speaking has no such reservations [...]. It draws together the industrial and entertainment – the latter being a particular form of culture, of cultural production – so much so that they can often be indistinguishable. (2004, 1)

When such definitions are thought together with poverty – or other forms of human misery – ethics once more wags its finger: Should depictions of poverty be allowed to entertain audiences? And should poverty be marketable and actually sell?

But there are also other ways of seeing the relationship between popular culture and poverty: Popular culture is perceived as having a special proximity to its audiences (Glover and McCracken 2012, 4) and addresses these audiences' desires and anxieties more immediately than a more high-brow cultural production would. In this light, popular representations may therefore also have a greater immediate relevance for and impact on their recipients' understanding of poverty – whether negatively, by confirming stereotypes, or positively, by affecting a change in the recipients' imagination of poverty. Because of the large numbers of people it may potentially reach, and which it actually "values" (Gelder 2004, 20), popular-cultural production also possesses a special potential to perform what Jane Tompkins has referred to as "cultural work",[1] and it can thus "be thought of as a significant arena for cultural commentary that is far from being automatically crude, debased and anti-rational. Instead, it can be at the heart of public debate" (Luckhurst 2012, 74). This chapter will pursue these tensions and ambivalences for recent popular-cultural production in the United Kingdom, first in a more general sketch, and then with special attention to examples of genre fiction.

---

1 In her discussion of American nineteenth-century popular novels such as *Uncle Tom's Cabin*, Tompkins conceives these novels "as doing a certain kind of cultural work within a specific historical situation [...]. I see their plots and characters as providing society with a means of thinking about itself, defining certain aspects of a social reality which the authors and their readers shared, dramatizing its conflicts, and recommending solutions" (1985, 200). Popular fiction therefore performs cultural work precisely because it "connects with the beliefs and attitudes of large masses of readers so as to impress or move them deeply" (Tompkins 1985, xiv).

2 Articulations of Poverty and the Popular on Contemporary Cultural Markets

There is ample evidence that poverty – and more generally social inequality and class difference – are part of today's popular-cultural production, and that it does sell, even in the most obvious corners of 'entertainment'. *Billy Elliot* (2000), for instance, the internationally successful film whose rags-to-riches story is set at the time of the 1970s Miners' Strike and the impoverishment to which it gave rise, has been transformed into a musical that has attracted large audiences in London's Theatreland since 2005. Television, as a fast-lived cultural market where the pressure to succeed commercially is most urgent, is likewise a home for popular productions about poverty. The sitcom *Little Britain* (BBC Three 2003–2004 and BBC One 2005), which exposes a white underclass and has been identified by Owen Jones as a prime example of a new class contempt for 'chavs' (2011, 1), has enjoyed wide popularity not only in Britain. Television 'reality shows' that permit celebrities to 'experience' homelessness (such as BBC One's *Famous, Rich and Homeless*, 2009), or rich people to display their charity (such as *The Secret Millionaire*, Channel 4, 2006–2012) have likewise attracted – and entertained – large numbers of viewers.[2] Early in 2014 the Channel 4 documentary series *Benefits Street* depicted the life of the residents of one of the UK's most benefit-dependent streets in Birmingham, raising wide attention and controversial reactions. A less sensational example is *Call the Midwife*, the BBC One adaptation of Jennifer Worth's memoirs about her 1950s life as a midwife in London's poor East End after the Second World War.[3] The series attracted eight million viewers with its first episode in January 2012 in a Sunday night slot preferred for heritage productions and struck a reviewer as having "the right balance [...] between social document and rose-tinted nostalgia", with "just enough grit to balance out the sugar" (Raeside 2012). Its blend of poverty with resilience, humour and period atmosphere was so successful that a second series was soon in the making. It is also significant that BBC One's webpage for its updated version of the Robin Hood mythology as adventurous family entertainment (*Robin Hood*, 2006–2008) offers a clip under the caption "What's Best for the Poor?". It is taken from the series' first episode, "Will You Tolerate This?", and described as a "[d]ramatic reconstruction of a discussion on answers to poverty in medie-

---

2 On such programmes, see Helen Hester's chapter on 'poverty porn' in the present volume.
3 Significantly, the expensive adaptation was only commissioned after Worth's memoirs had proved bestselling on the book market.

val Britain" in which "Robin Hood suggests the use of charity to feed the poor which would lead to improved spending power by the poor, therefore increasing markets. Whilst the Sheriff of Nottingham thinks the best answer is to increase hunger amongst the poor, increasing the motivation to work" ("Robin Hood"). That the presence of poverty in popular culture is noted and reflected not only by critics but also the 'general audience' is attested by a user-based source in the internet: the database "TV Tropes" lists various categories into which viewers have divided television representations of poverty; they range from "Barefoot Poverty" and "Homeless Hero" to "Just Like Robin Hood", "Rags to Royalty", "Riches To Rags" and "Slumming It" ("Poverty Tropes" 2013).

A look at the highly commercialized and competitive UK book market in the early twenty-first century[4] similarly yields a wide selection of poverty-themed publications,[5] and many can be characterized as popular in so far as they explicitly target the general reader and are written accessibly and sometimes even in straightforwardly appealing ways. Thus the life-writing segment not only offers the reader 'misery memoirs' which, as in the case of Peter Roche's bestselling *Unloved* (2007), display drastic social exclusion and neglect before they suggest that misery can be overcome,[6] but also books that convey such a message more cheerily. For instance, *A Street Cat Named Bob: How One Man and His Cat Found Hope on the Streets* by James Bowen, a busker and former heroin addict, climbed bestseller lists in 2012 and delighted readers with both its optimism and its portrayal of the human narrator's feline companion. A reader's comment in the on-line book club Goodreads[7] describes *Street Cat* as "a wonderful feel good *true* story" that "sure pulled at my heart strings and made me realise everybody should experience the love of a pet at least once in their lives" ("Dem's Review", 4 February 2013). In the fiction segment, J. K. Rowling has a less comforting story to tell in *The Casual Vacancy* (2012). Rowling's status as a 'celebrity author' (English and Frow 2006, 41) guaranteed that her novel about class conflict and social precarity in an English town facing the 'problem' of a council estate would get

---

4 On the dramatic commercialization of the British literary marketplace since the mid-1990s, see Squires, who notes "hundreds of thousands of new titles every year jostling for places on bookshop shelves and in the bestseller lists". She concludes that "[t]he reversal of the traditional book economy [...] towards a short-term, mass-market logic has been profound" (2007, 26). Also see Todd on "the biggest change in the book trade since the end of World War II" (2006, 20).
5 For a survey of this market, see Korte and Zipp (2014), where some of the examples mentioned in this chapter are also treated in more detail.
6 On Roche, see the readings offered by Korte (2012) and by Regard (2012).
7 On Goodreads.com, people can rate and review the books they have read. More than 4,000 books carry the tag "poverty".

wide attention (and be profitable for the author and her publisher).[8] The milieu of people living on the margins of society is depicted in drastic detail and with an almost clichéd familiarity:

> boarded windows daubed with obscenities; smoking teenagers loitering in the perennially defaced bus shelters, satellite dishes everywhere, turned to the skies like the denuded ovules of grim metal flowers. [Howard] often asked rhetorically why they could not have organized and made the place over – what was stopping the residents from pooling their meagre resources and buying a lawnmower between the lot of them? But it never happened: the Fields waited for the councils, District and Parish, to clean, to repair, to maintain; to give and give and give again. [...] So Howard was forced to draw the conclusion that they were choosing, of their own free will, to live the way they lived, and that the estate's air of slightly threatening degradation was nothing more than a physical manifestation of ignorance and indolence. (Rowling 2012, 60 – 61)

While this passage is focalized through the perception of a bigoted middle-class shop owner whose class prejudice is clearly meant to be satirized, the apparently hopeless destitution of the estate is equally familiar when perceived by a social worker:

> A pile of refuse was heaped against the front wall: carrier bags bulging with filth, jumbled together with old clothes and unbagged, soiled nappies. Bits of the rubbish had tumbled or been scattered over the scrubby patch of lawn, but the bulk of it remained piled beneath one of the two downstairs windows. A bald old tyre sat in the middle of the lawn; it had been shifted some time recently, because a foot away there was a flattened yellowish-brown circle of dead grass. After ringing the doorbell, Kay noticed a used condom glistening in the grass beside her feet, like the gossamer cocoon of some huge grub. (Rowling 2012, 65)

Rowling's novel is meant to critique a middle class to whom council estates and their inhabitants are a burdensome social other, and it attempts to counter such tunnel vision with a multi-perspectival narrative that also gives room to more socially responsible positions and the view of characters who live on the estate themselves. However, Rowling's novel at the same time reproduces stereotypical ideas and images with which middle-class readers – i.e. the majority of readers (Head 2006, 243) – may associate the poor, and it cannot fully avoid the pitfall that even a well-intentioned portrayal may expose the poor to a voyeuristic gaze.

---

8 Arguably, *The Casual Vacancy* was intended by its author as a 'literary' novel; it falls under 'popular' fiction, however, when this is thought of as "those books that everyone reads, usually imagined as a league table of bestsellers whose aggregate figures dramatically illustrate an impressive ability to reach across wide social and cultural divisions with remarkable commercial success" (Glover and McCracken 2012, 1).

Most of the examples I have mentioned so far do not deserve to be labelled as 'poverty porn' like some of the television programmes discussed in Helen Hester's contribution, but they may invite their better-situated readers to go armchair slumming. Indeed, encouraging such 'slumming' was a major issue in the controversial reception of Danny Boyle's Oscar-winning *Slumdog Millionaire*,[9] especially after the film had become a blockbuster. Associations of poverty portrayals with slumming have not been restricted to decidedly popular cultural productions, but because such productions are meant to be particularly accessible and appealing, they are also particularly susceptible to criticism that they encourage a socially disengaged gaze and gratify their recipients' voyeuristic impulses. Against this, one might claim, as Helen Hester does for 'poverty porn' television, that the popular representation of poverty, because it is calculated to be accessible, may also have a special potential to "prick the consciences" of middle-class audiences. In this vein, a recent contribution to development studies (Lewis, Rodgers and Woolcock 2013) acknowledges the power of popular cinema to promote the understanding of development issues. Such use of popular forms to spread knowledge and raise awareness of poverty is, of course, not new. It was common in the nineteenth century, when popular culture in the modern sense emerged.[10] Charles Dickens, who was and saw himself as a popular writer,[11] is an obvious case in point. His bourgeois readers' philanthropic sentiment was to be roused and shaped not only in novels such as *Oliver Twist*, where they could find their fictional avatars in charitable characters such as Mr Brownlow and the Maylies, or *Bleak House* with its scathing critique of a 'telescopic' philanthropy directed away from one's own society. Dickens pursued the same goals with his journalism and notably his magazine *Household Words* (1850–1859). This publication, intended as a "comrade and friend" to its readers, as Dickens writes in his "Preliminary Word" (1850a, 1), turned to poverty frequently, not least in prominent articles written by Dickens himself[12] or his trusted staff writers, one of whom was George Sala. These articles often addressed their readers directly, and here the reporter-narrators served as avatars for the middle-class readers, as in Sala's "The Key of the Street" (1851), where the reporter describes how he has lost the key to his house and is therefore obliged to find a place to sleep in the street or in a shelter, thus encountering the

---

9 For a summary of this criticism, see Banaji (2010).
10 See also the contributions by Frenk, Rostek and Regard in the present volume.
11 Dickens's relationship to the popular and mass culture is discussed by John (2010) and Rodensky (2009).
12 For instance, Dickens's "A Walk in the Workhouse" (1850b).

people who have to do so habitually.[13] Sala's article begins with an open reference to their precarity, and then asks the reader to join the reporter on his nightly adventure into unknown territory:

> It is commonly asserted, and as commonly believed, that there are seventy thousand persons in London who get up every morning without the slightest knowledge as to where they shall lay their heads at night. However the number may be over or understated, it is very certain that a vast quantity of people are daily in the above-mentioned uncertainty regarding sleeping accommodation [...]. Come with me, luxuriant tenant of heavy-draped four-poster – basker on feather-bed, and nestler in lawn sheets. (1851, 565–566)

What this brief excursus into nineteenth-century journalism suggests, just like Rowling's *The Casual Vacancy*, is the importance of how texts about poverty, and especially popular texts, configure subject positions from which their audiences can engage – cognitively, emotionally and attitudinally – with the poor people and the poverty about which they read.[14] In what follows, this chapter will explore different forms of such configuration for 'popular fiction' in its narrow sense.

3 Poverty in Popular Genre Fiction

Demarcations between 'literary' and 'popular' fiction have become blurred as the literary market becomes increasingly profit-orientated. But what the contemporary book market most clearly understands and treats as popular fiction is genre fiction, i. e. fiction "primarily based upon a limited number of forms or genres of narrative pleasure, such as suspense, romantic complications, bodily horror or futuristic speculation" (Glover and McCracken 2012, 2). To Ken Gelder, genre is a crucial factor in the logic of popular fiction:

> Whereas genre is less overtly important to literary fiction, the field of popular fiction simply cannot live without it, both culturally *and* industrially [...]. After all, popular fiction is not just a matter of texts-in-themselves, but of an entire apparatus of production, distribution

---

13 As Blake notes: "By inverting the class status of the writer from middle class urban spectator to that of homeless beggar, Sala refashioned himself as one of the first social investigators of the nineteenth century" (2009, 24).

14 On the importance of this positioning of readers, see Carolyn Betensky's contribution to this volume, and her *Feeling for the Poor*, which discusses an ethically problematic response to nineteenth-century social-problem novels: "If reading about social problems contributes to the idea that caring about suffering others is valuable in itself [...] then reading is an ethically ambiguous activity" (2010, 189).

(including promotion and advertising) and consumption – or what I call, more broadly, processing. (2004, 1)

However, popular fiction encompasses different genres, and it therefore offers various ways of configuring (middle-class) readers' positions and reactions towards poverty that may encourage both stereotypical perception and defamiliarizing or even subversive ways of seeing.

An ideologically conservative and formulaic approach to poverty characterizes the – often conflated – genres of popular historical romance and family saga, which both address a female readership. The rags-to-riches trope seems almost an inevitable component of the genre recipe. Catherine Cookson used to be the queen of the genre, and her novels are still well-represented in British libraries as well as on the book market, but she also has best-selling successors like Penny Vincenzi. In Vincenzi's novel *No Angel* (2000), as in many other popular narratives set in the nineteenth and early twentieth centuries, poverty is part of the general period flavour. More intriguingly, *No Angel* develops its rags-to-riches theme in the household of a publishing firm during the years before the First World War and thus allows its author to let characters discuss literature, including Charles Dickens. The working-class lover of one of the firm's owners characterizes *Oliver Twist* class-consciously as "some nonsense about a little chap being sent to the workhouse and working as a pickpocket before being reunited happily with his high-born family", and proclaims that this "would never happen, not in real life" (59).[15] Such meta-comments might lead one to expect that Vincenzi's approach to social inequality and poverty might strive to come closer to 'real life'. However, her indebtedness to genre conventions appears to perpetuate the pattern of *Oliver Twist* rather than depart from it.

The novel's child character is a girl, Barty Miller, who originates from a low-born family from Lambeth, one of London's traditionally poor quarters.[16] Help for the girl comes from the novel's high-born protagonist, Lady Celia, who has married into the bourgeois publishing dynasty of the Lyttons and who raises Barty from her humble life to become a member of her household. In contrast to her highly conservative mother,[17] Lady Celia is not afraid of transgressing

---

15 All page references for Vincenzi refer to the 2006 edition of the novel.

16 Charles Chaplin grew up here and was inspired for his later portrayal of the Tramp in films that are an iconic instance of a popular treatment of poor life; see Korte (2010).

17 Lady Celia's mother is at first full of prejudice against the labouring classes and the poor: "Barty's academic success baffled Lady Beckenham, who regarded the lower classes as intrinsically unintelligent. Fascinated by, as well as disapproving of what she called Celia's ex-

class barriers, as her own marriage already indicates, and Vincenzi characterizes her explicitly as a modern woman interested in social reform:

> She had read the writings of such people as Sydney and Beatrice Webb, George Bernard Shaw and H.G. Wells and found that what they had to say about social injustice made absolute sense to her. She and Oliver had agreed that he would vote for the Labour Party in the next election, and spent long evenings in the small downstairs sitting room at Cheyne Walk discussing the rise of socialism, the increasing role that the state should play in improving the lot of ordinary people, and how to combat the poverty which underpinned the wealth of the upper and middle classes. It was for Celia, at least, largely an emotional reaction; part of her stormy move away from her roots, a discovery of yet another new world which appealed to her idealistic heart. (21)

But Celia is not only an idealist; in order to become socially engaged, she joins the Fabian Women's Group, and it is as a member of this group that she befriends Barty's mother Sylvia, whose living conditions she is meant to study for a report intended to document "exactly how poverty damages people, damages them permanently" (46). Since women like Sylvia need not only political but material support, Celia gives Sylvia what she requires for her children and takes Barty into her own luxurious home. The beautiful and intelligent girl (in an act of social selection that contradicts her progressive ideals, Lady Celia has picked the most endowed from Sylvia's offspring) will thus receive a good education and a better chance in life.

The novel makes it clear that Sylvia and Barty are deserving objects of Lady Celia's philanthropy, being 'innocently' poor, undemanding and absolutely respectable. Sylvia's children are healthy, clean and sent to school. Barty is willing to make the best of the opportunities she is given in the Lyttons' home, but she also feels painfully estranged from the family she has left behind in Lambeth and is aware of the fact that she will not be able to return to them: "she wasn't like them, not any of them any more" (578). Barty's act of class-passing is one-way and cannot be reversed, but it also cannot be complete since she is widely perceived as a social trespasser. Barty thus begins to reject the gratitude which everybody expects her to show: "the worst thing of all was being told all the time, over and over again, how grateful she should be and how lucky she was. Every one said that: not just her mother, who was bound to, of course, but Nanny and Lettie and Truman [i.e. servants in the Lytton household] and every now and again, even Aunt Celia" (111). All in all, the novel presents Barty's advancement as a clear exception.

─────────

periment, she had expressed huge surprise at Barty being able to learn her letters or remember the simplest thing" (178).

It is Barty with whom readers of *No Angel* are most of all invited to feel, and it is through her perception that they are also meant to develop compassion for Barty's mother, who dies early from an untreated illness. When Barty revisits her late mother's modest home, the focalization lets the reader share Barty's outrage against an unfair society still strictly divided between rich and poor:

> She stood there, looking round the room: so small, so dark, so shabby, yet imprinted with her mother's presence, with the small defiant touches of charm and prettiness which she had brought to it [...]. And then the sadder things, the shabby coat, hanging on a hook behind the door and Sylvia's black hat, the worn-out boots, the old cradle, which again, Celia had given her, used now to store clothes in – all neatly folded and clean. The threadbare curtains, the unravelled doormat. Barty thought briefly, angrily of the rooms in Cheyne Walk, refurbished year after year, rugs, curtains, covers, all changed in the name of fashion: it was all so unfair. So dreadfully, dreadfully unfair. She blinked hard, brushed away the tears. (638–639)

Barty is no longer a lower-class character when she has these thoughts. Upper-class philanthropy has put her into a social position between her original family and her adopted one, and this turns her into the only significant character through whom middle-class readers of Vincenzi's novel are likely to find their own social status and attitudes configured. Thanks to her advancement, Barty is neither poor nor rich; she stands between social extremes like the majority of the novel's readers, and this is important for the way in which the novel projects possibilities for social change and indicates who the agents of this change might be. If Barty is read as the novel's avatar for middle-class readers, then her position is marked as one from which nothing can be effectively done socially to combat inequality and poverty. The girl is perceptive to social injustice, and the novel's readers can feel with her for her estranged family and the injustice they still experience, but Barty's position is quite obviously not one of influence. In the world of *No Angel*, the upper classes and their philanthropy are presented as the sole agency to effect any significant change in the situation of the poor.[18] Without Lady Celia's intervention, Barty would never have become a young woman with the prospect of university education. The poor need the rich, the novel spells out – they can neither help themselves, nor is there a middle class that would intervene in a significant way. This configuration may be seen to befit a piece of historical fiction that appears to have no immediate bearing on the readers' own social behaviour. However, since this fiction is read today, it might help to perpetuate a historical attitude towards the poor in the

---

18 This pattern is repeated when one of Barty's brothers returns disabled from the First World War and does not receive efficient help until Lady Celia's mother intervenes.

social imaginary. With the middle classes hardly playing a role in the action, *No Angel* might even suggest that poverty *only* concerns the poor (existentially) and the rich (philanthropically) and thus encourage a disengaged positioning of the middle-class reader which makes it possible to enjoy the novel as a historical 'romance' remote from her own immediate reality.

Strikingly, one can find a similar constellation in instances of contemporary crime fiction. Even where crime fiction is indebted to social realism, it is not exempt from perpetuating social tropes, such as the idea that poverty and crime go hand in hand and that lower- or 'under'class milieus are prone to generating crime. It seems almost ironic that this notion is confirmed in a piece of crime fiction that was precisely meant to counter stereotypes and do justice to the character of an underprivileged boy from a London council estate. Elizabeth George, the internationally bestselling crime writer, wrote *What Came Before He Shot Her* (2007) as a supplement to her successful and class-themed Inspector Lynley series (from 1989).[19] The novel is an attempt by its author to write a fully fledged social novel in order to provide the background story to the 'regular' Lynley novel in which Lynley's pregnant wife is shot. *What Came Before He Shot Her* tries to explain this crime, and it does so in the manner of council-estate fiction,[20] being set in a world which many middle-class readers will not know from their own experience and even shun because it is assumed to be dangerous.[21] Indeed, Elizabeth George constructs her reader as other to her characters' world, doing little to undermine familiar notions of council estates.

---

19 George is an American writer, but she makes her money with crime fiction about Britain, and notably with crime novels in a specifically British tradition that emphasizes the class theme. An ongoing theme in the Lynley series is the contrast between the aristocratic Lynley and his working-class assistant Barbara Havers. Scaggs notes George's affinity to the British whodunnit tradition and writes about her investigator figure: "Without a trace of irony, in addition to being a Detective Inspector, Thomas Lynley is also the 8th Earl of Asherton, and in many ways can be viewed as an updated version of Sayers's Lord Peter Wimsey" (2005, 53).

20 Susanne Cuevas defines "council estate novels" as a distinct genre of fictions which "focus on characters whose destinies are shaped by the social milieu of the council estate and are set in and around the streets of council estates" (2008, 385). In her acknowledgements, George thanks Courttia Newland, a British fellow writer reputed for his novels about black urban communities, because his "introduction to Ladbroke Grove, West Kilburn, North Kensington and the housing estates therein proved invaluable to [her] work" (George 2007, 644).

21 Precisely this is emphasized and challenged right at the beginning of a 'typical' piece of estate fiction, Alex Wheatle's *The Dirty South* (2008). The first-person narrator of this novel (who is in prison) provocatively addresses his reader as a social (and racial) other – and as an other with inadequate prejudices about London's allegedly dangerous parts: "Before all you know-it-all pussies start thinking that this is the story of some young black guy who didn't know his paps and lived in a Brixton ghetto – you're wrong. Yeah, I lived in Brixton, or Bricky as we call it. But

Her novel is focused on Joel, a mixed-race, twelve-year-old boy who is arrested for killing Lynley's wife – although he has only been used as a scapegoat by gangsters spawned by the desolate environment of the North Kensington estate to which he and his siblings are brought at the novel's beginning. Their family is dysfunctional, and the children are dropped off by their grandmother, who intends to return to the Caribbean with her lover, at their aunt's home on the estate. This aunt has left poverty behind, owning a small terraced house and a car. She is working in a Charity Shop until she can make enough money with her medical massage business. This job gives rise to occasions for Kendra to muse about poverty and charity, including a dubious charity that is mingled with obvious class contempt:

> She went on ironing. She laid a pair of black trousers on the ironing board and examined them top to bottom. She shook her head and held them up for Joel to see. A greasy stain dripped down the front of them, elongated into the shape of Italy. She tossed them to the floor, saying, 'Why do people think *poor* equals *desperate* when what it really means is wanting something to make you *forget* you're poor, not something to remind you you're poor every time you put it on?' She went back to the pile of clothes and snatched up a shirt. (619 – 620)[22]

Kendra is willing to care for Joel and his siblings, but she is eventually overwhelmed by her unexpected responsibility. In contrast to the historical scenario of Vincenzi's *No Angel*, George's contemporary setting (like that of Rowling's novel) includes social services that should provide assistance. However, their powers are shown to be too limited to give the support that Joel's family actually needs, and the same inefficiency is diagnosed for voluntary aid: Ivan, a middle-class man, organizes art workshops for the estate's children but completely underestimates the power of gangs. When Joel gets into trouble with a gang member who terrorizes his family, he therefore knows that it is useless to turn to Ivan for help, and since he does not trust the police, he turns to a more powerful gangster, who is behind the killing of Inspector Lynley's wife.

---

in a nice street. Leander Road, just behind Tulse Hill estate. Bricky does have decent streets but with all that fuckery stereotyping and media shit, you well-booted living in Berkshire and wherever wouldn't know that... Actors, bankers, librarians, secretaries, doctors all live in my road. Even gay people or chi chi men as we call them on the road. So I ain't the product of a grimy sink ghetto. Nor the product of a single mother family... Sure, Bricky does have its ghettos. Tulse Hill estate where a trailer load of eastern European people and white trash families live" (Wheatle 2009 [2008], 1–2).

22 Page numbers for the novel refer to the 2007 paperback.

George draws the environment with which Joel has to cope as too negative to give the boy a chance. He is intelligent, responsible and good at school, but once he gets into the estate's criminalized milieu, his fate seems predetermined, as the novel's very first sentence implies with naturalist certitude: "Joel Campbell, eleven years old at the time, began his descent towards murder with a bus ride" (1). Just as Vincenzi employs the rags-to-riches trope, George falls back on a poverty-generates-crime trope which Dickens already draws on in *Oliver Twist*. Indeed, Dickens is referred to in the novel's second paragraph when the narrator describes Joel's bus journey through North Kensington, where a prison "loom[s] over all of this like something designed by Dickens" (1). This reference to Dickens constructs a link between impoverished life and crime, but it also evokes the image of a child thrown innocently into misery – and in this case, without effective help from the middle classes that Oliver Twist enjoys from Mr. Brownlow and the Maylies. Indeed, George's crime novel conspicuously resembles Vincenzi's historical fiction in the notable absence of a significant role in which a middle-class reader could detect an avatar for her- or himself. Those characters in George's novel who try to assist Joel's family are either social workers, a contained professional group obliged to provide help, or characters who are in marginalized positions themselves. For instance, the novel seems to imply that Ivan's status as a gay man might motivate his engagement for underprivileged children. A tendentially distanced reader position is also encouraged by the fact that the novel presents its estate in familiar images and thus risks confirming stereotypes. *What Came Before He Shot Her* may be the effort of a writer to raise the social awareness of her regular readers, but what readers are made 'aware' of is, arguably, a reiteration of what they already know. Like Vincenzi's novel, George's tie-in to estate fiction seems to support an assessment that popular genre fiction tends to work with formulas and clichés. But popular fiction need not be associated with formula and can actually have quite a subversive impulse.

Kaye Mitchell emphasizes that popular fiction "offers both the means of consolidating or reinforcing older, more conservative or traditional norms and identities in the face of these new challenges, *and* the means of negotiating new paradigms and helping us to cope with the particular anxieties – and opportunities – that they might occasion" (2012, 123). Crime fiction is a case in point because, in contrast to George's novel, it also complicates and destabilizes ideas about simple connections between underprivileged life and crime. In Minette Walters's *The Shape of Snakes* (2000), for example, the death of a black woman is revealed to be an act of hatred committed by white "trash" (Walters 2000, 347) who live in council housing in her street, while the crime is investigated and solved by a woman who lives on the 'better' side of the same street.

She finds the victim and is deeply touched and haunted by her fate. The crime in a seemingly 'typical' milieu is thus shown to concern the middle classes, and a middle-class character is employed as an intermediary between the action and the world of the middle-class reader.

An even more radical positioning of a middle-class audience, which provides a significant contrast to Elizabeth George's treatment of the council estate, is attempted in a science fiction film also set on a London estate.[23] However, *Attack the Block* (UK 2011, dir. Joe Cornish) plays with tropes of estate fiction – as well as sci-fi and blaxploitation films – in order to destabilize middle-class prejudice. The film at first seems to confirm all clichés connected with its setting: a gang of black and white boys mug a white woman, the nurse Sam, who returns to her flat in the estate, where she is clearly out of place. However, *Attack the Block* then sets out to undermine clichéd notions – and its own social-realist setting – when the estate is attacked by vicious aliens from outer space. This unlikely attack relativizes all dangers associated with council estates and poor criminalized youth, and these dangers are turned into virtues when the boys fight the aliens and save their block. Sam, the audience's avatar, learns to appreciate the boys' cleverness, wit and courage, and is lectured by them about today's telescopic philanthropy. When Sam proudly reveals to the boys that her boyfriend is currently in Ghana, "helping children" and "volunteer[ing] for the Red Cross", she does not get the admiring response she expects: "Oh, is it. Why can't he help the children of Britain? Not exotic enough, is it? Don't get no nice suntan." By that time, circumstances have already forced Sam to join the boys' fight against the aliens, and when, in a final ironic twist of the action, the police hold the boys – and not the aliens – responsible for the havoc on the estate, Sam takes their side. She has learned that estate boys also have values, and she has fought with them against a common enemy. More importantly, having encountered real aliens, Sam no longer considers the estate 'alien' territory, and she is no longer an alien there. With its last images, however, the film avoids too harmonious a note, showing two of the young heroes under arrest in a police van, while a protest song is heard in the background. *Attack the Block* is popular genre cinema with an obvious message. However, the film uses genre formulas only to undermine them, and its parody of genre conventions as well as middle-class prejudices is unashamedly entertaining. The film engages the spectator's sympathy not through an appeal for compassion or social outrage but,

---

23 In general, as alternative world fiction, science fiction and fantasy have a high potential to subvert readers' preconceptions. For a more detailed discussion of the film see my essay "In the Ghetto" (Korte forthcoming).

first of all, by presenting its young characters as likeable children with their own sense of community, pride and agency. It has the potential to make its audience see – like the middle-class character in the plot – that problems on an estate can be attacked, and that the middle classes can play an active role in this 'fight'.

As we have seen, different kinds of popular fiction perform different kinds of cultural work, and the way in which they manage to engage their mainly middle-class audiences seems to hinge essentially on how they configure positions for these audiences. Even if not all instances of popular fiction will succeed in actually reaching large audiences, they are calculated to be accessible to many people, and are therefore of special significance for the formation – or possible reconfiguration – of the public imagination of the social world, including images, valuations and social feelings. That popular fiction is designed for pleasure and entertainment, works with tropes and conventions, and is produced with an eye on the market, may give rise to ethical misgivings, especially when it portrays the social world in clichéd ways. But depending on how it positions its readers, and uses conventions creatively, genre fiction can unsettle and complicate reader dispositions just as well as some aesthetically more complex fiction. Poverty and the popular can then make quite effective bedfellows.

Works Cited

Attack the Block. Dir. Joe Cornish. Prod. Nira Park and James Wilson. UK Film Council and Film4 Productions, 2011.

Banaji, Shakuntala. "Seduced 'Outsiders' versus Sceptical 'Insiders'?: *Slumdog Millionaire* through Its Re/Viewers." *Participations: Journal of Audience and Reception Studies* 7.1 (May 2010): 1–30.

Betensky, Carolyn. *Feeling for the Poor: Bourgeois Compassion, Social Action, and the Victorian Novel.* Charlottesville: University of Virginia Press, 2010.

Blake, Peter. "Charles Dickens, George Augustus Sala and *Household Words.*" *Dickens Quarterly* 26.1 (2009): 24–41.

Cuevas, Susanne. "'Societies Within': Council Estates as Cultural Enclaves in Recent Urban Fictions." *Multi-Ethnic Britain 2000+.* Eds. Lars Eckstein, Barbara Korte, Eva Ulrike Pirker, and Christoph Reinfandt. Amsterdam: Rodopi, 2008. 383–398.

Dickens, Charles. "Preliminary Words." *Household Words* 1.1 (30 March 1850a): 1–2.

——. "A Walk in the Workhouse." *Household Words* 1.9 (25 May 1850b): 204–207.

English, James F., ed. *A Concise Companion to Contemporary British Fiction.* Oxford: Blackwell, 2006.

English, James F., and John Frow. "Literary Authorship and Celebrity Culture." *A Concise Companion to Contemporary British Fiction.* Ed. James F. English. Oxford: Blackwell, 2006. 39–57.

Gelder, Ken. *Popular Fiction: The Logics and Practices of a Literary Field.* London: Routledge, 2004.

George, Elizabeth. *What Came Before He Shot Her*. London: Hodder and Stoughton, 2007.

Glover, David, and Scott McCracken. "Introduction." *The Cambridge Companion to Popular Fiction*. Eds. David Glover and Scott McCracken. Cambridge: Cambridge University Press, 2012. 1–14.

Head, Dominic. "The Demise of Class Fiction." *A Concise Companion to Contemporary British Fiction*. Ed. James F. English. Oxford: Blackwell, 2006. 229–247.

John, Juliet. *Dickens and Mass Culture*. Oxford: Oxford University Press, 2010.

Jones, Owen. *Chavs: The Demonization of the Working Class*. London: Verso, 2011.

Korte, Barbara. "Dealing with Deprivation: Figurations of Poverty on the Contemporary British Book Market." *Anglia* 130.1 (2012): 75–94.

——. "New World Poor through an Old World Lens: Charlie Chaplin's Engagement with Poverty." *Poverty and the Culturalization of Class*. Eds. Michael Butter and Carsten Schinko. *Amerikastudien/American Studies* 55.1 (2010): 123–141.

——. "In the Ghetto: Inequality, Riots and Resistance in London-Based Science Fiction of the Twenty-First Century." *Resistance and the City: Challenging Urban Space*. Eds. Christoph Ehland and Pascal Fischer. Amsterdam: Rodopi, forthcoming.

Korte, Barbara, and Georg Zipp. *Poverty in Contemporary Literature: Themes and Figurations on the British Book Market*. Basingstoke: Palgrave Pivot, 2014.

Lewis, David, Dennis Rodgers, and Michael Woolcock. *Popular Representations of Development: Insights from Novels, Films, Television and Social Media*. London: Routledge, 2013.

Luckhurst, Roger. "The Public Sphere, Popular Culture and the True Meaning of the Zombie Apocalypse." *The Cambridge Companion to Popular Fiction*. Eds. David Glover and Scott McCracken. Cambridge: Cambridge University Press, 2012. 68–85.

Mitchell, Kaye. "Gender and Sexuality in Popular Fiction." *The Cambridge Companion to Popular Fiction*. Eds. David Glover and Scott McCracken. Cambridge: Cambridge University Press, 2012. 122–140.

OED. "Poverty, n." Def. I.1.a. *The Oxford English Dictionary*. Online Edition 2013a. http://www.oed.com/view/Entry/149126?redirectedFrom=poverty#eid (5 November 2013).

——. "Popular, adj." Def. 1, 3.a., 4.a., 7.a. and 7.b. *The Oxford English Dictionary*. Online Edition 2013b. http://www.oed.com/view/Entry/147908?redirectedFrom=popular#eid (5 November 2013).

——. "Popular culture, n." *The Oxford English Dictionary*. Online Edition 2013c. http://www.oed.com/view/Entry/147908?redirectedFrom=popular#eid (5 November 2013).

"Poverty Tropes." *TV Tropes*. 2013. http://tvtropes.org/pmwiki/pmwiki.php/Main/Poverty Tropes (July 30, 2013).

Raeside, Julia. "Is Call the Midwife Perfect Sunday Night Television?" *The Guardian* 26 January 2012. http://www.theguardian.com/tv-and-radio/tvandradioblog/2012/jan/26/call-the-midwife (16 October 2013).

Regard, Frédéric. "Purloining the Image of Trauma: Photography, Testimony and Self Articulation in Peter Roche's *Unloved*." *Trauma and Romance in Contemporary British Literature*. Eds. Jean-Michel Ganteau and Susana Onega. New York: Routledge, 2012. 107–123.

"Robin Hood". *BBC One*. http://www.bbc.co.uk/programmes/p0128wdc (11 April 2014).

Rodensky, Lisa. "Popular Dickens." *Victorian Literature and Culture* 37 (2009): 583–607.

Rowling, J. K. *The Casual Vacancy*. London: Little, Brown, 2012.

Sala, George. "The Key of the Street." *Household Words* 3.76 (6 September 1851): 565–572.

Scaggs, John. *Crime Fiction.* London: Routledge, 2005.

Squires, Claire. *Marketing Literature: The Making of Contemporary Writing in Britain.* Basingstoke: Palgrave Macmillan, 2007.

Todd, Richard. "Literary Fiction and the Book Trade." *A Concise Companion to Contemporary British Fiction.* Ed. James F. English. Oxford: Blackwell, 2006. 19–38.

Tompkins, Jane. *Sensational Designs: The Cultural Work of American Fiction 1790–1860.* New York and Oxford: Oxford University Press, 1985.

Vincenzi, Penny. *No Angel.* The Spoils of Time Trilogy 1. London: Headline Press, 2006 [2000].

Walters, Minette. *The Shape of Snakes.* London: Macmillan, 2000.

Wheatle, Alex. *The Dirty South.* London: Serpent's Tail, 2009 [2008].

Helen Hester
Weaponizing Prurience

1 Introduction: Positioning Poverty Porn

The term 'poverty porn', which has gained currency in contemporary journalistic discourse, embodies a nexus of ideas regarding media representations of poverty and precarious lives. This chapter questions why it is that poverty comes to be linked with ideas about pornography and the pornographic, and interrogates some of the underlying assumptions about how audiences engage with depictions of poverty in twenty-first century Britain.

The usage of the phrase 'poverty porn' is in fact fairly various. The earliest example I have located appears in a review of the film *Angela's Ashes* (1999) from a January 2000 edition of the e-newsletter *Need to Know*. The term itself is not defined, but is used to summarize the film's depiction of impoverished, "salt-of-the-earth Oirish folk" (Need to Know 2000), and is obviously intended to represent a negative value judgement: *Angela's Ashes* is positioned as a work of "ponderous vomit-packed poverty porn" (Need to Know 2000). More recently, 'poverty porn' has been used to describe other works of fiction, from Danny Boyle's award-winning 2008 film *Slumdog Millionaire* (Jones 2009; Miles 2009) to the "aesthetic of suffering" allegedly preferred and encouraged by the Caine Prize for African Writing (Habila 2013). Whilst this chapter will touch on some of the broader examples of so-called poverty porn, its focus will primarily be upon one particular manifestation of the phenomenon – a manifestation grounded not in the realms of literature and cinema, but in contemporary British reality television.

A number of journalists have used 'poverty porn' as a pejorative label for certain types of reality television, particularly those which seek to represent "abject whites".[1] This is the term that Chris Haylett uses to describe "a mass of people, in mass housing, people and places somehow falling out of the nation, losing the material wherewithal and symbolic dignity traditionally associated with their colour and their class" (2001, 352). Gerry Mooney and Lynn Hancock (2010) are amongst those who have noted that reality TV programming depicting the urban working classes is "increasingly being referred to as the 'poverty porn'

---

[1] The market research agency YouGov recently characterized poverty porn as "reality TV programmes that document the daily lives of the unemployed urban poor living on housing estates" (Dahlgreen 2013).

genre". They cite such examples as the British talk shows *The Jeremy Kyle Show* (ITV, 2005–present) and *Trisha Goddard* (ITV, 1998–2004, and Channel 5, 2005–2010), as well as reality series such as *Secret Millionaire* (Channel 4, 2006–present), in which a wealthy individual goes undercover within impoverished communities to witness 'how the other half lives', and to distribute money to those individuals and causes found to be sufficiently worthy.

The 'poverty porn' label has also been applied to documentary series focussing on the lives of people reliant upon government benefits, especially those who live on British council estates. The most recent example is the four-part observational documentary series *Skint* (2013) which, as the show's website puts it, offers "stories of people who are in long-term unemployment, have never worked, or are growing up without any expectation of working" ("Episode Guides" 2013). The series, which is set on the Westcliff estate near Scunthorpe's once-thriving steel works, has proved something of a hit for Channel 4,[2] but (as we shall see later in this essay) some journalistic commentary has problematized this popularity by suggesting that the show is "consumed as hardcore 'poverty porn'" (Machell 2013).

The forerunners of *Skint*, including BBC Scotland's *The Scheme* (2010–2011) and BBC Northern Ireland's *The Estate* (2012), generated similar kinds of coverage upon their broadcast. Typical plotlines revolve around single or underage motherhood, drug and alcohol addiction, and anti-social behaviour of various kinds, and they might, therefore, be seen as raising awareness of some really important issues. Despite this, however, the *Guardian* journalists Iain McDowall (2011) and Jane Graham (2009) have both separately discussed whether *The Scheme* should be viewed as poverty porn. Graham (2009), for example, focuses on the question of "whether the programme's portrayal of heroin addicts injecting, teenage criminals confessing and 16-year-old pregnant girls considering abortion should be lauded as an unusually honest reflection of modern life, or seen as exploitative 'poverty porn'".

Given that none of the issues touched upon here – addiction, crime, abortion and even underage pregnancy – involve the explicit representation of sex acts or overtly eroticized bodies, we are presented with a particularly crucial question: Why is it that these series are aligned with (and even labelled as) a species of porn? As much as *The Scheme* and programmes like it might be seen to intersect with certain kinds of biopolitics, they are never framed or contextualized as being primarily grounded in the sexual. We might think of this as being one of

---

2 As Neil Midgley (2013) notes, the series proved popular with viewers, beating "ITV in the 9.00pm slot on Monday night, with 2.8 million viewers".

the basic definitional criteria of pornography, and yet it is markedly absent here. Indeed, it is worth noting that none of the works of poverty porn that I have mentioned so far would correspond to the characterization of the "pornographic" set out in the Criminal Justice and Immigration Act 2008, which states that a representation is pornographic if it is "of such a nature that it must reasonably be assumed to have been produced solely or principally for the purpose of sexual arousal" (HMSO 2008).

So what is it about certain representations of poverty which makes them so available for consideration as pornographic? What, in the absence of sexual explicitness, aligns them with an idea of porn? One possible point of confluence can be found in concerns about the possible exploitation of participants. Neil Midgley's (2013) piece on *Skint* for *The Telegraph*, for example, raises the issue of informed participation, stating that "Reality TV is like sex: a lot of it takes place between consenting adults [...]. But sometimes it's exploitative – and it's not always easy to see where the dividing line is." Midgley's most significant concern, however, has less to do with the individuals in front of the camera and more to do with those sitting at home in front of their television screens. This is suggested by his apparent distaste at the idea of viewers "staring voyeuristically at people who are a bit poor or a bit thick", and is embodied in his final, admonishing sentence: "don't present other people's suffering as entertainment" (Midgley 2013).

One of the key factors behind the emergence of the term 'poverty porn', I would argue, is an anxiety not simply about the representations themselves, but about the imagined reactions of those viewing them. With reference to *Skint*, and to its reception both by the general public and within the British broadsheet print media, the following pages will explore the interpretative anxiety provoked by the series, framing this in relation to the assumed conceptual incompatibility of compassion and prurience. I will then attempt to think through some of the ways in which prurience functions and, rather than dismissing this as a response which needs to be stifled in the service of a sufficiently ethical response to the suffering of the other, consider its potential usefulness as a rhetorical device and even an activist tool.

2 Prurience, Pornography, Precarious Lives

The idea of prurience – along with the related notion of voyeurism, in the pejorative sense of "watching other people's suffering or problems" (Collins English Dictionary, def. 2) – emerges frequently in reactions to poverty porn, and anxiety about viewer engagement can be seen to characterize a significant percentage of the public's response to the genre. A recent poll conducted by the online market research agency YouGov, for example, sought explicitly to address the topic of poverty porn, and found that "nearly half of the public (45 %)" thought that shows such as *Skint* were "in bad taste" and that they served to "make a spectacle out of poor people's lives" (Dahlgreen 2013). A similar concern with audiences marks many of the journalistic attempts to characterize and problematize the genre. In an article for the *Herald Scotland*, Pat Kane (2010) accuses contemporary audiences of needing "a prurient, affluence-confirming superiorism from our non-fiction TV", and concludes his discussion by claiming that "[t]he thing about porn is that it's easy to watch, you know what you're getting, and the payoff is instantly satisfying. Poverty porn is no different."

One could argue that these kinds of perspective link televisual depictions of poverty with a very particular set of anxieties about porn. That is, they understand media texts to be pornographic when the motives of those watching them are positioned as sordid, troubling and profoundly suspect. This is evident in Holly Young's (2012) suggestion that, in the case of poverty porn,[3] we never "move from passive news consumption to active engagement with the issue" because the separation between viewing subject and viewed object works to "emphasise the voyeuristic nature of the enterprise and confirm it as something more akin to consumption than education". A similar point is made by Andrew Billen in relation to *Skint*: whilst the series might draw upon (and profess to belong to) a tradition started by "left-wing documentary directors wishing to change society", it is also positioned as part of an emerging genre "in which the underclass is paraded for our entertainment rather than moral edification" (2013, 38). We can see, then, that those texts which come to receive the designation 'poverty porn' are seen as pandering to prurience by stressing the viewer's distance from the scenes represented and by facilitating an unethical passivity before representations which are framed and marketed as entertainment.

It would appear that those critics who see the pornographic in poverty porn effectively deny the possibility that watching these shows might provoke thoughtful critical reflection. For them, viewers engage with this kind of imagery of poverty in the same way that they supposedly engage with porn – that is, as little more than an entertaining and affecting spectacle, which may agitate a queasy appetite for titillation but which does not puncture the protective shield of passive voyeurism. Whilst this perspective demonstrates an extremely limited

---

3 Young (2012) is discussing yet another manifestation of poverty porn here: specifically, "disaster tourism". Her comments, however, share much common ground with journalistic discussions of reality television, and indicate at least a partial collective understanding of what constitutes poverty porn.

understanding of the viewer engagements experienced in relation to porn (which are much more various and nuanced than is typically assumed),[4] it does draw upon a pervasive unease about the pleasures of these texts. Specifically, it suggests an anxiety that, whilst shows like *Skint* may claim to offer "an insight into [the participants'] lives, highlighting social issues" ("Episode Guides" 2013), the actual responses experienced by and courted within viewers are likely to be somewhat less reputable. There is an anxiety, in other words, that the appearance of sympathetic concern or social consciousness may mask a distinctly unwholesome enjoyment of the spectacle of suffering.

Indeed, many of these examples of reality television arguably offer little in the way of an obvious incitement to political intervention. We are invited to witness people's struggles and sufferings in a manner that puts us under no obligations at all. As such, it would be easy to argue that an apparent intellectual or sentimental concern regarding the treatment of some of our society's most vulnerable people is viewed as concealing a politically disengaged pleasure in encountering genuine accounts of human suffering. It is precisely this idea of a passive and prurient interest on the part of the viewer which allows non-sexually explicit poverty porn to be linked with the pornographic. As the Porn Studies scholar Linda Williams notes, the notion of prurient interest first appeared in a legal context in 1973's *Miller v. California* Supreme Court case, where it was described as "persons, having itching, morbid, or lascivious longings of desire, curiosity, or propensity" (Williams 2008, 122). It is precisely this notion of prurience that I feel is at play here. Poverty porn comes to be viewed as a kind of porn because it facilitates a somehow lascivious enjoyment of accounts of socially precarious lives; accounts from which we ourselves are sufficiently distanced that we do not have to confront the reality or the politics of what we see.

In poverty porn, we see popular anxieties about the pornographic being conducted through a new and different object; a certain type of text comes to be positioned as pornographic because it can be seen to provide experiences of voyeuristic titillation and prurient pleasure. It is not insignificant, I think, that this idea of a passive response to representations of precarious lives can be related to a particularly pernicious understanding of the underlying causes of poverty. It effectively posits the neoconservative notion that the unequal distribution of wealth and resources is *fundamentally* resistant to change, because poverty itself is the fault of the poor. The middle-class viewer could not intervene even if she or he wanted to, because the poor somehow opt to live in a state of poverty, and

---

4 For a more detailed account of my understanding of pornography in its conventional sense – that is, as adult entertainment – see Hester (2014).

'welfare cultures' are self-generating, rather than the result of structural inequalities, governmental policies or the circulation of political discourses.

This is something that Owen Jones remarks upon in his influential text *Chavs: The Demonization of the Working Class* (2011).[5] He notes that "demonizing the less well-off [...] makes it easier to justify an unprecedented and growing level of social inequality", and links this with a lack of concerted intervention seeking to rectify the situation: "to admit that some people are poorer than others because of the social injustice inherent in our society would require government action. Claiming that people are largely responsible for their circumstances facilitates the opposite conclusion" (2011, 37). Jones attributes the pernicious popularity of this idea of personal liability for one's circumstances to the legacy of Margaret Thatcher's emphasis upon individual self-improvement over collective action (2011, 47), and goes on to argue that the "demonization of working-class people is a grimly rational way to justify an irrational system. Demonize them, ignore their concerns – and rationalize a grossly unequal distribution of wealth and power as a fair reflection of people's worth and abilities" (2011, 182–183).

There is certainly an argument to be made that *Skint*, for all its claims to get "behind the headlines [...] and show the real impact of worklessness" ("Episode Guides" 2013), plays into this popular mythology of personal responsibility for poverty. As Haylett remarks,

> The hallmark of this approach is the attribution of normative characteristics to those living in poverty, most especially an inability to defer gratification (self-indulgence), ambivalence about law-abiding behaviour (violence and criminality), fateful approaches to self-advancement (lack of ambition), over-fecundity (having more children than are affordable), loose attachments to conventional family life (family instability) and beyond those social failings a range of psychological traits of a more pathological nature. (2001, 362)

From the outset, *Skint* displays many of the tropes identified here; the opening episode, first broadcast at 9pm on Monday, 13 May 2013, introduces viewers to "the wall" on the Westcliff Estate – the unofficial social hub where, in the absence of any other suitable communal space, locals typically gather. According to a young male resident called Fergie, the wall is where locals meet to "drink

---

5 Jones also touches upon the poverty porn genre in his work, though he does not directly label it in this fashion: "Reality TV shows, sketch shows, talk shows, even films have emerged dedicated to ridiculing working-class Britain. 'Chavtainment' has reinforced the mainstream view of working-class individuals as bigoted, slothful, aggressive people who cannot look after themselves let alone their children" (2011, 122). The term itself does appear in his 2013 article on the topic, however.

beer, smoke weed" and socialize (*Skint: Episode 1*). Fergie stresses that it is the place to come to obtain restricted substances – "Class A's to class C's. It's an illegal shop" (*Skint: Episode 1*). Scenes of people consuming (in the dual sense of both ingesting and spending precious money upon) these substances feature frequently throughout the series, along with scenes of heavy alcohol consumption. This provides plenty of fodder for ideas regarding poverty as self-inflicted through indulgence and criminality.

The opening episode also introduces us to one of the series' central, anchoring characters – a man called Dean, who has (in the words of the narrator) "been on the social for a year now" (*Skint: Episode 1*), and whose wife is currently pregnant with the family's seventh child. The intersection of Haylett's notions of self-indulgence and over-fecundity seems to be emphasized within the programme, with the voiceover stressing that "feeding a family, especially one as big as Dean's, on what the social pays is always a stretch" (*Skint: Episode 1*). To illustrate this, the viewer is then presented with scenes of Dean buying black-market meat from the boot of a car. Whether or not the programme's attribution of "normative characteristics to those living in poverty" is deliberate (Haylett 2001, 362), one could certainly argue that it channels certain mythologies about "abject whites". In so doing, *Skint* risks reinforcing the stereotype of "an undeserving, beer-swilling, drug-taking poor, sticking their fingers up at the taxpayers they're living off" (Jones 2013).

To some extent, then, *Skint* might be accused of contributing to the kind of thinking that Haylett identifies: the kind of thinking that enables (and even encourages) a disengaged response to representations of poverty because it stigmatizes the poor. By positioning a life of deprivation as a kind of choice, made by people who are already somehow predisposed to make such lifestyle choices, and by blaming an existence of struggle upon the very people who are struggling, this approach to social inequality frees a middle-class audience from any kind of burdensome ethical responsibilities. As such, it enables this audience to enjoy the experience of prurience without the threat of personal obligation.

3 The Role of Compassion

This all suggests a rather negative reading both of *Skint* and of poverty porn more broadly. For journalists, as well as for the general public, it is a regime of representations of which we should be highly suspicious (and, if nothing else, correlating a representation with porn serves this function – a red flag to the good bourgeois subject that the material should be approached with mistrust and not a little distaste). But it is worth returning again at this stage to the idea that the term 'poverty porn' has a wide range of applications. The term connotes not only leisure or entertainment-based phenomena – in fact, a number of bloggers and international relations scholars apply 'poverty porn' to a set of texts which explicitly *refuse* viewer passivity and which instead stress our obligations and invite our intervention. This includes things like charity fundraising initiatives, aid appeals and social action campaigns: for example, Siena Anstis (2012) links the infamous Kony 2012 viral with "poverty porn messaging",[6] whilst Matt Collin (2009) argues that poverty porn (along with "development porn" and "famine porn") can be defined as "any type of media, be it written, photographed or filmed, which exploits the poor's condition in order to generate the necessary sympathy" required to gain support for a given cause. These are materials which seek to puncture the protective screen of the representation, provoke critical and ethical engagement, and motivate viewers to change their perspective or feel more acutely. It is evidently not just supposedly mindless entertainment which gets tagged as poverty porn, then; texts which ostensibly invite action also receive this label. So what are the pseudo-pornographic qualities linked with these texts? They do not encourage our blank passivity before the image, and yet for some commentators, they retain a link with voyeurism, prurience and the pornographic.

The idea that certain forms of poverty porn might encourage reflection and even action, returns us to the idea of the educational possibilities of shows such as *Skint*. Whilst many journalists dismiss a concern with contemporary social issues as a fig leaf for less ethical forms of viewer investment, a significant minority of the public do seem to attribute an instructive or edifying value to this type of reality television. The aforementioned YouGov public opinion poll on poverty porn found that "nearly a quarter" of respondents said that such shows are "interesting and entertaining, and give people an opportunity to see how the poorest people in our society live" (Dahlgreen 2013). Certainly, *Skint* does seem to invite empathic reflection upon the lives of its subjects. In the third episode of the series, we witness the struggles of Dean's eldest stepson, 16-year-old James, to find gainful employment. With few jobs available, and in the absence of the

---

6 This half-hour long documentary about the Ugandan rebel leader Joseph Kony was a provocative human rights based campaign that was widely watched and shared online. However, the campaign has been accused of neocolonialism, its 'clicktivist' tactics have been questioned and its content has been subjected to intense criticism for misrepresenting reality and the views of northern Ugandans.

qualifications required to get into college, the army is positioned as one of his only options.[7]

We see James completing his application, choosing between various potential career paths within the armed forces, and dropping off his medical forms, all the while discussing the fact that he's always wanted to be in the army and claiming that he's "not really [...] bothered about dying or anything" (*Skint: Episode 3*). The sardonic voiceover encourages the viewer to be more sceptical about this professedly freely-made life choice, however, remarking that "maybe there's a bit more to this army thing than James realizes", and "Who knows? By next year, James could be off getting shot at rather than fighting with his family" (*Skint: Episode 3*). Although this representation of a young man attempting to take up the only opportunities available to him is eventually undercut by the revelation that he failed to turn up for his interview, the show briefly opens up a space for engagement. The viewer is prompted to think about what a dearth of suitable employment prospects really means for residents of the Westcliff estate, especially school leavers and those who have never been in a position to work before. At the same time, however, we could argue that middle-class taste judgements are also being brought to bear here: a squaddie is a role that carries little in the way of either cultural or economic capital and as such, it is implied, could only ever be an acceptable choice for the most desperate.

We can see that poverty porn – even in its more obviously entertainment-based manifestations – is available for framing as educational due to its capacity to raise awareness of other people's lives, and can be seen to place a collective burden upon the viewing public to look at and to reflect upon an experience of poverty from which they would otherwise be alienated. One might argue that the value of these programmes lies precisely here – in their ability to make precarious lives visible and thereby to prick the consciences of middle-class viewers. Poverty porn, then, can be seen to encourage more than mere passivity in its audiences. Campaigning materials – and, in a looser and less direct fashion, issues-based reality television – seek to provoke an emotional response and to literally affect a change (however temporary or limited the actual form of that change may be; an adjustment in perspective, for example, or a commitment to financial donations). In other words, these types of poverty porn can be framed not as attempts to pander to prurience, but as useful ways of generating compassion and raising awareness.

---

7 As the voiceover notes: "Wherever there are no jobs, there's usually an army recruitment office. Mind you, even they're getting picky nowadays" (*Skint: Episode 3*).

This observation raises three issues: the limits of compassion, the possibilities of prurience, and the need to think about these two concepts together. First, regarding the topic of the limits of compassion, it is important to acknowledge that the attribution of an ethical usefulness to this kind of awareness-raising is in itself problematic. The experience of compassion should not be viewed as a politically useful ethical act in and of itself. Whilst sympathetic and empathic feeling – feeling *for* or *with* the other – can make us tremblingly alive to the sufferings of individuals, it may in fact mask underlying issues. That is, it can blind us to wider, more significant, but less personalized or immediately heart-wrenching structural inequalities. Indeed, we might see this as the inverse of the manoeuvre that Owen Jones identifies in *Chavs*, in which the "plight of some working-class people is commonly portrayed as a 'poverty of ambition' on their part. It is their individual characteristics, rather than a deeply unequal society rigged in favour of the privileged, that is held responsible" (2011, 10 – 11). Whilst certain manifestations of neoliberal ideology seek, as we have seen, to individualize the experience of poverty in order to downplay the contribution of class to one's socioeconomic prospects, poverty porn shows such as *Skint* seek to personalize poverty in order to secure a compassionate viewer reaction. Both approaches rely upon a focus on the individual – whether deserving or undeserving, worthy of scorn or sympathy. This serves to give the abstract idea of poverty a human face, but it does so at the expense of dealing with less interpersonally legible factors. The issue is reduced to the level of the atomized individual viewer feeling in response to the depiction of an atomized individual subject, and this detracts from both the complex nature of the social factors behind poverty conditions *and* the vital importance of rationally-driven collective action for effecting social change.

Secondly, I would contend that, whilst the usefulness of compassion is often overrated, the possibilities of prurience have been somewhat under-estimated. There is an evident suspicion of prurience within the media response to poverty porn – a suspicion that journalists rarely have the time or space to critically interrogate. To assume that all kinds of voyeuristic curiosity are inherently undesirable not only works to render value judgements axiomatic,[8] but also neglects to consider the role played by the libido in terms of human curiosity.[9] As Joel Aronoff notes, much of Freud's thinking on the topic links curiosity to his "general conception of drives" (1962, 40), and he suggests that it is precisely through a

---

8 That these value judgements are moralistic in character is surely implied by the term 'poverty porn'.

9 I would like to thank Carolyn Betensky for encouraging me to develop this line of thinking.

sexually over-coded desire to see and know that we "come to investigate the world and arrive at all kinds of abstract knowledge" (1962, 41).[10] We might therefore argue that there is a prurient element to much of what constitutes our interest in the wider world, and that to stigmatize prurience is to unquestioningly assume that there is a wholly disinterested mode of engagement available to the viewing subject.

Certainly, a voyeuristically curious engagement with depictions of poverty should be problematized if this represents the end point of the supposedly ethical encounter with the other. But what if this curiosity could actually be utilized as part of a wider process of engagement? What if prurience could be weaponized and deliberately manipulated as part of a wider rhetorical toolkit? If we accept, in the wake of Freud's insights, that the notion of a wholly 'pure' mode of engagement, untainted by the libido, is a fallacy, then we must remain open to accepting the possibility that prurient affect might in fact be a fairly standard by-product when it comes to the experience of sympathy.

My final point is a fairly basic one – that compassion and prurience are not mutually exclusive, and that we need to think about the ways in which these two concepts interact and talk to one another. Articles on poverty porn seem to want to hold these ideas in distinction, as if any twinge of prurience automatically overwhelms and smothers sympathy, and yet the need to hold these concepts apart has resulted in real interpretive uncertainty in the case of programmes like *Skint*. As we have seen, *Skint* both reinforces crass judgements about those who live in poverty and calls on the viewer to reflect with compassion upon the struggles of one northern English community: it tends to vacillate between presenting the affecting spectacle of the poor as chav caricatures and representing the residents of the Westcliff estate in a more nuanced and multi-faceted way. Images of the civic-minded Dean fixing his neighbour's window, for example, contrast with scenes of his 'unconventional' parenting – scenes which seem designed to invite the audience's hostile judgement. Whilst preparing to depart on a family holiday in episode three, the camera captures Dean's stress and frustration ("Just fucking do it and shut your fucking mouth. Fuck off. For fuck's sake. Fucking bollocks! You are not taking a fucking football, fuck off. Fucking idiot") – before cutting to two of the family's very young chil-

---

10 Aronoff compares Freud's biological explanation for curiosity to his social one. Even when conceiving of curiosity as a form of coping mechanism or social-problem solving, however, Freud's explanation retains its ties with the sexual and reproductive functions of the body. The child develops a fascination with conception upon the arrival of a rival sibling: in order to "prevent the occurrence of another such calamity, the child begins to search and to enquire into the causes of this catastrophe" (Aronoff 1962, 43).

dren playing together and rhythmically shouting the words "Fuck, fuck, fuck" (*Skint: Episode 3*). Indeed, episodes of *Skint* typically end with a preview of what to expect in the next instalment, and these previews seem like unabashed attempts to court a prurient interest in chav culture – a montage of quick cuts of violence, drinking, arguments and illegal drug consumption, set to a jaunty, fast-paced guitar soundtrack.

This ambiguous treatment of its subjects is reflected in the divergence of opinion amongst critics. Indeed, it is not only that some feel compelled to defend the show whilst others embrace the opportunity to denounce it; some critics struggle to reach any kind of consensus at all about what sort of show it is. *Skint* may feature scenes of urban deprivation and criminal behaviour amongst benefit-dependent housing estate residents, but can it really be said to be poverty porn if viewers are not sure if they are supposed to condemn or condone the people it represents? Indeed, individual critics appear to really struggle with personal ambivalence when reviewing the series. Andrew Billen of *The Times* notes that:

> The poverty is real and shocking but it can be an effort to feel sympathy for some of its Scunnie victims. Last Monday, Dean responded with perhaps justifiable outrage that his wife, Claire, was not to be compensated by the State for her complex pain syndrome, but his cause was undermined by his T-shirt's slogan: 'F*** moderation. Let's get wasted.' (2013, 39)

He ultimately concludes that "[i]f pornography dehumanises and degrades its subjects, this new genre of poverty programming cannot really be said to be pornographic. But it remains troubling" (2013, 39). John Niven's article for *The Daily Record* captures a similar sense of uncertainty about the show, leading him to declare that *Skint* "was uncomfortable viewing, as it should have been, straddling the difficult line between poverty porn and genuine insight" (2013, 41).

We can see from the journalistic response to the series, then, that *Skint* resists any attempt to impose definitive value judgements, as responses of both compassion and prurience are courted in the viewer. The provocation of these seemingly incompatible reactions is what thrusts the critic into a position of hermeneutic instability, and is part of what renders this example of poverty porn so troubling. The fact is, of course, that it is the insistence upon artificially maintaining a distance between these two modes of engagement – the attempt to hold compassion and prurience apart – which leads to interpretive anxiety in the first place. It is evident that the affective experience of compassion does not necessarily disbar a simultaneous prurient interest, and that the assumption of mutual exclusivity is erroneous. From my perspective, however, it is not just a question of asking why these two things can only co-exist so uneasily, but also whether, given the prominence of prurience in certain kinds of issues-driven (and even 'activist') texts, this denigrated response might actually facilitate certain forms of political engagement.

4 What Can Prurience Do?

Leo Bersani and Ulysse Dutoit make some enlightening comments about the difficulties associated with sympathy in their excellent book *The Forms of Violence* (1985). In this volume, they suggest that a trace of sexual pleasure inevitably infiltrates any experience of sympathy, arguing that

> there is a certain risk in all sympathetic projections: the pleasure which accompanies them promotes a secret attachment to scenes of suffering or violence. We are not, it should be stated, arguing (absurdly) 'against' sympathy. Rather, we wish to suggest that the psychic mechanism which allows for what would rightly be called humane or morally liberal responses to scenes of suffering or violence is, intrinsically, somewhat dysfunctional. The very operation of sympathy partially undermines the moral solidarity which we like to think of as its primary effect. Our views of the human capacity for empathetic representations of the world should therefore take into account the possibility that a mimetic relation to violence necessarily includes a sexually induced fascination with violence. (Bersani and Dutoit 1985, 38)[11]

This emphasis upon the interpenetration of prurience and sympathy, and its concomitant insights about the dysfunctional operations of the sympathetic or empathic response, has obvious implications for any discussion of poverty porn. All attempts to provoke sympathy, according to this reading, have the potential to segue into sexuality. This may go some way toward accounting for the ease with which the idea of porn has attached itself to things like poverty; the experience of being moved by the sight of precarious lives allows for the possibility of prurient enjoyment. It appeals to that dysfunctional psychic mechanism which smuggles certain forms of sexualized affect into the experience of sympathy. This reinforces the idea that a surfeit of emotional or sympathetic response,

---

11 To be clear, this does not necessarily mean that compassionate responses to scenes of suffering are automatically linked with recognizably genital forms of arousal. Bersani is very clear, throughout much of his work, that sexuality should be understood as a form of generalized intensity that occurs whenever "the body's 'normal' range of sensation is exceeded, and when the organization of the self is momentarily disturbed by sensations or affective processes" (1986, 38).

just as much as a dearth, can be seen to invite an interrogation of the viewer's motives and drives.

Poverty porn can evidently function as a site for the potential interpenetration of prurient and sympathetic impulses. It can be seen to draw upon a pervasive 'unwholesome' interest in the sorrowful or the horrific, even whilst openly addressing itself to concerns of a less denigrated kind, and to incorporate potentially eroticized affects into materials with awareness-raising or activist intentions. This may strike us as a highly problematic scenario. For one thing, it encourages in the viewer a transgressive investment in the suffering depicted, thereby undermining the ethical force of the text's affects. That is to say, titillating and troubling works of poverty porn can be seen to court, in a circuitous form, the very interests that they may be attempting to combat. If we get a prurient thrill from watching suffering, then one might assume that we are invested in that suffering; if we on some level enjoy scenes of poverty, then why would we be invested in attempting to combat that poverty? However, I would suggest that there is something slyly pragmatic about this rhetorical strategy. Certainly many people may be intrigued by poverty porn out of a transgressive prurient interest in enjoying the spectacles of precarious lives that they provide. At the same time, however, these materials crucially provide a mechanism via which one may disavow one's lascivious or morbid fascination at the very moment one indulges it.

Campaigning materials are, after all, works with expressly social, rather than pornographic, intentions, which set out to address themselves to reputable and high-minded concerns. In other words, certain varieties of poverty porn pander to prurient interest whilst simultaneously allowing the viewing subject to deny this fact, and thereby to placate her superego. They allow us to disown those motives to which – as a result of the legacy of shame surrounding *Miller vs. California*'s "itching, morbid, or lascivious longings" – we do not wish to own up. The viewer can assuage any sense of guilt or culpability, and go some way toward concealing the full extent of transgressive prurient interests from the self. In the case of *Skint*, of course, this may boil down to little more than the idea that middle-class viewers with diverse motives can justify their spectatorship by professing to watch in the interests of education and understanding, rather than to enjoy the spectacle of carnivalesque bad behaviour. However, this idea of prurience could get more purchase in the case of texts with more overtly and unambiguously activist intentions. That is to say, a voyeuristic curiosity about which the subject feels conflicted could easily be framed as a useful tool to manipulate.

What does this possibility of simultaneously entering into both prurient and reputable forms of engagement suggest? Does an admixture of prurience always undermine political intentions, or might it in some way work as a device to affect and manipulate the viewer in desired ways? It is my contention that, whilst the sexual undertones of poverty porn may mobilize a certain prurient interest, they may also play an unacknowledged role in the mobilization of sympathy itself. By activating the morbid, conflicted desire to witness suffering whilst providing a mechanism by which the presence of this desire can be robustly denied, the affecting depictions of suffering found within certain works of poverty porn provide something of a service. Their explicit appeal to the sympathetic impulse acts as something like an indirect form of licensed transgression.

Under these limited conditions, we allow ourselves to succumb to a forbidden desire to take pleasure in scenes of poverty, precisely because we can to some extent mask the full force of this desire from the self. This may prove polemically expedient, for whilst, as Susan Sontag notes, "painful, stirring images supply only an initial spark" (2004, 92) when it comes to meaningful political action, and may not necessarily prompt any form of useful reflection at all, the powerful desire to be able to disown and disavow the transgressive pleasure elicited by these texts may indeed work to promote political engagement or to encourage charitable giving. Even in less ambiguous cases than *Skint*, then – even in texts which are not burdened with the imperative to entertain – prurience is available to be mobilized for rhetorical and political ends.

This idea is in some ways reminiscent of Adam Smith's comments in his famous *The Theory of Moral Sentiments* (first published in 1759) regarding that which is "generous" and "noble" within human nature: "It is not the love of our neighbour, it is not the love of mankind", he argues, "which upon many occasions prompts us to the practice of those divine virtues. It is a stronger love, a more powerful affection, which generally takes place upon such occasions; the love [...] of the grandeur, and dignity, and superiority of our characters" (Smith 2004, 158). We are attracted to an inflated idea of the self, then, and our attempts to behave honourably may be a by-product of precisely this attraction. Actions of generosity, sympathy and self-sacrifice may, by this reckoning, in fact stem from a self-interested investment in the image of our own noble characters, and this investment is therefore available to be exploited for political ends. By facilitating the exploration and enjoyment of prurient interest within the context of representations of precarious lives, activist materials may prompt both engagement and action. What better way to conceal the indulgence of an itching, morbid or lascivious longing than by converting it into a reputable – and, perhaps, admirable – impulse?

Marcus Wood argues that "the enlightened man of sentiment [...] can have his cake and eat it" (2002, 98), and the attempt to do just that, apparently so disingenuous, can be exploited in attempts to encourage forms of social change. Of course, there are still problems to consider here; namely, that much so-called poverty porn seeks (at best) no greater intervention than the donation of a few pounds a month, and encourages the viewer to think of those in poverty not as human beings with agency but as objects dependent upon our beneficent middle-class goodwill. My comments about the rhetorical power of prurience should not be interpreted as approval for and affirmation of any and all forms of poverty porn. I do think, however, that my examples work to outline an under-recognized potential – a potential which could be seized upon by contemporary activist communities. Instead of courting compassion and disavowing any less reputable affects, we might embrace and target the libidinal, the curious and the self-interested. If we were to abandon what Matteo Pasquinelli calls the "puritanism of activism" (2008, 25), new ways of using psychic excess could be mobilized – weaponized toward activist ends. Poverty porn, for all of its problems, teaches us a crucial lesson; it is not only anxiety about the discomforting immoderation of porn which can be transferred to other objects, but also pornography's intense power and appeal. Prurience, if correctly channelled, could be a real resource for contemporary leftist and activist rhetoric.

5 Conclusion: Prurience Is Not the Problem

Skint admittedly displays little in the way of activist ambitions, beyond a loose and ill-defined interest in raising awareness. The show's engagement with voyeuristic curiosity never exceeds the premise outlined in its mission statement – to provide "provocative and revealing stories" ("Episode Guide" 2013) about contemporary worklessness – and the prurient interest it courts is never fully weaponized. But whilst *Skint* does little to exploit this interest, the series (and the various responses to it) does provide a useful springboard for exploring provocation and revelation, and the relationship between them. *Skint*'s depiction of poverty brings together two seemingly irreconcilable concepts – prurience and compassion – in a way that generates interpretative instability. Indeed, as a result of erroneous assumptions about mutual exclusivity, the show comes to resemble a multistable perceptual phenomena. Critics can (depending on their viewpoints and intended readerships) view it through the lens of voyeurism or education, and they can vacillate anxiously between these two perspectives, but they rarely seem able to consider it as both simultaneously.

Whilst the series does little to channel viewer engagement into meaningful action, it does helpfully indicate something about our characterization of the ideas of prurience and compassion, and can be used to help think through the potential political usefulness of the morbid, itching and lascivious desire to see. As we have seen, prurience has its uses, and it is not particularly helpful to condemn it out of hand. Ultimately, the major issue with *Skint* seems to lie elsewhere. It is not, in fact, its appeal to prurience that represents its most substantial flaw, but its characterization of poverty, which is shaped by omission. The show equates being skint with being jobless, when in fact, as Owen Jones has pointed out:

> You don't need to be jobless to be poor in modern Britain. Poverty is generally defined as households with less than 60 per cent of the nation's median income after housing costs are deducted. Less than five million people lived in poverty on the eve of the Thatcher counter-revolution, or less than one in ten of the population. Today, poverty affects 13.5 million people, or more than one in five. (2011, 203)

In a climate of underemployment, in which there is a "widening gap between the hours that employers are willing to pay for, and the hours that UK employees wish to work" (Blanchflower 2013), it is wrong to attribute economic vulnerability solely to those surviving without work. Those who are in employment may also be experiencing financial hardship as a result of a drop in real wages, and *Skint* obscures this fact by 'othering' the poor as the workshy, the unemployed and the wholly benefit dependent. The series may not entirely demonize the Scunthorpe community it represents – it may open up spaces for compassionate viewer reflection within the fabric of the spectacle that it stages – but it certainly fails to challenge the myth that joblessness is the cause of poverty.

It is also worth noting that the show makes some rather loaded assumptions about what constitutes the worklessness that it takes as its central theme. It would appear that the physically slight, youthful-looking Tracey, who features heavily in the final episode, is classed alongside the rest of the series' workless subjects. However, in framing Tracey as workless, the show overlooks the paid labour that she regularly performs to support her drug habit – namely, it fails to identify the erotic labour that she performs as a sex worker as in itself a form of work. This is despite the fact that the notion of economic exchange imposes itself in relation to Tracey's body in a fashion which overtly references (and sexualizes) the show's prurient interest in poverty. When Tracey asks for the cameras to be turned off so that she can take drugs, the producer enquires "Why is that? Where do you inject?" Tracey replies, "In my groin. And if you want me to pull my pants down, I'll have to charge you" (*Skint: Episode 4*). Here, both producer and consumer are momentarily interpellated into the role of punter, and ideas about voyeurism and exploitation rise insistently to the surface, reminding us once again of prurient interest's potential as a manipulable territory of discomforting affects.

This exchange between Tracey and the producer is enlightening not just in terms of the dynamics of prurience but in terms of the (to my mind more pressing) issue of labour in the show. It explicitly situates certain forms of corporeal action and bodily display *as work* for which the young woman expects to be financially compensated; to offer her up as another example of worklessness therefore suggests a rather limited conception of what work is and means, and indicates that those forms of labour performed and remunerated within the informal economy are positioned as invalid and unrecognizable. This links back to our discussion of the teenaged James's interest in the army; the value of work that does not correspond to bourgeois judgements tends to be mocked, marginalized, diminished or totally ignored. This failure to properly acknowledge sex work as work – combined as it is with the failure to engage with poverty within working households – is the most problematic feature of this so-called 'poverty porn' series for me. Prurience has the potential to function as an activist tool, but it is hard to imagine how the implicit mythologizing of the 'right' kinds of labour could achieve anything other than shoring up the conservative ideas about work.

Works Cited

Anstis, Siena. "On Invisible Children's Kony 2012 Campaign." *Siena* 7 March 2012. http://siena-anstis.com/wp-content/uploads/2012/03/07/on-invisible-childrens-kony-2012-campaign/ (13 August 2013).

Aronoff, Joel. "Freud's Conception of the Origin of Curiosity." *Journal of Psychology* 54 (1962): 39–45.

Bersani, Leo. *The Freudian Body: Psychoanalysis and Art.* New York: Columbia University Press, 1986.

Bersani, Leo, and Ulysse Dutoit. *The Forms of Violence: Narrative in Assyrian Art and Modern Culture.* New York: Schocken Books, 1985.

Billen, Andrew. "Nothing to Do But Breed and Feed? The Rise of Poverty Porn: From *Honey Boo* to *Skint*, We're Suddenly Hooked on Watching the Poor." *The Times* 28 May 2013: 38–39.

Blanchflower, David. "There Has Been No Good News for Britain's Army of Underemployed Workers." *The Independent* 28 July 2013. http://www.independent.co.uk/voices/comment/there-has-been-no-good-news-for-britains-army-of-underemployed-workers-8735425.html (13 August 2013).

"Episode Guides *Skint*." *Channel 4* 2013. http://www.channel4.com/programmes/skint/episode-guide (13 August 2013).

Collin, Matt. "What Is 'Poverty Porn' and Why Does It Matter for Development?" *Aid Thoughts* 1 July 2009. http://aidthoughts.org/?p=69 (13 August 2013).

Collins English Dictionary. "voyeurism." Def. 2. *Collins English Dictionary.* Online Edition 2013. http://www.collinsdictionary.com/dictionary/english/voyeurism?showCookiePolicy=true (13 August 2013).

Dahlgreen, Will. "'Poverty-Porn' TV in Bad Taste?" *YouGov* 31 May 2013. http://yougov.co.uk/news/2013/05/31/poverty-porn-tv-bad-taste/ (13 August 2013).

Graham, Jane. "The Scheme: Gritty TV or Poverty Porn?" *The Guardian* 28 May 2009. http://www.guardian.co.uk/tv-and-radio/tvandradioblog/2010/may/28/the-scheme-bbc (16 June 2011).

Habila, Helon. "How Darling Escaped from Paradise: Has the Caine Prize Created an African Aesthetic of Suffering?" *The Guardian* 22 June 2013: 10.

Haylett, Chris. "Illegitimate Subjects?: Abject Whites, Neoliberal Modernisation, and Middle-Class Multiculturalism." *Environment and Planning D: Society and Space* 19.3 (2001): 351–370.

Hester, Helen. *Beyond Explicit: Pornography and the Displacement of Sex.* Albany: SUNY Press, 2014.

HMSO, United Kingdom. "Criminal Justice and Immigration Act 2008." *legistlation.co.uk* 2008. http://www.uk-legislation.hmso.gov.uk/acts/acts2008/ukpga_20080004_en_9 (9 January 2009).

Jones, Lesley-Ann. "Uplifting? Slumdog Is Just Poverty Porn." *Sunday Express* 15 February 2009: 56.

Jones, Owen. "Farewell, Shameless: Your Heirs Have Work to Do." *The Independent* 24 May 2013. http://www.independent.co.uk/voices/comment/farewell-shameless-your-heirs-have-work-to-do-8631498.html (13 August 2013).

—. *Chavs: The Demonization of the Working Class.* London: Verso, 2011.

Kane, Pat. "It's Not about People or Poverty: The Scheme Is Quite Simply Porn." *Herald Scotland* 23 May 2001. http://www.heraldscotland.com/comment/guest-commentary/it-s-not-about-people-or-poverty-the-scheme-is-quite-simply-porn-by-pat-kane-1.1029731 (13 August 2013).

Machell, Ben. "Last Night's TV: Shameless." *The Times* 29 May 2013. http://www.thetimes.co.uk/tto/arts/tv-radio/reviews/article3777133.ece (13 August 2013).

McDowall, Iain. "The Scheme Is Misleading 'Poverty Porn'." *The Guardian* 13 June 2011. http://www.guardian.co.uk/commentisfree/2011/jun/13/scheme-bbc-onthank-scotland (16 June 2011).

Midgley, Neil. "*Skint*: How Channel 4 Got It Wrong." *The Telegraph* 5 June 2013. http://www.telegraph.co.uk/culture/tvandradio/10100707/Skint-How-Channel-4-got-it-wrong.html (13 August 2013).

Miles, Alice. "Shocked by Slumdog's Poverty Porn: Danny Boyle's Film Is Sweeping Up Awards, but It's Wrong to Revel in the Misery of India's Children." *The Times* 14 January 2009: 26.

Mooney, Gerry, and Lynn Hancock. "Poverty Porn and the Broken Society." *Variant* 39/40 (2010). http://www.variant.org.uk/39_40texts/povertp39_40.html (16 June 2011).

Need to Know. "Geek Media." *Need to Know* 14 January 2000. http://www.ntk.net/2000/01/14/ (12 August 2013).

Niven, John. "Seven Children on Benefits? Cue Howls of Outrage. A Steel Plant Nearby, Where 30,000 Worked, Lies Empty? Cue Silence." *The Daily Record* 19 May 2013: 41.

Pasquinelli, Matteo. *Animal Spirits: A Bestiary of the Commons.* Rotterdam: NAi Publishers, 2008.

Skint: Episode 1. Channel 4, 13 May 2013.

Skint: Episode 3. Channel 4, 27 May 2013.

Skint: Episode 4. Channel 4, 3 June 2013.

Smith, Adam. *The Theory of Moral Sentiments*. Cambridge: Cambridge University Press, 2004.
Sontag, Susan. *Regarding the Pain of Others*. London: Penguin, 2004.
Williams, Linda. *Screening Sex*. Durham, NC: Duke University Press, 2008.
Wood, Marcus. *Slavery, Empathy, and Pornography*. Oxford: Oxford University Press, 2002.
Young, Holly. "Disaster Tourism: How Bus Trips to the Scene of Hurricane Katrina Make Profit From Loss." *The Independent* 9 October 2012. http://www.independent.co.uk/voices/comment/disaster-tourism-how-bus-trips-to-the-scene-of-hurricane-katrina-make-profit-from-loss-8203902.html (13 August 2013).

Biographies of the Contributors

Carolyn Betensky is Associate Professor of English at the University of Rhode Island, where she teaches courses on Victorian literature and critical theory. Another focus of her research is poverty, which culminated in her book *Feeling for the Poor* (2010).

Marie-Luise Egbert is affiliated as a Privatdozentin with the University of Leipzig. In recent years, she has taught at the University of Freiburg. Her research interests range from translation studies to poverty studies.

Joachim Frenk is Professor of British Literary and Cultural Studies at Saarland University, Saarbrücken. He specialises in early modern literature, in Victorian and contemporary literature and in cultural studies.

Helen Hester is a Senior Lecturer at Middlesex University (Mauritius Campus). She has published articles on gender and sexualities, transgression, and the abject body, and is the author of *Dirty Money: Pornography and the Erotics of Consumption.*

Eveline Kilian is Professor of British Cultural Studies and Cultural History in the Department of English and American Studies at Berlin's Humboldt University. Her research interests include Gender Studies, discourse analysis, subject formation and narrative, and metropolitan cultures.

Barbara Korte is professor of English literature at the University of Freiburg. Her research areas include travel writing, the literature of World War I and currently the literary representation of poverty.

Romain Nguyen Van is a PhD student at the University of Paris-Sorbonne IV. Having taught undergraduate students in British Literature at the Sorbonne, he now teaches undergraduate students in Lcyée Thiers (Marseille).

Frédéric Regard is professor of English literature at the Sorbonne. He has written books on several twentieth-century authors and the history of British literature. He has edited collections of essays on life-writing, exploration narratives and early Arctic voyages.

Marina Remy Abrunhosa is a PhD student at the University of Paris-Sorbonne IV, where she also taught undergraduate students in British Literature. She currently teaches British Literature and translation at a Classe Préparatoire aux Grandes Ecoles in Besançon (preparing students for the ENS selective-entry exam). Her research thesis focuses on George Orwell and James Greenwood.

Joanna Rostek is a lecturer in English Literature and Culture at the University of Passau. Her research interests include the economic discourse in nineteenth-century Britain, women's/gender studies, postmodern philosophy of history, and Polish migrant literature and culture in the UK and Ireland

Georg Zipp read for his MAs at the University of Sussex and at Freiburg University. He is currently completing a PhD project on poverty in contemporary Caribbean fiction. He was also involved in a research project on figurations of poverty on the British book market.

Index